The Environmental Protection Hustle

The Environmental Protection Hustle $\#$ b

Bernard J. Frieden

The MIT Press
Cambridge, Massachusetts, and London, England

This book was set in IBM composer Press Roman by Eastern Composition, Inc. Printed and bound by Halliday Lithograph Corporation in the United States of America.

Library of Congress Cataloging in Publication Data

Frieden, Bernard J
  The environmental protection hustle.

  Includes index.
  1. Housing–Environmental aspects–California.
2. Environmental policy–California. 3. Housing policy–California. I. Title.
HD7303. C2F74   301.31'09794   78–21512
ISBN 0-262-06068-X

To Elaine and Debbie

Contents

Preface

In the fall of 1975 I began a year in residence at the University of California in Berkeley to start writing a book on housing. I had just completed my term as director of the Joint Center for Urban Studies of MIT and Harvard University, where I had organized a new research program on national housing policy. It was clear from the work my colleagues and I had done at the Joint Center that the country was facing an unprecedented demand for new housing in the years ahead. The huge number of young families searching for suburban homes was already putting great pressure on the nation's housing markets while homebuilding during the 1974–75 recession had dropped to the lowest level since World War II. Finding ways to meet the country's housing needs was an obvious yet neglected priority for public policy.

As I began to explore the California scene, I realized that local policies as well as national ones were going to have big impacts on the availability of housing. California was leading the country in a new commitment to protect the environment against the sometimes unfortunate consequences of urban growth. New environmental concerns might lead to some conflicts with our long-standing commitment to provide good housing and homeownership opportunities for families of average income, but since both commitments were valid I expected to find local governments striking reasonable balances between housing and environmental goals. Yet the number of environmental controversies was remarkable, and the outcomes seemed anything but balanced. I decided to shift the focus of my research from national policies to local ones and to write a book about how the new local growth regulations were affecting housing prospects for the average family.

California is one of the best places in the country to study both environmentalism and housing. It offers rich experience in all dimensions of these fields, and, as important, its people are happy to help newcomers find out what is happening. I am much indebted to the many Californians—public officials, homebuilders, environmentalists, citizen activists, attorneys—who shared with me their points of view on housing controversies. Many of them will disagree strongly with my conclusions, but I know from our conversations that they welcome debate on the issues and enjoy the challenge of dissenting views. Individual interviews are acknowledged in the text, but a general note of appreciation is also in order.

Many University of California faculty members helped me get started with the study and gave me the benefit of their advice during our discussions throughout the year. Melvin Webber, director of the Institute of Urban and Regional

Development, my home base in Berkeley, was a steady source of encouragement as well as a perceptive interpreter of California. So, too, was the late William L. C. Wheaton, then dean of the College of Environmental Design. Others on the Berkeley faculty who informed, challenged, and assisted included T. J. Kent, Jr., Aaron Wildavsky, Francis Violich, William Alonso, Chester McGuire, Wallace Smith, Sherman Maisel, Kenneth Phillips, Richard Meier, Thomas Dickert, John Costonis, and Barry Checkoway.

Other Californians who were generous with their time, information, and comments included Maurice Mann, then president of the Federal Home Loan Bank of San Francisco and members of his staff, Sheldon Gans, Preston Martin, Claude and Nina Gruen, Ronald Grudzinski, Bruce Ricks, Ted Dienstfrey, and John Blayney.

After I returned to MIT to finish writing the book, several colleagues offered valuable comments on a first draft. I am indebted especially to Robert Fogelson, Lisa Peattie, and Lawrence Bacow of the MIT Department of Urban Studies and Planning and to D. Quinn Mills of the Harvard Business School.

Financial support from several sources made this work possible. A John Simon Guggenheim Memorial Fellowship, together with MIT sabbatical support, gave me the freedom to investigate housing issues in California in 1975 and 1976. The Lincoln Institute of Land Policy and its director, Arlo Woolery, then provided support that enabled me to complete the work I had begun in California.

The Institute of Urban and Regional Development at the University of California in Berkeley was a stimulating place to work and an open door to the resources of the entire University. Its director, Melvin Webber, and its staff were helpful in countless ways that made my year as Visiting Fellow a great pleasure. The staff of the MIT-Harvard Joint Center for Urban Studies and its current director, Arthur Solomon, provided similar help after my return. Christopher L. Roberts did an excellent job of producing successive versions of the manuscript. Penny Johnson, my secretary in the MIT Department of Urban Studies and Planning, took care of the final revisions and production chores in her cheerful and efficient way.

A large part of chapter 9 was originally written for a conference on urban growth sponsored by the MIT-Harvard Joint Center for Urban Studies in June 1977. It will appear in a forthcoming volume of conference papers and is published here with the Center's permission.

Finally, I am deeply grateful to my wife Elaine for her encouragement during the down periods of authorship, and for her many good ideas that helped shape the book. Together with our daughter Debbie, we shared the fun of exploring California as well as the sacrifices that research and writing demand of authors' families.

Cambridge, Massachusetts   Bernard J. Frieden
July 1978

Chapter 1
Regulating the American Dream

One of the big news stories of 1977 was the rising cost of homeownership. House prices, mortgage rates, and operating costs had all moved up so sharply since the late 1960s that young families trying to buy suburban homes were astounded at how much they had to pay. The high housing costs that had been a problem for poor people for years now were affecting well-off middle-income families who had to strain their budgets to pay for modest single-family homes. A Herblock cartoon captured the sense of confusion by showing a bewildered couple studying a real estate sign that read: "For Sale—Comfortable Middle-Income House for High-Income Family."

As the government released figures showing median sales prices for new homes approaching $50,000, and as housing analysts published their reports on what was happening to homeownership costs, the press and television took notice. Headline writers had a field day with the notion of a single-family suburban home as the focal point of "the American Dream." Articles were headed "Dream of Home Ownership Imperiled by Spiraling Costs"; "End of an American Dream: Decent Housing, Reasonably Priced"; and simply "Home Dream Now Nightmare." *Time* magazine's cover story, titled "Sky-high Housing," capped all this with an imaginative portrayal: on the cover, a small single-family home rose from its plot of land to hover among the clouds. Inside, a photograph showed a suburban mother and her children sitting on the bare floor of a room they couldn't afford to furnish after straining their budget to pay for their new house.

The news stories called national attention to the troubles of young families trying to find suburban homes they could afford. The great prominence of these stories, and their repetition throughout the year, suggests that they carried news of more than passing interest. There were special reasons for public attention and concern. One was the extent of the cost increases themselves, which created a shock effect. Another was the importance of homeownership to most Americans. Owning a home is not only a preferred housing arrangement but also a symbol of middle-class success. Price increases that make homeownership more difficult are a threat to the average family's hopes for a good life.

The increase in homeowner costs was striking, even at a time when inflation was ravaging consumer budgets generally. Between 1970 and 1976 the sales prices of both new and existing homes went up much faster than either family income or the overall cost of living. Meanwhile rising interest rates, energy costs, and local taxes sent the full cost of homeownership up even faster than sales prices. Monthly carrying expenses, including mortgage payments, fuel and utility bills, property taxes, and maintenance costs, were up by 102 percent for the median-priced new home, and 73 percent for the median-priced older home, while median family income was up by only 52 percent and the Consumer Price Index by 46 percent.[1]

Along with these increases in median home costs went the elimination of most low-priced homes. Except for mobile homes, houses selling for less than $20,000, new or old, almost disappeared from the market; and only a few were available below $30,000.

The full series of cost increases meant that most middle-income families could afford to buy a home only if they were willing to make great financial sacrifices. In 1970 nearly half the families in the country were able to buy the median-priced new or old home while still keeping total housing expenses to not more than 25 percent of their incomes. By 1976, using the same standard, only one family in four could afford the monthly cost of a median-priced new home and only one in three, the monthly cost of a median-priced old home.

The commitment to homeownership is deeply rooted and widely held. As long ago as 1931 President Herbert Hoover spoke of it as a national tradition: "Those immortal ballads, *Home Sweet Home, My Old Kentucky Home,* and *The Little Gray Home in the West,* were not written about tenements or apartments ... they never sing songs about a pile of rent receipts."[2]

Increasingly, families in the United States have chosen homeownership over renting: by the 1970s two out of every three families in the country owned their homes. Families, in their child-raising years particularly, choose homeownership. Among married couples with husbands aged 30 or older, fully 82 percent were homeowners in 1975.

Although other consumer tastes change from time to time, the goal of owning a single-family home in suburbia has kept its hold on the public. According to a 1974 Gallup poll, almost 90 percent of the people want to live in a suburb or a small town rather than in a city. Only 13 percent said they would prefer city living, down from 22 percent in a similar 1966 survey. Preferences for housing types were also clear. Three out of four people wanted to see future housing take the form of single-family homes located in open areas, and two out of three regarded a sizable piece of land up to one acre as an important element in choosing a new home.[3]

People who have not made their way to suburban homeownership are striving especially hard to get there. Other surveys have found most blue-collar and middle-income renter families living in city neighborhoods or suburban industrial towns registering resentment with their present housing, and voicing their eagerness to buy single-family homes in the green suburbs.[4]

Changes in the age profile of the American population are also creating unprecedented demand for single-family homes. People choose housing partly on the basis of their age and family makeup. Couples in the early years of marriage tend to live in rental apartments, but after they have children, most turn to single-family, suburban living. The huge baby-boom generation, born in the postwar years from the mid-1940s to the early 1960s, has now begun to reach this stage of family life. Only the leading edge of that generation has entered the potential homebuying market so far, with many more still to come. Between 1975 and 1985 households headed by people between the ages of 25 and 44—the prime homebuying years—will grow by at least 9 million, according to current demographic projections.[5]

An entire generation, the largest in our history, has a stake in homeownership costs and has already begun to feel the pressure of sudden increases. What do these young families do when they discover how expensive suburban homes are? So far, a very large number of them have decided to make financial sacrifices rather than give up the idea of homeownership. Despite high prices single-family construction reached near-record levels in 1976 and 1977. Most buyers of new homes already owned other houses that they were able to sell in a rising market in order to find money for the downpayment. People trying to buy homes for the first time were not so fortunate. Most of these families managed to raise the money they needed only by pooling the incomes of husbands and working wives. Families whose total incomes were near the national average of $15,000 were able to buy new houses only by taking on exceptionally heavy mortgage commitments that absorbed a third or more of their incomes for housing expenses.

Stopping Suburban Homebuilding

While one large group of people was beating the bushes trying to find affordable housing in the suburbs, another group, smaller but influential, was doing its best to stop suburban homebuilding wherever possible—or at least to make sure that whatever was built was expensive. This coalition against homebuilding consisted of suburbanites who feared it would bring higher taxes and damaging social consequences, environmentalists concerned about the impact of growth on the natural landscape, and local government officials sympathetic to these views.

Although local hostility to growth has attracted some national attention, very few reporters or researchers have connected it to the rising cost of new homes. These have been separate stories: headlines such as "Nation's Cities Fighting to Stem Growth" simply had nothing to do with the other headlines about the end of the American Dream. The growth control and environmental movements have had a very favorable press, stressing the widespread benefits they can achieve by protecting the quality of our common environment against the onslaught of the bulldozer.

A closer look at how the growth control and environmental coalition operates in local controversies shows that its effects are far less benign. It has made a clear and substantial contribution to the escalation of new home prices; yet its success in discouraging homebuilding has failed to produce important environmental benefits for the public at large. Instead it has protected the environmental, social, and economic advantages of established suburban residents who live near land that could be used for new housing.

This book investigates a national anti-growth movement by concentrating on California. Why California? First, the local politics of no-growth has reached a stage of maturity there—particularly around San Francisco—that makes it possible to see clearly who opposes homebuilding and for what reasons. Other parts of the country can also qualify in this respect, but California has a further advantage. The effects of local growth decisions on the cost and availability of housing are very hard to measure. Analytical techniques are not sensitive enough to trace the effects of regulatory policies unless there is a concentration of similar policies within a single housing market. San Francisco has had a massive concentration of growth restrictions, to an extent unmatched elsewhere. The controversies reported in the following chapters alone eliminated housing units equal to half a year's normal building volume in the San Francisco region. Other housing disputes not reported here bring the probable total to the equivalent of a full year's normal homebuilding wiped out by local opposition between 1970 and 1977. This regulatory squeeze was serious enough to show some of the ways no-growth politics affect housing consumers.

Why is California the outstanding national example of opposition to homebuilding? During most of its history California welcomed newcomers. Through the mid-1960s its local governments were making plans for more growth. By the early 1970s one community after another began putting up barriers to keep out new residents and electing officials who ran on no-growth platforms. Even such strongholds of local boosterism as San Jose rejected their earlier belief in the unqualified benefits of growth and reversed direction abruptly.

One of the reasons for this reversal on growth was the wave of urban develop-ment that swept across California in the 1960s. Builders worked overtime not only to keep up with the move to suburbia that the whole country experienced but also to make room for the huge migration that was special to California. The results were visible all over. To many people, continued growth looked like a threat to the qualities that attracted them to California in the first place—its spacious communities, magnificent scenery, and outstanding resources for the good life of outdoor leisure.

Resistance to growth began as a very reasonable political shift, concentrating on saving such priceless assets as San Francisco Bay and Napa Valley wine country. But as it gathered power, and as people discovered they could stop growth at little cost to themselves, the movement became a good deal less reasonable. Soon it turned into general hostility toward homebuilding for the average family, using the rhetoric of environmental protection in order to look after the narrow interests of people who got to the suburbs first. In short, the pendulum swung from one extreme on growth to the other, pausing for only a split second in the middle.

The politics of no-growth required the invention of new tactics to discourage homebuilding. Local government staff and consultants rose to the occasion. Their tactics included putting land into agricultural preserves, declaring mora-toria on new water and sewer connections, setting explicit growth quotas, establishing service boundaries beyond which there would be no extensions of utility lines, charging thousands of dollars in "hook-up" fees for each new house as a price for local public services, and creating a climate of hostility that encouraged all opposition groups to bring pressure against proposed new devel-opments. Residents opposed to growth tested and polished their own tech-niques, which included making strategic use of public hearings, putting develop-ment issues on the ballot for popular vote, and bringing lawsuits that could tie up housing proposals for years.

Wherever possible suburban governments used methods that cost their own taxpayers nothing and that shifted the financial burden of their policies to new homebuyers, to the state's taxpayers at large, or to the federal government. In Marin County, north of San Francisco, persuading the federal government to buy land for a national seashore was a key part of the plan for restricting new urban development. Once the federal government had bought the land, however, local residents decided that the environment was much too fragile to withstand recreational activity. As a result they blocked the construction of new roads to the federal lands, and they opposed recreational facilities within the national seashore that might have attracted visitors. This scheme amounts to charging the rest of the country for a plan to freeze local land from development, and then not letting outsiders come to visit the land they have bought.

One-Sided Governmental Reviews

Growth restrictions and environmental controversies quickly affected a very high proportion of all the homebuilding in the San Francisco region. Between 1972 and 1975 environmental lawsuits alone challenged developments containing 29,000 new housing units, in an area that normally builds only 45,000 units each year. And in the new political and legal climate, stopping homebuilding soon became easy—so easy that even a lone boy scout doing an ecology project was able to bring construction to a halt on a 200-unit condominium project in San Francisco.

A close look at the controversies around San Francisco also helps explain what makes the new no-growth policies so effective. Opponents of growth for whatever reason—tax worries, snobbery, concern for the environment—have been able to exploit weaknesses in an elaborate process of local development reviews. The process had built-in biases against homebuilding to begin with. Numerous governmental bodies have to pass on new development proposals, and most of them act only after conducting studies and holding public hearings. The long sequence of reviews gives the opposition plenty of time to organize their campaign and then hands them repeated chances to block new developments. All the cases described in the following chapters illustrate both the complexity and the duration of these reviews. The longest review took one development proposal through nine years of regulatory proceedings before county officials finally killed it.

The review process is highly political, and the people with the greatest stake in its outcome—housing consumers—play no part in it. People who want to buy new homes come from all over the metropolitan area. They are unorganized, and probably unorganizable, since there is no way of knowing who they are until they turn up to look at new houses. Local governments conduct the reviews, and they are responsive to their own constituents who already live in the community. The only person at the bargaining table who has a commitment to building is the developer. By default, he is left to represent the interests of potential buyers. He does not represent them very well, for two reasons. First, there are conflicts of interest between the developer and his clients. He is ready to make costly compromises at their expense if that is the only way to get his permit. More important, he carries little weight in local controversies. Both the public and local officials consider him not so much a legitimate businessman as a snake-oil salesman coming through town to fleece the natives. "Rapist of the landscape" is the usual term for him. With little political clout in local circles, and with even less respect, he is in no position to speak for anyone.

The public hearings on new development proposals demonstrate mainly that new housing has no local constituency. Some local residents do have a stake in construction jobs, and they account for most of the small support development proposals are able to generate. Most residents, however, and most of the public hearings are concerned with the possible damage or inconvenience new construction may cause the people already living in the community.

Local reviews do not provide a balanced interpretation of the consequences of growth. They consistently exaggerate the problems that new housing might create. The public hearings have a theatrical quality that encourages speakers to simplify and dramatize all issues, including those of growth impact. In addition, the technical studies that local governments sponsor in order to analyze development impacts are themselves unbalanced. They lean heavily on speculative assumptions about events that nobody can foresee very clearly, and the results owe more to value judgments and political orientations than they do to scientific research.

In the controversies described in this book, the official government studies were usually drawn up in a political climate hostile to new development, and the results showed it. By making "worst case" assumptions, these studies were able to forecast hazards and dangers that could be prevented only by blocking whatever homebuilding was proposed. When private consultants furnished reasonably balanced technical reports to one government agency, its own staff rewrote them to emphasize a whole series of negative impacts that were highly unlikely to happen, including an imagined threat to our national bird the bald eagle. These revisions gave the county government good protection against the inevitable lawsuits charging that their studies were inadequate. But they did not provide a factual basis that local officials could use to reach a fair judgment. In another case the environmental impact report made an issue of alleged danger to a rare snake whose presence in the area was never verified, and to a presumably rare red-legged frog that turned out to be neither rare nor endangered.

Redeeming Environmental Virtues?

The actual issues that lead people to oppose homebuilding are hard to discover. By far the most frequent objections that growth opponents raise have to do with environmental impacts. These range from harm to wildlife to destruction of natural resources to increases in air pollution. Yet to label all protest as environmentalism would be a mistake. Many growth opponents use environmental arguments to mask other motives, such as fears of property tax increases or anxieties about keeping their community exclusive. Environmental rhetoric has become a valued currency for public debate, with much greater voter appeal than arguments that appear more narrowly self-interested. As a result people who are not environmentalists in any sense often borrow it for their own purposes.

A large number of growth opponents are environmentalists, however. Local environmental organizations often give testimony against housing proposals at public hearings and often bring lawsuits to stop developments. Some groups seem to oppose almost any growth, others are committed to protecting only certain natural areas that interest them, while still others oppose only certain kinds of developments. Still, the prominence of these organizations in development controversies does not mean that all or even most environmentalists have joined the attack on new housing. Many environmentalists save their political activity for such issues as nuclear power or natural resources and take no part in local growth debates. And within the organizations that do take positions on community growth, there are diverse views: the national leadership is usually more willing to strike compromises between housing and environmental priorities than are local chapters. So the performance of environmental activists in California does not add up to an indictment of the environmental movement at large.

But neither is it true that the only growth opponents who use environmental arguments are impostors or members of fringe groups. Growth opponents often include respected local environmental organizations as well, who might be expected to offer cogent environmental reasons for their opposition. Yet the reasons they actually cite are a tangle of contradictions that must raise suspicions about their motives.

Sierra Club chapters, for example, have opposed some suburban housing on the grounds that it would generate unnecessary long-distance commuting; have opposed other housing near suburban job centers on the grounds that it should be located closer to the central cities; and have opposed new housing near the central cities on the grounds that it would use up scarce open space there. Another California environmental group, People for Open Space, has objected to housing in the valleys near San Francisco because the valley soil is better suited to farming, and it has opposed new construction on the hillsides because it claims hill developments will increase the chances of landslides, floods, and fires.

Environmental opponents also waver between judging new developments in terms of their region-wide impacts and judging them in terms of very local impacts. As a result they argue against some housing developments on the grounds that they are poorly located from a regional point of view, while they argue against others that are in better regional locations on the grounds that their local environmental impacts will be undesirable. Growth management studies usually take a regional perspective and argue for efficient use of land through compact development. Yet environmental activists try to limit growth by pressing homebuilders to cut the amount of housing in individual projects, and, therefore, to build at lower densities that make less efficient use of land. In one case environmentalists helped defeat a proposal that was favorable to both regional and local environmental considerations, apparently on the principle that the best development is no development at all.

Environmental opposition to homebuilding has almost no connection to mainstream conservation issues, such as reducing pollution and eliminating environmental health hazards. Housing proposals seldom conflict with these goals. (In the rare cases when they do, it is usually possible to solve specific environmental problems without blocking entire developments.) Stopping homebuilding usually accomplishes nothing for the public environment. It protects certain tightly regulated communities against change, but shifts development to other places where there is less resistance. The net environmental gain for the metropolitan area is zero, and sometimes less than zero. Environmental groups have helped to stop a series of housing developments located within short commuting distances of the main job centers around San Francisco. The result has been to push homebuilding farther out to scattered sites at the fringes of the urban area, where the new residents will use more gas and pollute more air while they drive longer distances to work.

A consistent environmental theme against homebuilding is simply the need to save open space. The ideological source for this position is not conservationism, which stresses the wise use of resources, but rather the preservation movement. The open space that local growth opponents want is usually for private preserves, not public parks. Preservationists form effective alliances with other resident groups whose concerns are to protect their own social and tax advantages. Together they use the rhetoric of public purpose in fighting new housing, but the goals they pursue are mostly ideological and private ones. They try to guard well-to-do suburbs against change, and the environment they protect is a local environment their affluent members can afford to enjoy.

Housing Consequences

Growth restrictions and housing controversies around San Francisco have combined to limit and delay new homebuilding, to raise its cost, and to restrict the places within the region where homebuyers with modest incomes can afford to live. Some local regulations have added to construction costs by reducing the supply of building sites and imposing high hook-up fees for public services. More generally, the new politics of no-growth have raised costs by creating delays, uncertainties, and pressures for developers to make expensive revisions in their plans. At a time of rapid national escalation in building costs, delays wiped out opportunities to build when it was still possible to produce homes that middle-income families could easily afford. The demands of growth opponents compounded the inflationary effects of delay by forcing developers to make big reductions in the amount of housing and to increase the amount of open space within their projects. These compromises inevitably raised the development cost per home to the point where moderate-cost housing was no longer feasible.

In Oakland a controversy that lasted from 1971 to 1976 led one homebuilder to cut 90 percent of the housing from a middle-income development he originally proposed and to convert most of his land into estate lots for luxury homes. In Alameda four years of controversy led another developer to eliminate two-thirds of the units he proposed, and to market the remaining third at three times the original price.

Local growth policies help explain why the San Francisco area has had much greater increases in housing prices than the rest of the country. New home prices almost doubled in metropolitan San Francisco between 1970 and 1977. The slow pace of new construction, despite a surge of housing demand, fueled a speculative boom in 1976 and 1977 that sent the average price for a new home over $75,000. This was nearly one and one-half times the national average, and it was the highest price level in any of the major metropolitan areas. The high price of new homes led to increasing demand for older houses and helped drive their 1977 average price up to $71,000, which was also one and one-half times the national figure for existing home sales.

Other Fallout

Growth policies have had far-reaching consequences, including some that boomeranged against the communities responsible for them. Marin County, for example, deliberately avoided tapping new sources of drinking water in the early 1970s because growth opponents were afraid that more water would encourage more development. Beginning in 1975, northern California had three abnormally dry years. Marin County with its very limited water supply was hit first and hardest. Water rationing began there early in 1976, and the rations were cut to a bare minimum by 1977. Although the national press attributed Marin County's shortage to unusual weather, the drought in Marin County was largely man-made, a result of its own growth-control policies.

Conspicuous among the victims of the water shortage were the county's dairy farmers. Earlier the county had placed their land in a special agricultural zone that permitted housing developments only if each house was on a lot of at least 60 acres, as part of a plan for restricting growth. Dairy farmers had objected to the zoning but were outvoted. Now, unable to sell their land for urban development, they had to pay exorbitant costs to bring water for their cows in rented tank trucks.

Marin County's policies, which included a water hook-up moratorium in most places where new housing was feasible, had exceptional success in deflecting growth. Not surprisingly, the county also had exceptional increases in the cost of single-family homes, both new and old. As the value of older homes escalated in a tight market, county assessors increased property valuations by as much as 40 percent. Property owners facing big tax increases were quick to protest the new assessments, but few seemed to realize that their problem was related to the county's growth policies.

The anger of Marin County's taxpayers was a prelude to the California taxpayer revolt that sent shock waves rolling eastward in the spring of 1978. Restrictive growth policies in both northern and southern California held up construction while housing demand took a sudden spurt after the recession of 1974-75. Lot shortages, and big increases in the time it took to get building permits, prevented homebuilders from responding to the turnaround in local housing markets. Families with mortgage money in hand waited in long lines to bid on the few new homes that were ready and then paid top prices for whatever they could find, new or old. Speculators soon moved in to turn a quick profit by buying houses for resale at even higher prices a few months later. In Los Angeles and Orange County, average sales prices for new homes jumped by almost 30 percent from 1975 to 1976. By 1977 San Francisco and Los Angeles led the country in home prices, with San Diego not far behind.

California's efficient assessors promptly marked up house valuations throughout the state to the newly inflated levels, creating windfalls in property tax collections for the cities and counties. Organizers of an initiative campaign had no trouble collecting signatures to put Proposition 13, a tax-limiting constitutional amendment, before the voters in June, 1978. It passed by a 2 to 1 margin, requiring a rollback of property valuations to the 1975-76 levels and setting a ceiling of 1 percent on future property taxes. The immediate fiscal result was a predicted cut in local property tax collections from $12 billion to about $5 billion a year. The immediate political results were a governmental crisis in California and a conviction among public officials across the country that they would have to reduce spending or face more taxpayer uprisings. But comments on Proposition 13 in the national press overlooked almost completely the role of housing inflation in getting the taxpayers fighting mad and the local growth policies that triggered this whole chain of events.

Beyond California, local governments in most parts of the country have also been inventing and applying new ways to limit growth. On the national scene the attack on homebuilding is not as new an event as in California. It follows on the heels of an earlier successful movement to exclude housing for poor people and minority groups from the suburbs. Suburban interests formerly managed to defeat legal challenges to their exclusionary zoning and to block federal policies that aimed at opening the suburbs to subsidized housing. Now a new alliance combining environmentalists with the old protectors of the suburban status quo has come up with techniques for keeping out not only the poor but even the middle class. These new devices have not been very successful so far in stopping homebuilding across the nation, but the evidence suggests that they have restricted its location and made it unnecessarily expensive.

Local growth controls are important contributors to the recent increase in house prices, but by no means the dominant cause. The basic cost-push comes from factors such as high interest rates, energy prices, and rising costs of building materials and labor. While policy-makers and economists search for national strategies to cope with the underlying inflation, local restrictions are working to make that inflation worse for housing than it is for most consumer items. In addition to better strategies for containing inflation, the country also needs better local housing policies.

The Debate Over Regulation

The new restrictions surrounding homebuilding are also important for reasons that go beyond the nation's housing needs. They are part of a striking increase in government regulation that spread far across the country's economic life in the 1970s, reaching from job safety to energy supply to automobile design. Understanding what the new regulations do to housing can help clarify an emerging national debate about the meaning of government regulation for American society.

Most of the new regulations began with a promise to protect the public against some hazard. Their most noticeable outcome, however, has not been the promised protection but a growing number of rules and guidelines, hearings, inspections, permit requirements, administrative orders, and lawsuits. As a result the costs of regulations are becoming painfully clear, even to people who were sympathetic to their purposes and had urged them in the first place.

A case in point is Harvard University, supplier of top-level presidential advisors who helped recent administrations in Washington expand the federal role in domestic affairs. Even this citadel of academia has begun to have doubts about government regulation now that it has had a first-hand look at the enforcement procedures. The Harvard president's report for 1974–75 reviewed Harvard's relationships with the government and complained that "in a few short years, universities have been encumbered with a formidable body of regulations, some of which seem unnecessary and most of which cause needless confusion, administrative expense and red tape." According to the report, faculty members at Harvard spent a total of 60,000 hours complying with federal regulations during the academic year. For the university at large, the cost of administering five major government programs ran from 5 to 8 million dollars a year.

Similar encounters with bureaucracy have prompted many people to wonder whether the new regulations are accomplishing enough to justify the trouble and expense they cause. And there are no ready answers. Scholars who studied the older regulatory agencies found them often under the control of industries they were supposed to regulate. Yet this pattern of regulatory capture clearly does not apply to most of the new agencies, which are flourishing in an atmosphere hostile to compromise. Most of them were created only after a public and media outcry about some evil that demanded government intervention, such as pollution, health hazards, pension swindles, or dangerous consumer products. Most have broad powers to compel compliance, based on tough legislation passed over the objections of affected business interests. And the governmental resources committed to regulation are both impressive and costly. At the federal level alone, 100,000 employees and 83 agencies were at work regulating some private activity by the mid-1970s; as many as 34 of the agencies were created after 1960.[6]

Almost all the regulatory programs are achieving something, but many observers question whether they are achieving very much. Some analysts of public policy believe the benefits are mostly symbolic. Aaron Wildavsky, in a review of the massive clean-up program of the Delaware River Basin Commission, concludes that even this expensive five-state effort will leave the river still "unswimmable, unboatable, and unsightly." "That isn't much," he contends, "for around three-quarters of a billion dollars, not much, that is, if you value results. But if the process of cleaning—'Out, damned spot!'—is what you value, if the act of purification is what you aim at, then the whole thing is a rip-roaring success."[7]

Similarly, Merril Eisenbud, New York City's first environmental protection administrator, argues that the nation's environmental protection programs are directing huge sums of money into projects with small payoffs, while neglecting activities that would be far more productive. "We aren't keeping our eyes on what is truly important—the health and well-being of people—and on cost-benefit ratios—how much we can improve health with a given expenditure of money resources," he says. "What is amazing to me is how our American society, which venerates practicality and bottom-line reasoning, can have gone so far wrong."[8]

The debate over regulation raises many questions about purposes, priorities, and costs. Some have to do with the nature of the results. Others center on who benefits—whether the public at large or some special interest group. Equally important, and even more uncertain, is the question of who pays the bill for these benefits, Although the political rhetoric surrounding regulation usually speaks only of expenses imposed on industry, the indirect costs to consumers may also be very great. Further, critics are asking whether government action is creating problems of inequity by imposing substantial costs on some people in order to produce benefits for others.

An investigation of the new housing controls turns up disturbing evidence on all these points: the public benefits are small, costs to the consumer big, and inequities unmistakable. California's painful experience, as front-runner in the rush to regulate growth, amounts to a demonstration of how the new regulation can be turned against the average young family.

Chapter 2
From Pro-Growth to No-Growth in California

California, more than any other part of the country, has come to symbolize growth and the belief that growth is good. Its power to draw people from all over the world started with the gold rush. As the West was settled and the railroads reached California, its farmland, natural resources, climate, and economic opportunities kept the migrants coming in record numbers. Since 1900, California's growth has consistently been at least twice the national rate, and from 1940 to 1970 it grew more than twice as fast as any other state, nearly tripling its population in thirty years.

Californians have thrived on the growth their state attracted. Until recently they did their best to encourage more. A large part of the business community, including firms in construction, finance, land development, transportation, trade, and services, owed its prosperity to the high rate of population increase. And a strong current of civic pride and boosterism helped enshrine growth in the consciousness of many Californians. During the 1960s Californians demonstrated a special sense of excitement as their state overtook New York to become first in population in the country—a large electric sign near the Oakland Bay Bridge displayed the changing tally day-by-day.

Yet there has also been a growing undercurrent of doubt about the desirability of growth. In the late 1960s state government and many cities began taking steps to manage growth more carefully, to control the effects it might have on the natural environment, and in some cases to place limits on it. Public officials discovered unsuspected political support for proposals to control growth.

The turnabout of attitudes has been most complete in the San Francisco Bay Area. There, a drive for increased public control over the area's future development has had exceptional success. What the advocates of growth control have done with their success, however, raises troublesome questions about how the new politics of urban development will affect most people.

The Bay Area, like the rest of California, went through a binge of rapid growth between the 1940s and the late 1960s. From 1940 to 1970 its population increased more than two and one-half times to a total of 4.6 million people. During the peak growth years of the early 1960s there was a net in-migration of from 70,000 to 80,000 people each year.[1] Although the pace of growth was more moderate than in the land rush of southern California, it still brought with it the usual tract housing, suburban shopping centers, industrial parks, and new highways. The result was a highly visible change in the character of the region.

San Francisco's natural setting is remarkable for its variety, its distinctiveness, and its beauty. Its magnificent bay, rolling hills, tall mountains, seacoast, and towering trees create splendid panoramas that people can enjoy from vantage points throughout the region. The city of San Francisco itself, with its tightly clustered houses climbing the hillsides and overlooking the bay, is outstanding for its scenery. In short, the environment of the San Francisco area deserves to be protected. The growth of the 1950s and 1960s did not engulf it, but it did pose a threat for the future if similar developments were to continue unchecked. Those who sensed this threat were able to rally public opinion behind them, in large part because what was threatened was so highly visible and so widely enjoyed.

In little more than ten years the political climate turned quickly from support of growth, to control of growth, to hostility to growth. Several early steps had to do with the transportation system. In the late 1950s many San Franciscans objected to a proposed elevated highway along the waterfront, which would have cut off views of the bay and of the historic ferry terminal building from the downtown business district. This was one of the first of a wave of urban highway protests across the country. In San Francisco it succeeded only after construction of the Embarcadero freeway had already begun, but it stopped that highway in mid-air at the ferry terminal. In 1964 a similar protest blocked construction of a freeway through Golden Gate Park.

Concern over the impact of urban growth also led to the construction of the Bay Area Rapid Transit (BART) system, the first new subway system in the country since the turn of the century. When plans for the subway were first drawn up in the 1950s, civic leaders in San Francisco, as elsewhere, thought of "urban sprawl" as the major problem created by metropolitan expansion. Urban sprawl meant the type of development epitomized in Los Angeles, but actually taking place around most of the major cities wherever new suburbs were spreading across the land. When middle-income families, industry, and businesses joined the flight to suburbia, it also meant the decline of central cities. San Francisco's civic leaders became committed to the BART system as the centerpiece of their strategy for managing urban growth. It would protect and strengthen the economic vitality of downtown San Francisco while also channeling suburban development into a series of compact centers near the outlying transit stations. Compact, high-density growth would also be an effective way to protect the still-abundant supply of open space throughout the region.[2]

In 1962 voters in the San Francisco area approved a record bond issue for $792 million to get construction started. The BART system's history illustrates not only widespread popular concern for managing urban growth and a willingness to back that concern with tax money but also a less admirable tendency of many growth control plans to distribute costs and benefits unfairly. In the case of BART, extra funding from local sales taxes, as well as state and federal aid, supplemented the original property tax levy earmarked to pay off the bond issue. Residents of the three counties in the BART district pay most of the capital and operating costs through property and retail sales taxes. As a result of the regressive impact of these taxes, families with low and moderate incomes contribute much higher proportions of their earnings to the BART system than families in middle- and upper-income brackets. Yet, thanks to the system's successful design to attract long-distance suburban commuters, the passengers are mainly middle- and upper-income people. A recent analysis concludes: "The poor are paying and the rich are riding."[3]

The Bay and the Vineyards

Another campaign early in the 1960s brought a halt to a type of development that was especially damaging to the region's natural environment. Local governments and private developers had been filling the shallow waters along the shoreline of San Francisco Bay to create sites for industry, housing, and municipal projects. The bay itself—one of the most distinctive features of the area, a prized resource for recreation and beauty, and a contributor to the region's natural air conditioning in summertime—had become a source of inexpensive land for development. One study of proposed dredging and filling operations raised the distinct possibility that within the foreseeable future the bay would shrink to the size of a shipping channel.

A small group of prominent women associated with the University of California publicized the threat to the bay, organized citizen groups, and made contact with influential members of the state legislature. A coalition of conservation and civic groups worked effectively with legislative leaders to set up a special study commission in 1964 and, a year later, to get legislation establishing the Bay Conservation and Development Commission. The legislature gave this commission a three-year life with power to control filling and dredging in the bay and a mandate to prepare a long-term plan for its conservation. After another intense campaign, the 1969 legislature made the commission a permanent agency with authority to continue protecting the bay by restricting landfill operations.[4]

Another of the region's scenic delights and tourist attractions was also facing an uncertain future in the 1960s. This was the Napa Valley, renowned for the vineyards that produce some of California's best wines. Homebuilders were beginning to build suburban houses there, and the state highway department had plans for a freeway running the length of the valley. Napa County officials began to worry about vineyard land that would be taken for the highway as well as housing developments that the highway might encourage.

Their worries, however, had more to do with financing local government than with saving the scenery. The vineyards made up close to half of Napa County's property tax base. And in contrast to residential areas or even to industrial parks, the wine producers demanded very little from the county in the way of public service. One report spoke of the desirability of "maintaining and perpetuating an industry that generates a high tax revenue for the County without requiring or demanding any supportive service facilities in order to maintain its productivity. That is, the industry . . . generates a pure revenue tax."[5]

The county supervisors decided to create an agricultural preserve, taking advantage of recent state legislation that authorized reduced assessments for farmland whose owners signed agreements promising to withhold it from development for at least ten years. Establishment of an agricultural preserve was a way of reducing the pressure for land development by keeping property taxes low. Further, it was a way of stopping the freeway since the state highway department was prohibited from building freeways through preserves set up under the state law.

County staff recommended a rezoning from the prior one-acre minimum lot size to a new 20-acre minimum lot size. They based the new figure on a study that showed 20 acres to be the minimum land area needed for agriculture. The zoning they proposed would have permitted any agricultural activity (not only vineyards), or else one single-family house per 20-acre lot. At preliminary hearings "everyone and his brother" asked to have his property excluded from the zone.[6] The county supervisors made a few modifications in the zone, redrew it to cover 25,000 acres of the valley, and adopted the new zoning in April 1968.

Although the new zoning gave effective protection to the scenic and tax-producing vineyards, this action once again raised questions of equity because of the way it distributed costs and benefits. Most landowners were angry. They called attention to the fact that the study used as a basis for the zoning had found 20 acres to be the necessary minimum size for economically viable agriculture. Yet they pointed out that 79 percent of the parcels in the preserve were less than 20 acres in size. The owners of small, marginal vineyards lost opportunities to sell their land for development. Neighboring homeowners, on the other hand, had their scenic views protected, and, indeed, homebuilding on hillsides adjoining the preserve soon accelerated, with developers building expensive houses on one-acre lots. The suburban residents of Napa County who enjoyed most of the benefits were overwhelmingly in favor of preserving the vineyards, and they had the votes.

Within the preserve the owners of large vineyards who intended to keep on producing wine also benefited from the reduced assessments. The small landowners, however, paid the cost of the scenic preservation. A spokesman for the opposition described the costs and benefits this way:

The establishment of the Preserve is to the benefit of everyone outside of its boundaries and a detriment to everyone within who will "pick up the tab for it," except for the vintners. . . . The Preserve is for the benefit of the man who wants to drive through the Valley and see the joys and beauties of the vineyards, but who has no economic stake in it. It is for the benefit of the man who has a home on the hill and who likes to look down on the vineyards. It is for the benefit of the people outside the Preserves . . . their tax bills will be less . . . as a result of reduced population. It is for the benefit of the man outside the Preserve who wants to sell his land; his land has enhanced in value. . . . [7]

Moving Beyond Growth Management

By the early 1970s action to manage and control growth was turning into action to stop growth. In addition to the momentum generated by a series of successful campaigns around the San Francisco area, local groups by then were also able to make use of new programs created by state government.

One of these programs was a series of measures designed to protect farmland and other open space from urban development. In 1965 the legislature passed the California Land Conservation Act, better known as the Williamson Act, which was the basis for Napa County's protection of its vineyards. Its stated purposes included protecting prime agricultural land as well as preserving farmland for its value as open space. The act authorized cities and counties to set up agricultural preserves. Within these areas property owners could enter into agreements with the local government to continue the land in agricultural use for at least 10 years. After signing the agreement, the landowner was entitled to a preferential tax assessment and to compensation that would offset future tax increases.

This act, however, could not authorize any drastic reduction in assessments because California's constitution required that all property be assessed at fair market value. Therefore, in 1966 the state's voters approved a constitutional amendment permitting below-market assessments for land whose use was restricted to agriculture or open space. The legislature then spelled out a special method for assessing land under Williamson Act agreements on the basis of its agricultural income rather than its market value.

In 1969 the legislature extended the program by redefining the type of land that could be included in agricultural preserves. The new provisions changed the emphasis from preservation of prime agricultural land to preservation of open space. Then, to encourage more aggressive local use of the program, the state began to appropriate funds to compensate cities and counties for property tax revenues they would lose by reducing assessments within established preserves. By 1976 the state was spending about $16 million per year to reimburse local governments for some of the lost tax revenues. Local taxpayers made up for the rest of an estimated $60 million in Williamson Act tax losses.[8]

The Spread of Environmental Regulation

Public interest in environmental issues continued to grow, spurred on in part by national media coverage of "the environmental crisis," which by the late 1960s had replaced the earlier "urban crisis." In California particularly, environmentalism took on the character of a political movement. The building blocks for a movement were already there in the form of a large number of citizen groups concerned with conservation and environmental protection. Each political success encouraged more political action. In 1966 the conservation groups joined together for lobbying purposes and set up the Planning and Conservation League with a full-time legislative staff in Sacramento. The league operated effectively on behalf of nearly a hundred affiliated organizations whose legislative interests ranged from auto emission controls to protection of open space, billboard regulation, and state planning. The oldest environmental group, the Sierra Club, had its own lobbying operation with considerable influence in state government.

The legislature passed a series of laws that opened the way to increased public control of urban growth. In 1969 the Porter-Cologne Water Quality Act gave the State Water Resources Control Board the power to stop development in any area violating water quality standards. The board did not hesitate to use its power, or to extend it. In 1970 it tied up new construction in San Francisco and five other

Bay Area communities by blocking new sewer connections there until the waste disposal system came up to standard. In 1973 the board moved to stop growth in communities violating clean air standards. Using its authority to review state and federal grants for sewage treatment systems, it decided to block these funds from reaching areas with air pollution problems until the local governments took action to stabilize their population at present levels.

"This policy by no means forces communities to cut off growth," in the opinion of the board's vice chairman. "We're just saying that we can't use federal and state money to induce growth that pollutes the environment of already overloaded basins. The community can build as big a plant as it wants and make as many connections to it as it pleases, but it will have to pay those extra costs itself—and, of course, make sure that our regulations aren't exceeded in the process."[9]

Next the legislature passed the California Environmental Quality Act, which political observers interpreted as a legislative response to Earth Day. This 1970 law parallels the National Environmental Policy Act of 1969 in requiring environmental impact reports for projects likely to have a significant effect on the environment. As in the case of the federal law, this requirement proved to be a sleeper.

The California act required state and local government agencies to prepare environmental impact reports for projects they proposed, but environmental groups went to court to try to broaden this requirement to include private developments as well. In 1972 the State Supreme Court interpreted the intent of the act as applying to private projects as well as public ones.

The court's decision had a profound effect on local growth politics. It forced local governments to confront environmental issues directly whenever they had to make decisions about land development. The impact reports often set the terms of debate at public hearings on housing proposals, and the environmental review process gave local citizens opportunities to challenge developments they opposed, either at public hearings or in the courts.[10] By 1976 California was producing 4,000 environmental impact reports a year—four times as many as the federal government.[11]

The California Environmental Quality Act also produced a large number of lawsuits—at least 244 through 1975.[12] Recent cases typically involve charges that an environmental impact report is inadequate, but their real significance is that they are a way of putting pressure on local governments and private builders to come to terms with groups that oppose new development. "Lawsuits have a

number of advantages," according to a handbook prepared for local environmental organizations. "First of all, there is obviously a chance of winning the
suit. However, the mere threat of a suit can also be an impressive political
tactic. . . . And finally, suits can be an effective delaying tactic in order to force
compromises. Developers may want to postpone their project until the Court has
cleared their status, or the Court itself may issue an injunction or temporary
restraining order. Extensive delay may even force the developer to abandon his
plans due to financing difficulties."[13]

The California Environmental Quality Act also added a professional constituency to the interest groups that were already concerned with environmental
regulation. By requiring several thousand environmental impact reports each
year, the act generated new work for natural scientists, soils engineers, and other
technical specialists. People who prepare environmental impact reports organized
a new professional society, the Association of Environmental Professionals, early
in 1975. By mid-1976 they had 700 members, had made contact with state
legislators, and were keeping a watchful eye on new environmental bills in
Sacramento. They were concerned with improving the quality and usefulness of
environmental assessments, but they also had an obvious stake in establishing
their work as a continuing function of state and local government.

Protecting the Coast

Environmental causes do well at the ballot box as well as in the state legislature.
In 1972 an alliance of environmental organizations committed to protecting
California's thousand-mile coastline became convinced that the legislature was
not prepared to take effective action at that time. They decided to go directly to
the voters with an initiative campaign. A hurried signature drive succeeded in
putting an ambitious regulatory proposal on the November 1972 ballot. The
coastal zone initiative, known as Proposition 20, proposed setting up six regional
commissions, as well as a state Coastal Zone Conservation Commission, with
power to stop or regulate development up to a thousand yards inland and with a
charge to plan for the conservation of a much wider coastal zone before the end
of 1975.

The campaign over Proposition 20 was intense and often bitter. Its supporters
included the League of Women Voters, National Council of Senior Citizens, the
American Association of University Women, the University of California Student
Association, the California Congress of Parents and Teachers, as well as the

Sierra Club and several dozen environmental groups. It had the unprecedented endorsement of sixty members of the state legislature, including the assembly speaker and the senate president, as well as the support of both U.S. senators from California. Arguments in favor of the measure often sounded like a crusade against the California business establishment. Senate President James R. Mills wrote:

Over $1 million will probably be spent by wealthy special interests to defeat Proposition 20. Their campaign tactics are designed to deceive and confuse the voters. They want our few remaining miles of beaches left as they are—available for development by them in any way they want. . . .

Unless Proposition 20 is approved the "public be damned" attitude of the special interests will prevail.[14]

In the opposition were, indeed, numerous members of the California business establishment including the state chamber of commerce, manufacturers' association, and real estate association; Standard Oil of California together with other oil companies; Pacific Gas and Electric and other utilities; and many firms in real estate and manufacturing. Labor unions were also active in the opposition, including the Building and Construction Trades Council, the Council of Carpenters, and the Fishermen's and Allied Workers' Union.[15] The opposition tried to raise some important equity arguments. A labor union brochure, for example, spoke of the "loss of millions of dollars and thousands of jobs in needed development projects, jobs especially important to racial and economic minorities in the construction industry." Another opposition pamphlet argued that coastal zone conservation would lead to exclusion, rather than access, for the average person: "Only a favored few would benefit from the coastal "deep freeze," those with the physical and monetary resources to enjoy the beaches by backpacking and horseback riding and who would "lock up" the beaches from the general public; and those owners of established beach homes in exclusive areas whose property values would increase when people of moderate means are prohibited from sharing amenities."[16]

But arguments about social equity were suspect when they came from people who had a clear economic self-interest in promoting coastal development. Proposition 20 won by a majority of 55 percent, contrary to most expectations. The coastal zone commissions were soon in business, and although they permitted many developments to proceed (some with modifications), they blocked numerous others and took a very broad view of their mandate to regulate growth. In an Orange County decision, for example, they followed the example of the State Water Resources Control Board by imposing a growth limitation as the solution to a problem of declining air quality in the area. Before permitting the outfall line of a sewage treatment system to pass through the coastal zone, they insisted on reducing the system's ultimate capacity from a planned population of 220,000 to one of 174,000, thus lowering the limit for future growth.[17]

Coastal zone regulation also produced a controversy in San Francisco that came to symbolize the new style of growth politics and that struck fear into the hearts of homebuilders around the country as they learned of it at national conferences and trade association meetings. While writing a report on San Francisco's Lake Merced for an eagle scout project, 16-year-old Allan Riley discovered that a real estate developer was planning to build a 200-unit condominium project on its shore. He thought the development would be harmful to the lake and began to raise questions about it before several city agencies responsible for issuing the necessary permits. Despite his objections the city agencies approved the project early in 1973.

The passage of Proposition 20 the previous November, however, raised a question of whether the developer would have to go before the coastal commission as well. The housing was located well outside the thousand-yard coastal permit zone, but the boy scout discovered a minor provision that extended the thousand-yard zone further inland around the shore of any body of water that lies partly within a thousand yards of the ocean, as Lake Merced does. He went to court and got an injunction blocking a start on the project until the coastal commission could review it. With the help of two high school friends, he pursued the case doggedly before the regional coastal commission and then the state commission. Despite his objections that the project would be damaging ecologically, both commissions approved it.

At that point a San Francisco attorney volunteered her services to help the boys file a lawsuit against the coastal commission. Although construction had already begun, the court found the coastal commission had acted improperly in its handling of the case and ordered a review. The commission, though, decided to appeal the decision, and the boys went back to court to try to get another injunction stopping construction pending the outcome of the appeal. The judge refused to issue another injunction, but instead urged them to settle out of court. They agreed to drop their fight in exchange for an acre of property near Lake Merced worth approximately $50,000, plus $100,000 in cash which they put into a fund to finance environmental causes. Gerson Bakar, the developer, estimated the fight had cost him—and the families who bought his condominiums—a total of $400,000 in delays, legal fees, interest costs, and the final settlement.

What disturbed homebuilders around the country was the power shift that enabled a lone boy scout to block a major project for a year and a half, as well as the shift in values that made it possible for an eagle scout project to lead to this harassment.[18]

San Francisco Suburbs Change Course

The growing web of development controls in California, together with the emerging political strength of the environmental movement, created an atmosphere that encouraged many local communities to rethink their policies on growth. Several San Francisco suburbs were beginning to feel the pains of the rapid expansion they had experienced during the 1960s. Among them was the East Bay city of Livermore, whose population had gone from 16,000 in 1960 to 38,000 by 1970. The schools were getting crowded, the sewage treatment system was approaching its capacity, water reserves were not great enough to cope with peak demand days, and air pollution was becoming a problem.

A small group of long-time residents decided it was time to reverse the city's growth policies. They formed a citizens' committee, expanded their membership to 200, collected donations, and with outside legal help drafted an initiative to go on the ballot at the next city council election. Their proposal called for a moratorium on residential building permits until the city had found satisfactory solutions to its problems with schools, water, and sewage. It specified the solutions as no double sessions in the schools and no overcrowded classrooms as defined by the California Education Code, sewage treatment facilities and capacities that would meet the standards of the regional water quality control board, and a water supply adequate to meet anticipated demand with sufficient reserves for fire protection. In a single weekend they gathered three times as many signatures as they needed to put their measure on the ballot. In the election of April 1972 the voters passed the initiative by a comfortable margin and also elected two new city councilmen who took positions in favor of it.

A homebuilders' association promptly went to court to contest the ordinance, and in December 1972 the trial court declared it invalid. In addition to raising questions about the standards specified for solutions to the city's problems—the California Education Code, for example, authorizes local school boards to set their own standards for overcrowding—the trial judge noted that there was nothing in the ordinance requiring the city to try to solve these problems. The ordinance, in effect, allowed Livermore to freeze growth rather than solve its problems.[19]

Livermore appealed the decision and meanwhile figured out other ways to discourage growth. First, the city adopted an expensive set of development fees adding up to some $4,400 for a typical small house. These included a residential construction tax, city and county water fees, a park fee, storm drain and sewer connection fees, and a school fee of $850 per house. Second, Livermore used the tactic of limiting the expansion of utility systems in order to restrict further growth. Having identified a problem of inadequate sewage treatment capacity, the city then made plans for only a small increase in its system—too small to accommodate much additional housing.

Then local officials reviewed their policies on annexation of nearby territory. As interpreted by homebuilders trying to operate in the area, the new policy was to refuse to annex land developed for housing, while encouraging annexations of industrial or business development—a policy well calculated to protect the fiscal interests of present residents. Consistent with the annexation policy, city officials decided against extending water and sewer lines to land beyond the city limits.[20]

In December 1976, however, the initiative ordinance of 1972 got a new lease on life when the California Supreme Court upheld it. The majority opinion recognized "the growing conflict between the efforts of suburban communities to check disorderly development with its concomitant problems of air and water pollution and inadequate public facilities, and the increasing public need for adequate housing opportunities." Nevertheless, it held that such laws as the Livermore measure are "constitutional if they are reasonably related to the welfare of the region affected by the ordinance."[21] As a result the case was sent back to trial court for a determination of the regional impact.

Even San Jose

San Jose is the environmentalists' favorite horror story. They frighten each other and the public with the cautionary tale of how the beautiful, flowering orchards of the Santa Clara Valley were paved over to become part of the sprawling city of San Jose, with a Los Angeles-like appearance that has earned it a reputation as the northernmost part of southern California. The facts of the story are true, although people with different values reach different conclusions about it. A more balanced view comes from a well-known architectural guide to northern California:

Nowhere has more productive soil been paved over, more beautiful agricultural landscape transformed into endless tract houses, strip commercial development and wirescape—a garden demolished. Yet in its place has emerged a new garden for people. Santa Clara Valley now shelters hundreds of thousands of working people and their families. It provides them with nearly every imaginable service close at hand. And it blesses them, as it did the prunes, with a particularly salubrious climate only lately somewhat blemished by nitrous oxide emissions.[22]

An important element in the cautionary tale is that the residents of San Jose themselves welcomed, encouraged, and publicized the growth that brought such violent change to their environment. Before 1920 San Jose was a sleepy marketing center for an incredibly rich agricultural area that produced more than one-third of all the prunes in the world, as well as big crops of apricots and walnuts. Its chief growth booster was the manager of the local chamber of commerce, who made a film about the Santa Clara Valley in 1921 in order to promote his vision of San Jose as a dynamic and prosperous city and to attract the people who would make it grow. He called it "The Valley of the Heart's Delight."[23]

San Jose's population grew to about 70,000 before World War II and then took off at an incredible rate during the great California boom of the 1950s and 1960s. Industry—especially electronics, aerospace, and manufacturing—joined the rush, and San Jose went from 95,000 people in 1950 to almost 450,000 in 1970. During much of this period it was the fastest-growing city in the entire country. And, as a result of an aggressive annexation policy, San Jose increased its land area from 17 square miles in 1950 to 147 by the early 1970s. Growth on this scale created an economy that gave many people a stake in continued growth. Construction became a major industry, and retail trade flourished on population growth. The political leadership of the community, including the daily *San Jose Mercury-News,* maintained a long-standing commitment to continued expansion.

It was an important event, therefore, when San Jose began to take steps to discourage future growth, not so much because its measures were innovative or tough but because they meant that public opinion was turning against growth even in San Jose. In the 1960s there were signs that city services were not keeping up with the new demands. Schools were crowded, roads were becoming congested, and air pollution was becoming more noticeable. And the voters, troubled by rising tax rates, began to turn down bond issues for public improvements. Two pro-growth candidates for the city council were defeated in 1969 elections, and the pro-growth city manager retired soon afterward. In 1970 the city council declared in an urban development policy statement that its goal was to "insure that San Jose's future growth will proceed in an orderly, planned manner to achieve a balanced composition of industrial, commercial, residential and public uses."[24]

The city government also took a decisive step to control future growth. It divided the vacant land around San Jose into three districts: an urban service area, urban transition area, and urban reserve. The new development policy limits almost all future development to the urban service area. By redrawing its boundaries from time to time, the city can effectively control both the amount and location of new growth.[25]

School problems led to a more publicized citizen campaign for growth control in 1973. Parents and teachers who were dissatisfied with crowding and double sessions in some of San Jose's schools tried to persuade school officials and the city council to block new housing developments in areas where the schools were already overcrowded. Although they had some success in working out a new procedure to force negotiations among developers, school districts, and the city council, they decided to use a voter initiative to impose tighter restrictions. Their proposal was to prohibit the city council from zoning any additional land for housing in areas where the schools were already overcrowded (according to specified standards) or where the proposed development would create such overcrowding. Additional zoning would be permitted only if the developer entered into an agreement with the local school district to provide whatever extra classroom space was needed. Even where the standards were met, if the local school district objected to a zoning change on the basis of its school impact, rezoning would require a five-to-two vote of the city council instead of the usual simple majority.[26]

During a short campaign before the election, supporters of the initiative used simple arguments: "Stop! Control of City Hall by Developers. Rampant Growth. Double Sessions in Your Schools." The *San Jose Mercury-News,* on the other side, called the measure a "deep freeze," argued that it would put people out of work, and that it would say "newcomers unwanted." The newspaper urged "bond issues, not moratoriums" as a solution. The measure won a narrow victory at the polls, with stronger support coming from the newer parts of the city and from those areas where schools were crowded.[27]

The initiative campaign brought other political changes. Three city council candidates who supported it also won, and the following year San Jose elected a new mayor who campaigned on a platform of "managed, controlled growth."[28]

The new zoning restriction did not stop new building, but it probably slowed its pace and increased its cost. From April 1973, when the ordinance was adopted, through the end of January 1975, San Jose processed 135 zoning applications in 16 different school districts. Although some were disapproved, none were turned down for reasons related to school crowding. In all, the proportion of San Jose building permits going to areas with crowded schools dropped from 82 percent the year before the initiative was passed to 75 percent the following year, which may indicate that some developers decided to avoid heavily impacted areas.

Many builders were able to negotiate agreements with local school districts. Through the end of January 1975, 79 agreements were signed, producing a total of $315,000 in cash contributions from developers to six different school districts. These charges generally ranged between $120 and $320 per home. Most of the money was to go for renting portable classrooms as a temporary measure to relieve overcrowding.

Meanwhile, the crowding that gave rise to the initiative has become less serious. All six school districts were able to eliminate double sessions by the end of 1976. Whether this easing resulted more from new growth controls or from a decline in the school-age population, however, is not known.[29]

Despite the improvement in school conditions, San Jose continued to tighten the screws on future development. The city council extended the initiative ordinance beyond its original expiration date in 1975 and imposed development moratoria in two different parts of the city. Traffic congestion was the reason for one and flood hazards for the other. The moratoria together removed 3,400 acres from the defined urban service area. In addition, the council had second thoughts about a commitment it had made in 1970 to keep the urban service area large enough to accommodate five years of normal growth. The 1975 revision of the urban development policy concluded that "the city is no longer able to maintain a supply of developable land which accommodates five years of projected growth, and in fact may be unable to expand much beyond the existing area."[30]

This urban development policy greatly reduced the amount of vacant land available for development in San Jose. With the demand for new housing still very strong, the reduction in land supply undoubtedly increased lot costs for new homebuilding. In addition, the review procedures for new developments became more complicated, more time-consuming, and more uncertain. These factors, too, probably increased the cost of new homes.

A study commissioned by the Urban Land Institute compared the cost of building identical homes in San Jose during the pro-growth period of the late 1960s and during the period when the new growth controls were taking effect in the 1970s. Between 1967 and 1976 the price of one type of new home increased by 80 percent, from $25,000 to $45,000. The price of the other increased by 121 percent between 1968 and 1976, going from $22,000 to $49,000. On the basis of a careful breakdown of development costs, Claude and Nina Gruen estimated that at least 20 to 30 percent of these housing cost increases to the consumer resulted directly from San Jose's local growth management.[31]

Another study by the Rand Corporation found that the new growth controls also brought about important changes in the informal negotiations between local officials and homebuilders. These changes in turn had adverse effects on the quality of new developments. As one developer put it, "the bureaucracies are larger, the rules are more numerous, and there is no inclination to 'find the way' to do something. Today we have to do what there already is a way for."[32]

The Rand Corporation study found developers avoiding subdivision and housing designs that were subject to increasingly uncertain discretionary reviews. Yet this result ran counter to the goals of San Jose's growth management policy. One of San Jose's major goals was to reduce the urban sprawl created by single-family homes on free-standing lots spread across large land areas. One preferred alternative was to build planned unit developments with the homes clustered together and with common open space rather than large lots for individual houses. Another was to build moderate-density housing, such as town houses or condominiums. Five of the nine developers interviewed for the Rand study reported that they were avoiding planned unit developments because delays and difficulties of negotiating their plans with city agencies had become too costly. Also, many of the builders were reluctant to build moderate-density housing because the rezoning necessary for it led to prolonged hearings and hostility from neighboring residents. Thus the developers were returning increasingly to traditional single-family detached houses on separate lots in order to minimize their contacts with city officials.[33]

The new growth controls, then, increased the price that homebuyers had to pay in order to get into San Jose, while reducing the variety of housing types available to them. The campaigns and debates that led up to tighter growth controls gave almost no attention to the effects they might have on families who want to buy new homes. Whether the new regulations also produced the benefits of less crowded schools and more orderly growth still remains to be seen.

Petaluma: World Fame through Overregulation

When the British journal, *The Economist,* published a special section on the west coast in December 1975, its accompanying map of Washington, Oregon, and California showed just a few of the major cities in the San Francisco area: San Francisco, Berkeley, Oakland, San Jose—and Petaluma. That was a big gain in recognition for a city of 25,000 that until recently was known mainly as the chicken-and-egg capital of northern California.

What made Petaluma world famous was its unusual attempt to set an annual quota for new homebuilding, together with the court cases this quota system generated. Putting a ceiling on building permits was such a direct and obvious way of stopping new growth that homebuilders feared it would set a precedent for other communities around the country. To people concerned about exclusionary land use practices, Petaluma became a symbol of hostility to growth, just as earlier San Jose had come to symbolize enthusiasm for growth.

Like other communities prominent in the growth-control movement, Petaluma changed its policies abruptly, on the rebound from a period of rapid growth with very little regulation. Highway improvements during the late 1950s, combined with the outward expansion of the San Francisco Bay Area, brought it increasingly within commuting range of San Francisco even though it lies 40 miles to the north. Its population began to climb, going from 14,000 in 1960 to 25,000 in 1970. During the early 1960s new homebuilding averaged only about 250 units per year. In 1968, however, the city issued permits for almost 500 units and, after a drop back toward the 400 level in 1969, for 643 units in 1970 and 880 units in 1971.

Most of the new homebuilding was in the eastern part of town where easy zoning made it possible to build inexpensive homes on 6,000-square-foot lots. The sudden spurt of growth soon led to double sessions in the schools and complaints about inadequate parks and playgrounds. Further, the new growth was rapidly using up the capacity of the sewage treatment system.

In October 1970, city officials held an informal meeting with local developers to go over their construction plans for 1971. They learned that nine major homebuilders were planning to build another 1,200 housing units, all in the troubled area east of Highway 101. After consulting with the city manager and the planning commission, the city council put a temporary moratorium on new development early in 1971 in order to gain time to complete a planning study and work out a development policy. During the next year the city sent out a questionnaire to its residents on growth issues, appointed a citizens' committee to organize a development policy conference, adopted an official development policy, and met with homebuilders to discuss how to implement a proposed environmental design plan.

The council adopted a target of rolling the growth level back to an average of 500 units per year for the next five years. In April 1972 it approved construction of 500 units that had been held up by the moratorium, and later that year adopted its new residential development control system. The purpose of the new system was both to control the timing of growth, so that the city could phase in new schoolrooms and water and sewer capacity to keep pace with it, and to carry out a series of very detailed objectives spelled out in the newly adopted environmental design plan. These included balancing new development between the eastern and western parts of town, increasing the supply of apartments, encouraging some high-density housing near the central business district, providing for a wide range of sales prices and rents, and improving the quality of housing and site design.

Under the control system the city decided the total number of housing units to be permitted each year and then divided this quota into the number of units in east, central, and west Petaluma, and within each area into the number of apartment and single-family units. A residential development evaluation board then reviewed all development applications for the coming year and sorted them into the appropriate categories by location and housing type. Within each category the board ranked each proposal in competition with the others according to an elaborate point system.

Points were awarded according to the availability of each of a series of local public facilities and services (ranked from very poor to excellent); for the design quality of buildings, landscaping, and the site plan; for the provision of open space and foot or bicycle paths; for the provision of needed public facilities such as major streets or additional schoolrooms; for the extent to which the development promotes contiguous growth rather than leapfrogging; and for the construction of housing for low- and moderate-income families. The board then awarded its quota of building permits to the proposals within each category that had the highest point total.

According to Frank Gray, Director of Community Development, homebuilders objected most to having to compete with others for their allotments, but the competition had many advantages for the city. It enabled the council to see what the total building pattern would be for an entire year and to avoid scattered developments such as those that led to sprawl in San Jose. Also the city's small staff was able to process subdivision plans much more efficiently in a batch than if they had come in one at a time during the year.

The system got off to a rocky start because of outside events. In 1972–73, to end the moratorium, the city council awarded allotments to all units in the pipeline without using the allocation or point system. The new system did not go into full effect until 1973–74. Then, after a year, it was suspended because the Construction Industry Association of Sonoma County won a lawsuit against the city in Federal District Court. In August 1975, however, the U.S. Court of Appeals reversed the trial court decision, essentially on the ground that the Construction Industry Association lacked the standing to sue on behalf of people who might have been excluded from living in Petaluma. In 1975–76 and again in 1976–77, the system was back in full operation.

The major problem with this system was that it could not find enough developments to fill its various quotas for different parts of town and different types of housing. Even though developers were anxious to build in Petaluma, their proposals did not fit into the neat boxes laid out by the development control scheme. In particular, developers were not prepared to build as many units in western and central Petaluma as the city wanted. Thus in 1975–76, the city was unable to fill any part of its quota of 25 single-family units for central Petaluma, and in the west it was able to award only 91 units rather than the 150 units in its quota. Further, some developments fell by the wayside even after they received their allotments. They either failed to survive the later regulatory hurdles of subdivision control and building permit review or the developer abandoned them for reasons of his own. Thus for the three years when the system was in full operation, the control board authorized an average of 382 units per year rather than the intended 500, and of these an average of only 307 per year were either built or under construction by mid-1976.

The city's inability to get enough proposals to fill its quotas would not have been a problem if its actual intent were simply to discourage as much growth as possible. But if the city's intent was to keep growth on target, then the over-regulation created a problem. According to the community development director, "We don't want more than 6 percent growth per year; we also don't want much less. There are capital facilities—especially water and sewer—that need to be paid for and were built with 6 percent annual growth in mind, so we do want close to 6 percent growth."[34]

As a result of the residential development control system, Petaluma by 1976 no longer had a problem of too much growth. Instead it had a problem of underbuilding. Plans for 1977-78 were to reallocate 400 units that had been awarded earlier but never built and to monitor more closely in the future what happens after the allotments are made. But the entire system, which was initially adopted for a five-year period, was being restudied.

Gray nevertheless claimed other benefits for the system. It succeeded in shifting some development to the western sector, even though not as much as the city wanted, and it also increased the number of apartment units in the east. As an unanticipated effect the difficulty of getting new building permits encouraged rehabilitation of many fine old Victorian houses in the central and western parts of the city. The classroom shortage was no longer as severe in 1976 as it was in 1971, but a drop in the school-age population was probably as responsible for this as the control system. In Gray's opinion the competition for building permits improved the quality of site design and layout, and encouraged the addition of such features as bike paths and recreation areas. He conceded that these would at the same time raise the cost of housing to the homebuyer.

Interviews with local homebuilders revealed that city government spokesmen had been in touch with several to say that they were very eager to get more building, and that next year Petaluma would approve "almost anything" — a policy not exactly conducive to the careful growth management implied by the point-rating system. When one homebuilder told city officials how hard it was to build in Petaluma, they told him not to worry, they would get his plan through. "But," he says, "the fact is they can't because the system is too cumbersome."

Developers complained particularly about long processing times for development, often two years or more. These resulted partly from the fact that the control board had only a single processing cycle each year and partly from the fact that other regulators in the city government were slow and imposed extra requirements of their own. The building department, for example, asked one developer to build a bicycle path on public land adjoining his housing at a cost of $27,000. The homebuilder considered this an extra and unfair requirement that city staff imposed because "they think they have you by the 'throat.' " Developers also argued that the point system was very subjective. They contended that different members of the control board awarded their points very differently and that basically the individual members decided which development they liked and then awarded the points to make them come out high. As a result the point system failed to give very clear guides to developers.

The long processing times and uncertainties of review apparently did succeed in raising development costs, though. Homebuilders had to pay for very long options on land or had to pay carrying charges for long periods of time before they could build. Both homebuilders I interviewed estimated that comparable new homes cost $3,000 to $4,000 more in Petaluma than in nearby cities. Both, in fact, preferred to build homes in other cities in Sonoma County, even though they are farther away from San Francisco. One found that he was able to build a house of higher quality in nearby Rohnert Park than he could for the same price range in Petaluma.

Despite their reservations, however, both builders operated in Petaluma before the growth control system was instituted and both continued to build at least some housing there afterward. They were living with the system but not happy with it, and fearful enough of local vindictiveness so that neither wanted to be quoted.

Environmentalists in California are fond of saying that we live in an age of limits. The Petaluma experience suggests that there are also limits to the amount of regulation that can successfully be heaped onto homebuilders. Petaluma's growth controls were less than successful because homebuilders did not interpret market demand in ways that matched the city's highly detailed objectives. What the regulators wanted was not the same as what consumers would buy, at least as the homebuilders judged consumer demand. But the Petaluma regulations probably raised the cost of whatever new housing was built in the community, although the cost increases appear to have been less than in San Jose.[35]

Chapter 3
Better Living through Environmentalism

Many communities in northern California are making use of new tactics to protect their environment and control their growth, but none have matched the record of Marin County for thoroughness, dedication, and ingenuity. Marin County, a wealthy suburb north of San Francisco, is the best place to look for an understanding of what it means to stop suburban growth in the name of environmental protection. It means closing the gates to people who may want to move in and, where possible, even to people who may want to visit; turning to state and federal governments for help in paying the costs of exclusivity; and maintaining a tone of moral righteousness while providing a better living environment for the established residents. Finding policies to suit these purposes has not been easy, however, even in the favorable political climate of Marin County. Recent growth controls succeeded in blocking homebuilding in most parts of the county, but they created unusual strains of their own, including a man-made water shortage. A look at the Marin County experience, therefore, also raises the question of whether a community can isolate itself fully from the inconveniences of the outside world without damaging itself in the process.

An Environment Worth Protecting

Marin County's natural setting could inspire even lukewarm environmentalists to militant action in its defense. Its southern tip begins at the Golden Gate Bridge, just across the water from San Francisco. From there it extends 50 miles along the rugged cliffs and sandy beaches of the Pacific coast. Most of the county's built-up communities are in its eastern sector, bordering the northern rim of San Francisco Bay and connected to the city by the county's only major highway, Route 101. Between the seacoast and the suburban homes along Route 101 lies a picturesque hilly area used mainly for dairy farming. The county's scenic vistas include sculptured hills, green in the spring and yellow most of the year, covered in part by eucalyptus trees and chaparral growth; many views of the bay and the ocean; redwood groves near the coast; and clear air everywhere.

These attractions encouraged a wave of homebuilding in the county during the 1960s when the population grew from 149,000 to 210,000. Although this growth was noticeable, and to some people even worrisome, it did not crowd the county's vast land resources. As of 1970 only 7 percent of the county's land had been developed while 50 percent was still in agricultural use and 26 percent was open land in public ownership.[1] Concern over future growth led the eleven cities within the county to join together with county government to prepare a long-range development plan. After four years of studies, discussions, and committee work, the Joint City-County Planning Council adopted a plan in 1973 that set the basic framework for Marin County growth policy.

The plan tries to reduce population growth in Marin County but still allow a moderate increase—to 260,000 by 1980 and 300,000 by 1990. In the absence of special controls the planning staff projected that population would otherwise increase to 297,000 by 1980 and to 365,000 by 1990.

The planners proposed not only to limit the amount of new development but also to channel it very carefully into selected locations. They divided the county into three corridors corresponding to the main geographic zones. A coastal recreation corridor with 37 percent of the county's land area would be devoted almost entirely to publicly owned open space. An inland rural corridor with 39 percent of the county's land area would be preserved for agriculture. Almost all new development would go into the "city-centered" corridor which contains 24 percent of the county's land area. Even here, however, only an additional 7,000 acres would be committed to development between 1970 and 1990. This modest increase means that within the most built-up sector of the county developed land was only 30 percent of the total acreage in 1970 and would rise to no more than 38 percent by 1990.[2]

The county plan set very minimal growth targets, but a look at recent events in Marin County shows that even these would let outsiders have greater access to Marin County than most residents were willing to accept.

Shifting the Cost of Exclusion

The county's strategy for protecting its land from development relies heavily on persuading the state and federal governments to pay most of the cost. In the coastal recreation corridor most of the land is in public parks. The largest holdings are federal—Point Reyes National Seashore, the Golden Gate National Recreation Area, and Muir Woods National Monument—and there are also several state and county parks. The 1973 county plan makes a logical claim on federal and state support to pay for these areas: "Because recreational facilities here primarily serve people from beyond Marin County, they should continue to be the responsibility of federal and state governments."[3]

But will these recreational facilities primarily serve people from beyond Marin County, or will they primarily serve Marin County residents? Intensive lobbying by local conservation groups and public officials led to federal land purchases for

Point Reyes in the early 1960s and for the Golden Gate recreation area in the early 1970s. During the long campaign to get federal support, proponents argued that these unique coastal resources deserved protection so that visitors from all parts of the country could come and enjoy them. Now that the federal government has bought the land, however, environmentally concerned residents have discovered that the ecosystems are extremely fragile and will not be able to withstand many visitors.

As the National Park Service began to make detailed plans for visitor centers, parking areas, campsites, and picnic grounds, intense local lobbying continued—only now the lobbying was against any facilities that might encourage visitors. The county supervisor representing this district, Gary Giacomini, reported in 1976 that he spent 90 percent of his time negotiating between West Marin people and the federal government: "Many of them now think it was a mistake to have the federal recreation areas. They're afraid of having four or five million visitors a year. Federal people have proposed some compromise plans so that this won't be like Yosemite, but any plans that will bring in visitors upset West Marin people. Park Service staff say that since federal taxpayers bought the land, they are entitled to come and use it. They also say they wish they had bought out the three or four towns around Point Reyes so there would be no opposition."[4]

Another way to prevent outsiders from using the national seashore and recreation area is to make it hard for anyone to get there by car. Existing roads connecting the Golden Gate Bridge and Route 101 to the coastal corridor are narrow, winding, and slow. In the mid-1960s the state highway department proposed two new freeways to connect Route 101 to Point Reyes, but strong local opposition stopped both of them. One of the objections was that new interchanges along the proposed freeways would encourage unwanted home-building in open areas between Route 101 and the coast.

Federal officials then came up with a plan designed to meet this objection. They proposed building a special limited-access national parkway to go from the Golden Gate Bridge directly to Point Reyes with no interchanges along the way that might encourage development. This plan fared no better. Tremendous local opposition and virtually no expressions of support led federal staff to shelve it in 1971. With unwanted development no longer an issue, what were the objections this time? According to the county plan, "Many citizens felt that no new roads should be built anywhere in the county, and especially not in the fragile environment of West Marin." Yet behind the concern for a fragile environment was another concern about outside visitors: "There was also considerable controversy about whether the parks and open areas of West Marin should be seen primarily as facilities that should be accessible to the public, or as national resources that should be preserved in their original condition."[5]

The county government, however, did not take an open position against public use of the publicly owned recreation areas. It simply opposed improved access to these areas by car, for environmental reasons. County policy favored the use of bus service and possibly other forms of public transit to bring people to coastal recreation areas. Whether vacationing families are willing to load camping gear, picnic equipment, and children onto buses in order to visit Point Reyes remains to be seen.

As for the existing two-lane roads that wind across Marin County to the seashore, the county proposed keeping them in their present condition as scenic highways. The county planners added nervously, however, that although these routes would qualify as scenic highways under state criteria, they should not be designated as such: "Showing routes to West Marin as scenic highways on state maps and signs would inevitably encourage visitors to drive, either to reach the coast or as a recreational experience in itself."[6]

Such attitudes toward public open space are by no means unusual among Marin County environmentalists. Consider the case of two University of California professors, Thomas Dickert and Robert Twiss, who interviewed 600 hikers on watershed lands owned by the Marin Municipal Water District, and returned in a state of shock at what they learned. The majority of the hikers interviewed believed that "there are already far too many people making use of the open space in California and . . . nothing should be done to encourage more widespread use." They suggested making access difficult and eliminating such comforts as tables and benches in order "to keep out those who are insufficiently dedicated to the open spaces." Further, the researchers concluded, "they [the hikers] believe that love of the out-of-doors can be measured by the amount of effort people are willing to expend in getting where they want to go and the amount of discomfort they are willing to experience once they get there." However, when the interviewers asked what should be done to make the wilderness more accessible to the elderly or the handicapped, most respondents said flatly, "Such people would simply have to forego the wilderness experience."[7]

In view of these findings, if it is true that how much people love open space can be measured by the trouble they are willing to endure in getting there, then what Marin County offers the federal taxpayer is a remarkable challenge to establish his credentials as a lover of nature.

No-Growth in the Growth Corridor

The city-centered corridor in the east is the area designated to receive almost all the new housing that will be built in Marin County through 1990. But the only part of the plan carried out so far is the part calling for a big increase in public open space within this zone. The countywide plan aimed at keeping more than 60 percent of the city-centered corridor undeveloped, even by 1990. To ward off development pressures, it proposed adding 31,000 acres of public open space while permitting less than 7,000 acres to go into development.

The county government moved quickly to start acquiring open space. In 1972 a countywide vote established an open space district with authority to add ten cents on top of the regular tax rate. By 1976 this tax yielded a million dollars a year, which the regional open space district used to buy up ridges and hilltops in the city corridor. City governments within the corridor also began buying up open space, financing their purchases through a series of bond issues and, in some cases, with matching funds from the regional open space district.

Groups of homeowners living in the eastern corridor soon joined the drive to protect open space, after figuring out how to get other people to pay part of the cost while reserving the land for their own private purposes. The first of these groups consisted of well-to-do homeowners living in Lucas Valley, San Rafael, a modern, planned development of 500 homes plus elaborate community facilities that brought sales prices of about $80,000 by 1976. During the 1960s Lucas Valley residents blocked plans to rebuild an adjacent road into one of the freeways intended to serve Point Reyes National Seashore.

In 1971 a developer proposed building townhouses or condominiums on a hillside site overlooking Lucas Valley. The homeowners association met and discovered that many of its members valued their view of the open hills so much thay they were willing to consider buying the entire hillside area to keep it from being developed. The owner was willing to sell the land to the homeowners association at a reasonable price, and a citizens' committee began to investigate ways of buying and managing the hillside.

The committee decided first on a set of principles that any proposal would have to meet before they would submit it to community residents. These conditions included: taking the hillside land off the county tax rolls, so that home-owners would not have to pay additional property taxes on it; and making sure that each homeowner's payment for his share of the land purchase would be tax-deductible on both California and federal income tax returns. Removing the land from the property tax rolls meant that taxpayers throughout the county would have to pay more in order for Lucas Valley to get its open space. Making the payments tax deductible would mean that taxpayers throughout California and throughout the United States would help Lucas Valley buy its open space.

The implied notion of a partnership with other people, however, did not extend to the use of the land. Another basic condition was that the homeowners association should keep control of the land. Still another was that the land should be designated as open space, not a park. The homeowners' board of directors then took a more explicit position on the use of the hillside. Its main use was to be for the visual enjoyment of the Lucas Valley community. In addition, they proposed making it available for limited grazing to accommodate the horse owners among them and opening it for limited hiking, but with no facilities that might attract outsiders, such as picnic tables, water, toilets, or marked trails.

The residents got what they wanted. The county board of supervisors agreed to extend the authority of an existing county fire service district so that it could also buy and manage parkland. This county service district could finance the purchase through a bond issue at the favorable interest rate that tax-exempt municipal bonds command in the investment market. Each homeowner would pay his share by having the principal and interest on the bonds added to his property tax. As part of the property tax payment, it would be an eligible deduction on state and federal income tax returns. Since the hillside would become county property, the board of supervisors would be responsible for it. The supervisors, however, agreed that they would take no action affecting the land without advice from the homeowners association board of directors, thus leaving the local residents effectively in charge of their own open space. In April 1972 the proposed bond issued won more than 95 percent of the votes in a special Lucas Valley election.

The result was that Lucas Valley homeowners created a private preserve and got it exempt from real estate taxes. They financed it at a favorable interest rate, thanks to the federal tax subsidy given to local government bond issues. They were then able to reduce their state and federal income tax obligations by deducting its cost as though it were a property tax expense. In recognition of this splendid action, the Marin County Board of Supervisors passed a resolution commending Lucas Valley residents for "distinguished public service."[8] The idea spread quickly. By the end of 1973, four more homeowner groups approved similar open space bond issues, and many more did the same afterward.

The Man-Made Drought
There is an old story about a struggling businessman who moved his failing shop out of town but soon returned driving a big Cadillac. When a fellow storekeeper asked why the sudden prosperity, he explained that a flood had wiped out his new store and enabled him to collect a handsome insurance settlement. His impoverished friend pondered this news and then asked, "Tell me, Sam, how do you make a flood?" Nobody has yet figured out how to make a flood, but in Marin County they know how to make a drought.

While the county, the cities, and homeowner associations were all busy fencing off open space in the county's one corridor designated for growth, opponents of new development there turned to still another tactic for blocking homebuilding. They decided to create a water shortage.

Until recently most municipal water districts in the country operated on the assumption that their purpose was to supply as much water as their customers demanded. In growing suburban areas such as Marin County, the water district normally brought new sources into its system about every ten years. By 1970 the district had six reservoirs, all located within Marin County. It supplied water to the great majority of people within the county, including all but one of the communities in the city-centered corridor. Anticipating future growth, and continuing past practices of increasing the water supply in order to meet it, the Marin Municipal Water District began making plans to bring in more water from sources outside the county.

In 1970 the district proposed a $12 million intertie with the adjoining North Marin Water District which gets its water from nearby Sonoma County. Voters approved the bond issue, but by a narrow margin.

A year later the district proposed a much more ambitious project, the Sonoma-Marin Aqueduct, to tap into a vast new water supply from the Russian River in northern California at a cost of $110 million. Opponents quickly challenged the proposal, arguing that it would encourage unwanted population growth. According to William R. Seeger, then general manager and chief engineer of the water district, "We immediately were challenged first for planning too far into the future, and secondly, for anticipating a growth rate not in conformity with that being planned by groups concerned with maintaining the county in its present state of development."[9]

The bond issue lost badly at the polls. Seeger reflected on the outcome and concluded: "Those wanting to use the water industry as a population-control device in effect say that they cannot depend on the planning and zoning regulations, boards of supervisors, city councils, etc., to hold the line on low density. They feel that the only sure way to keep the growth curve down is by limiting utilities. We found this out in Marin County, Calif., the hard way. We lost a bond issue 9:1. After a consistent track record of passing six general-obligation bond issues since 1916, with substantial margins of support, we were shocked."[10]

In the aftermath of the defeat, water district board members decided to fill a vacant seat by appointing a conservationist who might help them come to terms with the new mood among their constituents. Then another critic of past water policies won election to the board in 1972. A year later another conservationist, who had been active in Sierra Club politics, ran for election in a campaign that presented the key issue as growth vs. no-growth and stressed his opposition to bringing in water from Sonoma County. When he, too, was elected, the conservationists had a three-to-two majority on the board. They immediately declared a temporary moratorium on new water connections and in June 1973 voted to extend the moratorium indefinitely.[11]

The board, meanwhile, delayed building the intertie that had been approved and funded in 1970 while it worked on still another Russian River water plan to put before the voters. As first formulated, the new plan called for a bond issue of $32 million, but an early revision brought the cost down to $23 million. Still, members of the county board of supervisors doubted whether the voters would approve such an expensive project, and they charged the water district directors with deliberately concocting a losing bond issue so that they could then justify continuing the water moratorium. County supervisor Michael Wornum called the proposal a "Trojan horse."[12] After a joint meeting with the county supervisors, the water board agreed to cut its plans still further to a $7.5 million bond issue. Despite a request from the board of supervisors, however, the water district directors refused to give a formal endorsement to their own proposal. As supervisor Gary Giacomini put it, "It was the worst-managed bond proposal I've ever seen."[13]

Even the scaled-down proposal quickly came under fire. The issue was not how much it would cost, but how much growth it might bring. The Committee to Save Marin, known locally as the Green Panthers, circulated leaflets urging voters to turn down the proposal on the ground that "Marin should not become another Los Angeles." Another opponent wrote in the Sierra Club newsletter: "If we vote no . . . we will be giving our county government the message that we want growth to be planned and limited and that, if the planners can't find ways to make their recommendations work, then we must rely on utilities (which previously have been used as planning tools to develop an area) to control development."[14] Predictably voters turned down the bond issue, this time by a margin of two-to-one.

The water moratorium continued, preventing local officials from issuing new building permits in the city-centered corridor except for one community that got its water from a different district. After many delays the intertie voted in 1970 was replanned. Construction finally began in September 1975, but meanwhile the moratorium stayed in effect.

By 1975, however, Marin County's water politics had repercussions that went well beyond stopping new development in the eastern corridor. A drought that began that year quickly depleted local reservoirs to dangerously low levels. The district turned to emergency measures, starting with limited water rationing in March 1976. Because reduced water use cut the district's revenues, it promptly announced a 27-percent increase in water rates. By February 1977 the water board cut the ration down to 47 gallons per person per day and put into effect a plan for strict metering, which imposed high charges on any family going over its limit. "It's worse than a crisis; it's a disaster," said the new general manager.[15]

The three conservationists who had dominated water policy in 1973 were no longer living in the county by 1976. One of them took the trouble to write to the Marin County weekly newspaper:

"No-growth" was never a part of my platform. "No-growth" was, instead, a facile label misapplied by local newspapers. My actions on the MMWD[Marin Municipal Water District] board were aimed at protecting the water supply of existing users. I felt that voters should not be manipulated into voting for water bond issues because of the spectre of dry faucets.[16]

The *Pacific Sun* drew a sober conclusion in retrospect:

Those who advocated new sources were accused of trying to foster the interests of developers, of trying to "Los-Angelesize" the county. Those who opposed new sources of water were accused of trying to go outside the law, to "zone with water." What was given short shrift were staff warnings that, without new sources, a dry year or two could put the district in severe difficulties.[17]

Later other communities in northern California also had to turn to water conservation and rationing schemes, but Marin County had the earliest and the worst shortage. Although the national media attributed all the local shortages to a prolonged drought, Marin County's problems were largely the result of its own growth control politics. At a public meeting immediately after the first rationing scheme and price increase were imposed, speaker after speaker attacked the district's policies. They charged the water board with creating its own crisis by failing to seek new sources. "You must stop engaging in the control of water to restrict Marin's growth," said one spokesman to loud applause. The directors replied, however, that county voters had twice defeated bond issues aimed at bringing in the water.[18]

Despite the seriousness of the water shortage, some environmental groups continued their tactic of opposing new water in order to stop growth. In February 1976 the Marin Conservation League told its members that it had joined a lawsuit to try to stop construction of the Warm Springs Dam, which would provide a large amount of water in nearby Sonoma County. The league explained that it opposed the dam "because it tickets 42,500 acre feet of water annually for MMWD [Marin Municipal Water District]—(enough for 85,000 homes)—water which voters twice said they don't want."[19]

In western Marin County, residents responded to the water shortage in characteristic fashion: they stepped up their efforts to keep out visitors who might use up their scarce water. In the summer of 1976 the coastal town of Bolinas made plans to celebrate the nation's Bicentennial by putting up a roadblock. Just before the 4th of July weekend, residents posted a sign at the edge of town reading, "Town closed: Water Shortage and Fire Emergency." Local businessmen objected, however, and painted over the part of the sign reading, "Town closed." Instead volunteers flagged down oncoming cars and asked the drivers to go away because of the water shortage. Later the director of the local utility district made a statement warning tourists that they could expect to find no public toilets working and no place to wash their hands and asking them to please bring their own drinking water. [20]

Preserving Farmland—with No Water

The water shortage also posed a direct threat to what the countywide plan was trying to accomplish in the inland rural corridor. There, about four-fifths of the land was used for agriculture—mainly dairy farming, sheep ranching, and some cattle ranching. The countywide plan aimed at keeping almost all of this land still in agricultural use by 1990. But agriculture is already economically marginal in Marin County; feed for cattle needs to be trucked in long distances from

California's Central Valley and elsewhere. Government action will be necessary to encourage farmers to stay in business.

The county's strategy consists of a combination of assistance and regulation. County government offers 25 percent matching grants as well as low-interest loans to help farmers build holding ponds and install pollution abatement facilities to keep their cattle from fouling the streams. Also, the county managed to enroll about 60 percent of its farmland under Williamson Act agreements that lower property tax assessments. The state reimburses Marin County for a significant part of the lost property taxes, and other property-owners in the county pay more to make up for the rest of the tax losses on farmland. As a result taxpayers all over California share the cost of preserving farmland in Marin County.

The agreements that farm-owners sign in exchange for their tax reductions keep their land undeveloped for at least ten years. Beyond that, however, the county has used its zoning power to give the farms much more protection than most farmers want. Between 1970 and 1972 the county rezoned most of its farmland from what had been a low-density residential zone with a minimum lot size requirement of two acres. The new agricultural zone specified an incredible minimum lot size of 60 acres for any parcel sold for a single-family home. (In the eastern states, courts have been uneasy about approving local zoning with lot sizes as large as five acres. Marin County, however, is living up to California's motto, "Give me men to match my mountains," by pioneering in zoning to match her mountains.)

County supervisor Gary Giacomini described the way farmers reacted to the 60-acre zoning: "They crowded in here [to the County Office Building], threatened to smash windows, threatened lawsuits and then started some."[21] Later, according to Giacomini, they discovered that the value of their land continued to increase, and dairy farmers, especially, were happy not to have people living nearby with dogs that scare the cattle. Most want to keep the agricultural zoning, he reported, and those that started the lawsuits later withdrew them.

The county's reason for the agricultural zoning is clear enough. According to Sol Silver, chief of advanced planning in the county planning department, "The county wants the open space and, as a result of having agriculture, it doesn't have to buy the land."[22] However, the man-made water shortage came close to undoing the farmland preservation strategy. Dairy farmers depend on water from nearby creeks for their cows, and the creeks ran dry in the summer of 1976. Normally the water district would have sold them water, but in 1976 it had no surplus water to sell. A few months earlier, in March, the county supervisors tried a familiar ploy. To get the federal taxpayer to pick up the cost of Marin's exclusionary policies, they declared a state of local emergency that would make the farmers eligible for federal aid. The state and federal governments took no immediate action, however, and there was no outside assistance available during the summer.[23]

Many farmers began to bring in water in rented tank trucks, but the cost was high. Their harassed representative, Supervisor Giacomini, had this to say at the end of June: "We are in the midst of a crisis. If they can't get water soon, they'll sell their herds and be out of business. Then we can't have 60-acre zoning."

In 1976 the water district took emergency measures to bring in additional water from nearby districts through a temporary pipeline, and then the voters overwhelmingly endorsed a $17 million bond issue for a new reservoir. But neither action was able to give any immediate relief to the rationing system, the dairy farmers, or the moratorium on new hook-ups.

The Results of Growth Control

Marin County's growth control tactics undoubtedly reduced the volume of new homebuilding there below what it would otherwise have been. Because many factors influence housing markets, there is no sure way to trace the effects of specific growth restrictions; yet the evidence at hand strongly suggests that Marin County has succeeded in deflecting new housing to other parts of the San Francisco area.

The county is a highly desirable place to live, and during the 1960s it attracted a substantial amount of homebuilding. Between 1960 and 1969, 5.3 percent of all the new housing built in the nine-county San Francisco region went into Marin County. As other areas more accessible to San Francisco and to suburban job centers exhausted most of their vacant land, the normal course of metropolitan expansion would have given close-in Marin County, which had a huge supply of buildable land, a larger share of the region's new housing in the 1970s. Yet between 1970 and 1976 Marin County's share actually dropped to 4.7 percent. People wanting to live north of San Francisco and unable to find homes in Marin County are likely to look next in Sonoma County, which lies north of Marin and is still farther from San Francisco and the job centers of the East Bay and southern peninsula. Between 1960 and 1969 Sonoma County's share of new homebuilding was 4.5 percent. From 1970 through 1976, however, its share doubled, to 9.2 percent of the total.[24]

If there is strong demand for housing in any community and if there is very little construction to absorb this demand, then people who want to live there will probably have to pay premium prices for whatever housing is available. This is indeed the case in Marin County. In the early 1970s sales prices for both new and old single-family homes were consistently higher in Marin County than in any other county of the San Francisco area. By the end of 1974 the average single-family sales price (for new and old homes combined) was $55,700 in Marin County, compared to a Bay Area average of $45,600.[25]

New single-family tract houses also sold for much higher prices in Marin County than in the rest of the region. Of the tract houses completed between 1972 and 1974, 62 percent in Marin County sold for prices of $45,000 or more, compared with only 36 percent in this price category in the rest of the region.[26] These figures do not prove that growth controls alone are responsible for the high prices in Marin County since the county was also a high-price area in the 1960s. But growth restrictions in the 1970s surely contributed to the rapid cost increases.

If these interpretations are correct, and Marin County's policies have shifted some growth northward to Sonoma County and also have helped raise housing prices within Marin County, who has been hurt? Most families of average income who wanted to live in Marin County have been unable to do so. If they moved farther out from the city to Sonoma County as an alternative, they are probably commuting longer distances as a result. Other families who were able to afford Marin County houses probably paid more as a result of growth controls than would otherwise have been the case.

Did the citizens of Marin County fare well in this process? Some who owned their homes and considered them an investment were probably pleased to see their value go up steadily. Those who rented, however, and those with modest incomes who wanted to move to better homes, faced a budgetary strain if they wanted to buy in Marin County. County residents were slow to recognize the connection between growth controls and housing costs. Yet in time the rising cost of housing made a noticeable impact. By 1976 the *Pacific Sun,* Marin County's weekly newspaper, organized a citizen task force to look into how local people were coping with "the tremendous increases in the cost of keeping a roof over their heads in this county."[27]

Another little-noticed effect of restricted homebuilding is the rising value of older homes in a tight market. This effect does attract attention, however, when the assessors revalue older property as they did in Marin County in April 1976.

In some areas assessments increased by as much as 40 percent. Property owners facing bigger tax bills promptly besieged the county assessor's office to protest the new valuations.[28] Eventually, the passage of Proposition 13 in June 1978 protected homeowners from additional tax increases by rolling back assessments to the 1975–76 level and limiting the tax rate to 1 percent. This meant that Marin's residents could safely continue to restrict the county's growth without feeling much pain in their pocketbooks.

Stopping growth, Marin County style, has produced a few results that make even established residents unhappy, as well as other results that impose serious costs or limit choices for other people in the San Francisco area. The greatest cost, however, may be a subtle one: the legitimation of arrogant public policies designed to keep the average citizen from enjoying a good suburban life. Marin County's growth-control tactics draw their basic support from a climate of opinion that views the county as a heroic, beleaguered fortress fighting to stave off the forces of commercialism while preserving the higher values of dedication to environmental purity. A county planning department report, for example, was titled "Can the Last Place Last?" In this view present residents have almost unlimited rights to control the land and the environment around them in the cause of higher values, regardless of the consequences for others.

It is easy to justify selfish protectionism in the name of preserving environmental values. The Marin Ecumenical Association for Housing made this discovery when it tried to build 100 units of low- and moderate-income housing for the elderly. The association took an option on a former Dominican brothers' priory and made plans to remodel it. The neighbors immediately organized petition campaigns and brought two lawsuits, challenging the county's right to grant a permit for low-income housing in their area. After three years of litigation the housing association temporarily let its option lapse while waiting for a guarantee of federal financing. Neighborhood opponents immediately took advantage of this lapse to buy the property for $100,000 more than the housing association had offered.

"We paid dearly for our principles," the attorney for the neighborhood group explained. "This is a beautiful residential neighborhood. The use projected was inconsistent with the neighborhood and with what the neighbors wanted. We decided to preserve the character of the neighborhood. We had an opportunity to put our money where our mouth is." The neighbors explained that they were worried about inadequate sewage and water pipes, lowered property values, and the fact that the elderly residents would be too isolated from recreation, transportation, and shopping.[29]

Protecting the environment against low-income old people is only a step re-moved from the moral righteousness that surrounds other self-serving action in Marin County. Further, environmentalists outside the county reinforce the legitimacy of exclusionary policies by praising them as environmentally wise and courageous. According to the Stanford Environmental Law Society, for example, the lesson of the county's water politics is that the "voters of Marin have illustrated that they will not permit their public resources and services to be needlessly wasted, nor senselessly expanded, precipitating undesirable increases in population."[30]

After Marin County's water policies boomeranged, the most prominent environmental writer in the San Francisco area depicted the county as heroically paying the price for growth control. "The people of Marin," Harold Gilliam wrote in his column in the *San Francisco Chronicle*, "were among the first in any county in the U.S. to perceive the limits to growth and the fallacy of waste, and to translate the perception into action." In a county whose developed area is only 7 percent of its total land and whose median family income ranked fourth highest in the nation in 1970, this exaggerated conception of limits must raise questions about whether there is also a responsibility to share resources with the rest of society. But Gilliam's view is otherwise, and he speaks for many environmentalists when he writes:

Let it be proclaimed from the housetops: Our prodigal waste of limited re-sources cannot continue. Every step toward an ethic of conservation increases the chances that our children will inherit a civilization that can sustain itself. We may hope that the Marin experiment succeeds and inspires emulation else-where.[31]

Chapter 4
Raising Housing Costs by Environmental Politics

The clearest way to discover the effects of no-growth politics on homebuilding is to trace the history of housing developments that have been blocked or delayed as a result of local opposition. Finding examples poses no problem in northern California: the region is a graveyard of big development proposals. Contrary to a widespread belief, however, when housing proposals generate stiff opposition, developers do not usually persist with their original plans and simply raise prices enough to cover the cost of delays, legal proceedings, or other regulatory expenses. Instead, they compromise with their critics by cutting the number of moderate-cost houses in their plans and substituting a smaller number of houses that only high-income families can afford.

Making Moderate-Cost Homes into Luxury Estates

One typical controversy involved housing proposed in the foothills of Oakland, on a site offering superb views of San Francisco Bay, of the city of San Francisco across the water, and of the Golden Gate Bridge to the west. It was close to major freeways leading to the Oakland Bay Bridge and downtown San Francisco, and to other major routes serving the entire Bay Area. It was also the last large tract of open land in Oakland still in private ownership, and, therefore, its future was bound to attract the attention of groups concerned with open space.

In 1971 Challenge Developments, a California subsidiary of Alcoa, bought the land and made plans for a residential community of 2,200 families, with the housing divided almost evenly between single-family town houses and condominium apartments. The plans included a small lake to be created by damming a stream at the bottom of the valley, with a local shopping center and most of the apartments clustered alongside the lake. Of the total 685 acres more than two-thirds were to be set aside for parks and open space, with the housing concentrated on the rest. Challenge Developments expected to build for a middle-income market, with town house sales prices averaging $33,500 and condominium apartments averaging $23,750.

The proposal required city government approval as a planned unit development, but it seemed to pose no serious obstacles from the city's point of view. Just three years earlier the city council had adopted a statement of development policy for this area that included very explicit standards. The council's resolution called for keeping two-thirds of the property as open space, building a mix of housing types for a population not to exceed 6,500, and putting in a valley road and a ridge road as the main elements of a new circulation system. The plan met all these requirements, with room to spare: more than 70 percent of the land was set aside for open space, and total population was expected to reach only 5,400. The proposed circulation system included a major street along the ridge and a connecting road to the valley, but it did not require a street running the full length of the valley.

The developer had stayed well within the bounds of established city policy, but after 1968 public attitudes toward growth and toward open space had changed enough to make those established policies very shaky. When the city planning commission began to hold public hearings early in 1972, strong opposition emerged. An organization of nearby residents, "Citizens against Mountain Village," took the lead, while the San Francisco chapter of the Sierra Club, as well as many individuals, all joined in the opposition. Opponents focused on the fact that the project would make big changes in the landscape. The plan required cutting and filling along the most prominent ridgeline to create a platform for the new road as well as grading several large building pads where most of the houses would be concentrated. The main arguments against Mountain Village were that it would destroy the last large open space in the city that was still in private hands, would ruin a pleasant view of the ridge and a wooded ravine, would impose heavy school costs not covered by tax returns from the development, and would destroy a habitat for wildlife—principally deer, fox, opossum, gophers, salamanders, and several kinds of birds.

Midway through the public hearing the city planning department prepared a staff report summarizing the major issues.[1] Granting that the proposal was in conformity with existing city development policies, the planning department nevertheless noted that it raised new questions about the characteristics of acceptable development there, and about the advisability of any development. The report also commented that grading along the ridge was likely to be noticeable from a large portion of the city, but that the initial scars would disappear over time as the developer completed his landscaping. Also, the impact on wildlife and vegetation would be substantial, and "this ecosystem, though not of irreplaceable value, constitutes one of the last remaining natural areas in Oakland." As for school costs, the planning department found that a new school would be needed to serve the people of the area, noted that the school district did not have the funds to buy a school site or to build a school, and suggested that the most desirable way to finance it would be for the developer both to supply the site and build the school.

The city planning department recognized that much of the opposition to Mountain Village was basically opposition to growth rather than a concern over specfic negative impacts of this proposal. Its report presented a quick summary of the "no-growth" position as well as the counter-arguments that might be advanced for a "keep-growing" policy. The basic question it posed was "even if, upon analysis, it were found that there would be few negative implications resulting from the proposal . . . , would it not be better to retain the total area as open space?" The answer, according to the city planning department, depended more on one's values and philosophy than on an analysis of the consequences of building Mountain Village.

Still the department suggested a compromise between "no-growth" and "keep-growing" policies. According to this view there was a legitimate need for more housing in the city and in the region, and a close-in site, such as the property in question, was a better location for housing than either an outlying suburb far from jobs, or an already built-up and crowded neighborhood. Also, if the city were to buy more land for parks and recreation, low-income neighborhoods had more pressing needs than the area around Mountain Village, where people lived on spacious single-family lots and where there already were several large regional parks. This point of view led to the conclusion that, unless there was clear evidence that Mountain Village would damage the environment or overburden city services, the city should work with the developer to make whatever changes seemed desirable and should then approve the project.

Although the staff report avoided making a recommendation on the proposal, the compromise position it outlined did suggest a reasonable way of moving ahead. Further, the planning staff welcomed the offer by Challenge Developments to turn over 480 acres of its property for a city recreation area and characterized this land as having "the magnitude of a regional park." Before taking final action, the planning commission asked the mayor and city council for advice on whether Oakland might be able to come up with funds to buy the entire site as public open space. They learned that the city would be unable to raise enough money to buy the land even if it were able to get federal matching funds. With this information in hand, and after five public hearings, the planning commission approved the Mountain Village application in July 1972.

Having survived the first governmental review, the proposal moved next to the Oakland City Council. The council asked the city manager to do another staff study of the Mountain Village development, this time analyzing how much it would cost the city and the Oakland school district to provide services for the residents, and how much local tax revenue the project might generate. The manager's study found that Mountain Village would have a very favorable impact on the city's finances. After the development was complete, new tax revenues would exceed new service costs by a substantial margin, ranging from $400,000 to more than $600,000 per year, depending on the assumptions used for the forecast.[2]

For the Oakland school district, however, Mountain Village was likely to produce a deficit. A school enrollment forecast showed that a new elementary school would be needed for the area, as well as some expansion of existing junior and senior high schools, at a total cost of some $2.1 million. After the development was complete, school operating costs were still expected to exceed new school district revenues from Mountain Village by a margin ranging from $67,000 to more than $300,000 a year, depending on the exact assumptions. School officials described this to the city manager as "a tremendous burden . . . in light of our present crucial financial situation." They suggested that Challenge Developments pay for all new school construction and that the city of Oakland consider using its own resources to cover the annual operating deficit.[3]

The city council held its own series of public hearings where opponents of the project registered the same objections once more. A Sierra Club representative outlined the likely environmental impact and asked the city council to put off its decision until a more thorough environmental and economic study could be made. The council, however, appeared to be following the compromise position suggested by the earlier planning staff report and attempted to deal with whatever problems the proposal raised, while moving toward eventual approval. In October the council adopted a new requirement for a bedroom tax ($100 for each bedroom in a new home) to raise additional funds that would help offset the school costs.

Meanwhile an unforeseen event created fresh complications. Since 1970 the California Environmental Quality Act had required all governmental reviews of construction projects to give specific consideration to their environmental impacts. Most state and local officials believed the act did not apply to private developments but only to government projects. On September 21, 1972, as the council was completing its work on Mountain Village, the California Supreme Court handed down its decision in the Friends of Mammoth case, ruling that the Environmental Quality Act applied to private as well as public projects.

To comply with the Environmental Quality Act, the city planning staff quickly prepared a memo on Mountain Village and recommended that the planning commission endorse the proposal as consistent with the conservation element of Oakland's newly adopted general plan. The city planning commission promptly ruled that the project was in accord with the conservation element, and six days later the city council accepted this ruling and issued the necessary permit for a planned unit development.

At this point Mountain Village seemed to be moving ahead with reasonable speed. Despite neighborhood and Sierra Club opposition it had won local government approval after less than a year of review. The controversy over Mountain Village entered a new phase, however, when the opponents who were unsuccessful in dealing with city government turned instead to the courts. Less than a month after the city council action, Citizens against Mountain Village brought a lawsuit against the city and against the developer, charging that Oakland had failed to comply with California Environmental Quality Act requirements, and also with a minor provision of the Oakland planning code that required the council to make a specific finding whether residents of a new development would be adequately served by existing or proposed public services. The Sierra Club organized a wine-tasting event to raise legal funds, and filed an *amicus* brief in support of Citizens against Mountain Village. The lawsuit delayed further action, and then in June 1973 the court ruled against Oakland, holding that its conservation element did not meet the requirements of the California Environmental Quality Act and that, in addition, the council had failed to make the required finding that school facilities would be adequate for project residents.[4] Complying with the court order, the city council rescinded its earlier approval.

While the case was in court, Challenge Developments conducted lengthy negotiations with school superintendent Marcus Foster and members of his staff to try to find a solution to the problem of school costs. In August 1973 Challenge offered to supply a school site plus the site improvements needed for school construction. A month later project opponents brought a lawsuit against the school district and the developer to prevent the transfer of the school site without a public hearing. Then another unforeseen event further derailed the project. In November 1973 Marcus Foster was assassinated. Negotiations over school problems came to an abrupt halt.

Revision

With growing uncertainty surrounding the Mountain Village proposal, Challenge Developments shifted staff time and energy to other and more promising projects but still kept trying to get the necessary approval for Mountain Village. In 1974 they started work on an environmental impact report that would comply with the California Environmental Quality Act. Early in 1975 they completed a draft report, but city planning department staff members believed that a great deal of additional work would have to be done to meet the statutory requirements.

The outlook for Challenge Developments was very discouraging. Opponents of the project had already shown their determination to harass the developer through legal action wherever they could find an opening. Earlier, Challenge executive T. J. Lannen had tried to arrange a meeting with opposition leaders to see whether they could reach an agreement or strike a compromise. They were unwilling even to meet, however. Lannen anticipated further trouble ahead, and Challenge decided to review the entire project to see whether they could revise it in some way that would make it more acceptable to the opposition. First, they considered making a moderate reduction in the amount of housing, but the high cost of making this hilly site suitable for building would have to be spread over a great many homes if the project was to be economically feasible. Challenge then considered a more drastic cut in the number of houses—enough to eliminate the need for a four-lane ridge road and for most of the expensive and objectionable grading and filling of land.

In February 1976 they submitted a rough version of a new plan to the city. Originally they had proposed building some 2,200 housing units on the site. Now they proposed building from 150 to 200 single-family homes and dividing the rest of the land into 100 lots ranging in size from three to fifteen acres, which they would sell as sites for estate homes. City officials discussed the new plan informally with neighborhood opponents and Sierra Club representatives and brought back the word that they would no longer oppose it. "This is the most you can expect," according to Lannen. "You don't get any medals from the Sierra Club unless you plant grass."[5]

Winners and Losers

What were the results of the political controversy over Mountain Village? The developer and his opponents eventually struck a compromise, but middle-income housing consumers paid a heavy price for it. The original proposal would have offered very desirable living arrangements for some 2,200 families who could have enjoyed the environment of the Oakland hills and magnificent views of San

Francisco Bay. The cost would have been very reasonable, since most of the housing was to sell for $33,500 or less. By contrast the 1976 plan provided for no more than 300 families, and priced out those with average incomes. From 150 to 200 single-family homes remained in the plan, but the new price was expected to range from $40,000 to $60,000 per home. The plan also offered 100 lots for "estate homes" with the lots alone priced from $35,000 to $75,000. Families paying these land prices could be expected to build houses costing from $100,000 to $200,000.

From the point of view of the housing consumer, the end result was a deep cut in the amount of housing available—to a little more than one-tenth of the original volume—combined with a drastic increase in price (see table 1). What started as middle-income housing came out instead as luxury homes.

The compromise plan restricted the housing to a small group of well-off people, but did it generate compensating environmental benefits for the community at large? Its main environmental outcome for the public was to restrict access to the open space in question as much as it restricted access to new housing. The original proposal offered the city of Oakland 480 acres of open space for recreation. The compromise plan carved up almost all this land into private homesites, making bigger lots for the reduced number of families who would buy or build homes there. It was true that the new plan preserved more open space from development, but at the same time it closed that land to the public. It would be open space to look at but not to use. The main beneficiaries of this environmental preservation were the immediate neighbors, whose views would remain unspoiled.

The revised plan then gave the neighborhood and environmental opponents

Table 1
From middle-income to luxury homes: Mountain Village, Oakland

	Housing units		Price
1972 plan	23	single-family rowhouses	$40,000 (average)
	1,080	single-family rowhouses	$33,500 (average)
	1,080	apartments	$23,750 (average)
Total:	2,183	units	
1976 plan	100	lots for estate homes	$35,000–$75,000 (for lots only)
	150–200	single-family rowhouses	$40,000–$60,000
Total:	250–300	units	

most of what they wanted: there would be little cutting and filling to mar the landscape, most of the site would remain open, the small number of families moving in would make few demands on the school system, and the high value of their homes would lighten the property tax load for homeowners already living in Oakland. The loss of the city park and the elimination of moderate-cost housing were a small price to pay, especially since somebody else was paying it.

The people with the greatest stake in this controversy—potential homebuyers—were neither involved nor represented. So the developer and his opponents compromised at the expense of someone who was not there: the housing consumer.[6]

Chapter 5
Creating A Development Deadlock

As homebuilding turned increasingly into a political issue, a growing network of government regulations provided opponents with ready-made opportunities to block or delay new developments. Each regulatory agency became a potential pressure point for the opposition; yet none of them was willing to give much weight to the interests of housing consumers. As more people learned how to use government channels to block growth, what was once only an obstacle course soon turned into a mine field. A recent controversy in Alameda illustrates how the regulatory system discourages oppositon groups from negotiating with a developer and invites them instead to create deadlocks at the expense of the housing consumer.

Alameda is a quiet community of 70,000 people on the eastern shore of San Francisco Bay, just across the water from downtown San Francisco. Its neighborhoods of aging single-family homes form a middle-class enclave bordering on the industrial and low-income areas of the city of Oakland. Most recent housing in Alameda was built on filled land along the bay shore, facing San Francisco. During the 1960s Utah International, Inc., completed an expensive landfill operation to create a 900-acre site for future construction on Bay Farm Island, a tidal marsh at the southern edge of Alameda. Late in 1969 the company announced plans for a residential development of 11,000 housing units to hold an eventual population of more than 28,000 people. This announcement produced a storm of opposition from Alameda residents, which led Utah International to shelve it for the time being.

The development proposal described in this chapter took shape in 1972 when Utah entered into a joint development venture known as Harbor Bay Isle Associates. In May 1972 Harbor Bay Isle Associates presented the city with a new plan calling for 9,055 housing units (mostly condominium apartments), plus offices, an industrial park, and neighborhood stores. The plan set aside about one-fifth of the site for open space, consisting of an elaborate system of lagoons, a marina, a recreation strip along the shore, two parks, and three school sites. The housing was intended for middle-income families, with prices expected to range from $21,000 to $37,000 per unit.

Almost every large development has to deal with unforeseen events, as well as with the many troubles that can be anticipated. In this case the unforeseen event came within a month. For some time the state highway department had been planning to build a second bridge across San Francisco Bay, just south of the Oakland Bay Bridge. This "southern crossing" would have provided easy and direct access between Bay Farm Island and downtown San Francisco. Utah International, as well as many other business firms, had made plans that would depend on the construction of the bridge. However, the bridge itself became the center of a controversy, which resulted in the state placing the question of whether to build it before the voters in a special referendum. In June 1972, to the surprise of most observers, a majority voted down the bridge proposal, and one of the key public works assumptions behind the Harbor Bay Isle plan was suddenly gone.

The developer, nevertheless, moved ahead to try to get city approval. In the summer of 1972 the planning commission held four public hearings on Harbor Bay Isle's request for rezoning. Crowds of more than five hundred turned out, mostly to voice their opposition. The main issues that surfaced were the high density of the new residential community and the traffic it would generate. The complaints about density grew out of concern about the huge number of new-comers this single development would bring to a relatively stable community. Harbor Bay Isle's anticipated population of 21,000 would increase the size of Alameda by almost one-third. The traffic issue resulted mainly from the elimina-tion of the southern crossing. Alameda is an island connected to Oakland and the East Bay highway network by a tunnel and several bridges. Commuting traffic from Harbor Bay Isle threatened to tie up existing connections unless they were widened or unless new bridges were built. The planning commission listened to these objections and then approved the development only after rezoning the site to a lower density than the developer had requested.

This compromise on density did not go far enough to satisfy Alameda resi-dents. Before the city council could take final action on the rezoning, opponents proposed a city charter amendment prohibiting further apartment construction in Alameda. In March 1973 the voters approved the amendment and forced Harbor Bay Isle Associates back to the drawing board.

Six months later the development group presented Alameda with a new plan. They cut the amount of housing almost in half, down to a total of 4,950 units, mostly single-family homes plus some duplex houses. The price per house went up correspondingly. The May 1972 proposal had been for a price range of $21,000 to $37,000 per unit. Now the low end of the price range began where the high end had been a little more than a year earlier. The September 1973 plan anticipated sales prices of $38,000 to $57,500 for the single-family homes and $70,000 for the duplex houses.

Conflicts beyond Alameda

Alameda officials now had a proposal to consider that should have been less objectionable than the earlier one. Despite the reduction of population and density, however, continued public resistance to a large influx of newcomers as well as concerns about traffic bottlenecks made approval uncertain. In addition, the possibility that planes from nearby Oakland Airport might produce high noise levels over Harbor Bay Isle began to emerge as an even more formidable issue—one that multiplied the regulatory obstacles by bringing a series of government agencies from outside Alameda into the spreading conflict.

Part of the Harbor Bay Isle property faces Oakland Airport to the south, and another part lies under the flight path of planes taking off from its main runway. Despite the nearness of the airport, the developer's first technical studies indicated that airplane noise was not likely to be a major problem. As a result of federal regulations, newly built planes have much quieter jet engines than those that went into service earlier. The increasing use of new planes and the retirement of old ones would reduce noise levels substantially. Further, California regulations mandated additional reductions in airport-generated noise, and Oakland Airport put new noise-abatement climb procedures into effect in the summer of 1972. Evidence that airplane noise was not a serious problem was available in an adjacent neighborhood where there were few complaints on this score, and where new town houses were selling briskly for about $50,000 each. As a precaution, however, Harbor Bay Isle Associates decided to use the part of their property facing the airport for an industrial park and to soundproof the buildings in it.

Oakland Airport officials, by contrast, maintained that airplane noise would be a serious problem for any future residents of this area. Harbor Bay Isle Associates hired an aeronautical consultant who began to meet with airport staff members and to review the technical studies that supported their conclusions. These conclusions, he discovered, resulted from forecasts of an enormous increase in passengers using Oakland Airport, from an assumption that there would be many night flights and frequent emergency operations in the northern part of the field, and from a projection that the older and noisier jet planes would still be flying for many years while the newer and quieter ones were phased in very slowly.

There were good reasons to question these expectations. In terms of passenger traffic, for example, Oakland Airport is a quiet place. In 1975 it handled about two and one-quarter million passengers as a result of having increased its annual volume by an average of only 16,000 passengers per year during the previous six years. Yet airport staff members were using projections that anticipated a 500 percent increase to 13 million passengers by 1980, and to 24 million by 1985.

Similarly, the consultant could not believe the figures airport planners supplied on how many old planes would still be using Oakland's runways in the future. He told Ronald Cowen, President of Harbor Bay Isle Associates: "It would appear that there are simply not enough DC-8-60 type airplanes in the world to afford 22 takeoffs and 22 landings per day at the Oakland International Airport. . . . meanwhile, the McDonnell Douglas Corporation has dismantled all of its DC-8 assembly facilities, and there will never be any more such aircraft than there are today."[1]

Airport officials, apparently troubled by the prospect that more people living nearby would mean more complaints about noise, dismissed studies that disagreed with their own. Early in 1973 Maurice Garbell, Harbor Bay Isle's aeronautical consultant, prepared a report entitled *The Harbor Bay Isle Development and the Oakland International Airport: A Classical Example of Airport-Neighbor Compatibility*. During a meeting of the regional airport systems study committee, Lynn Lee of the Harbor Bay Isle staff handed copies of it to Walter Abernathy, Deputy Executive Director of the Port of Oakland, and Donald Flynn, Director of Airport Planning. Garbell, in a subsequent letter to Abernathy, recounted the episode as follows:

We make further note, for the record, that you and Mr. Donald C. Flynn . . . leafed through our above-identified report—you for two minutes and 24 seconds, and Mr. Flynn for four minutes and 13 seconds—while the . . . meeting was in session and that immediately following your inspection of that report, the two of you handed the following holographic evaluation of it to Mr. Lee:
"If horseshit were music, this would be a symphony."
Might we ask you to favor us with a designation of the specific item or items in our report . . . to which your above-quoted written comment . . . applies.[2]

Another consultant soon reviewed the situation and concluded that airport noise might indeed be a problem in the future. Following the requirements of California law, Alameda and Harbor Bay Isle Associates commissioned an environmental impact report on the proposed development to replace an earlier one prepared for the original plan. The new report noted the substantial dispute over future noise levels and concluded that there was a question as to whether Oakland Airport would be able to stay within the state's mandated noise limits in the next 10 to 15 years without cutting back its operations below the levels to which it aspired.

Both the developer and the airport were blocked from taking what might otherwise have been reasonable steps to avoid a noise problem. If the noise over Harbor Bay Isle reached the maximum level permitted by state regulations, then those regulations permitted only a single kind of residential development: apartment buildings with special acoustical treatment to reduce interior noise levels. But the recent amendment to Alameda's charter enacted in response to the earlier proposal explicitly prohibited new apartment buildings.

Oakland Airport, on the other hand, might have been able to handle increased traffic without adding to the noise over Harbor Bay Isle by building a new runway that would allow planes to take off over the bay instead of over the land. A runway long enough for jet planes, however, would require filling some land in the bay. The Bay Conservation and Development Commission had been established a few years before with the mission of protecting San Francisco Bay by regulating landfill operations, and the commission staff had recently gone on record as opposing any landfill undertaken only for the purpose of reducing aircraft noise.[3]

Still another factor increased the probability of future conflicts over airport noise. The consultants who wrote the environmental impact report found other studies showing that college-educated, well-to-do people, such as the expected residents of this development, were more likely than others to complain about airport noise. Even if the noise stayed within the levels permitted by state regulations, nearby residents might still bring pressure on the airport to limit its flights. The environmental impact report found it "very probable that the seeds of noise aggravation and complaints are being built into this project."[4]

The environmental impact report considered several alternatives more favorable to the airport than residential development, but most of these were farfetched; and even they offered no satisfactory solution to environmental problems. The most extreme possibility it considered was to break the protective dike that had been built around the site and to return the landfill material to the trench below the bay from which it had originally been removed. Returning the fill material to the borrow pit, however, would have created a significant problem of sedimentation in the bay. Still another possibility was to carry the fill out through the Golden Gate and to dump it in the open ocean, but the report conceded that this would be prohibitively expensive, perhaps twice the cost of the original dredging and fill operation.

From an ecological point of view, the most attractive alternative was to leave the site alone. Without development or maintenance, the action of water and wind would eventually breach the dikes and fill in the drainage ditches. In time the area would revert to coastal dunes and a salt marsh. But the developer had spent $13 million to fill the site in the first place, as well as substantial holding costs and other expenses since then. Leaving the land alone would mean public purchase of the property at a price that would have to take these costs into account.[5]

The Alameda City Council had little interest in protecting Oakland Airport's right to grow, but it was responsive to its constituents who wanted to limit the amount of new housing. In March 1974 it rejected the developer's request for rezoning but in May approved rezoning at a still lower density for the first phase of the project. In a less complicated regulatory climate, this decision would have allowed Harbor Bay Isle Associates to start construction. In the California regulatory climate of the 1970s, it simply moved the development along to the next stage where other governmental bodies would now have their chance to block it.

First, the Alameda County Airport Land Use Commission had the authority to set boundaries for residential zoning based on state airport noise guidelines. In June this commission found the approved zoning for the first phase "not in the best interests of the airport" and sent it back to the city council for reconsideration. The city council could override this finding only by a four-fifths vote, and in August it endorsed the rezoning once more by the necessary margin.

Paralysis through Lawsuits

Oakland Airport had still other channels open to it for stopping the development. Late in 1974 the airport brought a lawsuit against Alameda and Harbor Bay Isle Associates, alleging that the environmental impact report and Alameda's general plan were both inadequate and that the city's approval of the first phase was, therefore, invalid. The case went to trial, and Harbor Bay Isle Associates realized they might lose. They also realized that the same law that gave Oakland Airport an opportunity to challenge their environmental impact report made it easy for anyone to challenge any environmental impact report. Oakland Airport was busy with plans to expand its terminal to meet the flood of new passengers it was expecting. The airport itself was required to file an environmental impact report on its expansion plans. Harbor Bay Isle Associates started a lawsuit of its own, charging that Oakland Airport's environmental impact report was inadequate.

In the summer of 1975 Oakland Airport won its case. The Alameda County

Superior Court found the city of Alameda's general plan inadequate on several grounds, including its failure to consider the consequences of the decision not to build the southern crossing and its failure to consider Oakland Airport as a factor influencing Alameda's land use.

In the case of the environmental impact report, the court's finding of inadequacy was really a comment on the impossibility of maintaining an orderly review process when the developer was constantly forced to keep revising his plans. Two environmental impact reports had already been prepared for this proposal. The first was scrapped when the charter amendment prohibiting apart-ment construction in Alameda forced the developer to withdraw his original plan. The second was prepared to accompany the new plan of September 1973 for single-family housing. A well-known consulting firm prepared it, and it was a thorough, balanced report. But the Alameda City Council had refused to approve the zoning needed for this new plan. Instead it had authorized a lower-density zoning for the first phase of the project. The court now held that, because of the latest density reduction, the developer would either have to pre-pare a third environmental impact report, or as an alternative he could prepare a full plan for all phases of the project based on the new zoning and then hope the city would find enough similarities in it to the September 1973 plan so that the present environmental impact report might still apply.

Next Harbor Bay Isle Associates had their day in court at the expense of Oakland Airport. In April 1976 the San Francisco Superior Court found the air-port's environmental impact report inadequate. The decision also gave support to what the developer had contended all along: the airport's studies were using very questionable projections of future growth. The opinion noted that even the airport's own environmental impact report referred to these projections as "exaggerated" and "no longer considered realistic."[6] The court then called a halt to any further work on the airport's terminal expansion until an adequate environmental impact report was prepared.

Now the circle of frustration was complete. Every group involved in the con-troversy had learned to use effective blocking tactics. Alameda's aroused citizens had prevented the developer from building apartments that could have complied with state noise regulations. The Bay Conservation and Development Com-mission had blocked the airport from solving its noise problems by building a new runway heading into the bay. The County Airport Land Use Commision had blocked the city council's decision to let the development start with a low-density first phase. But the city council then overrode the Airport Land Use

Commission ruling by a four-fifths vote. Then the airport blocked the developer by successfully challenging his environmental impact report as well as the city's general plan in court. The developer in turn blocked the airport expansion by winning a lawsuit that found the airport's environmental impact report inadequate.

Still Harbor Bay Isle Associates had strong motivation to try to move ahead despite the "no exit" situation that surrounded them. They had already invested $40 million in this venture and had continuing carrying costs of $10,000 a day.[7] In April 1976 Harbor Bay Isle Associates prepared a new plan, reducing the density still further to comply with the zoning that the city council had approved for the first phase. Now they proposed to build 3,170 houses, mostly single-family detached. Once more the prices ratcheted upward. In the September 1973 plan, the upper end of the range for single-family homes was $57,500 Now $55,000 became the lower end of a new range that extended as high as $165,000. The average price for the new homes was expected to be around $65,000. Further, the developer commissioned work on a new environmental impact report, the third for this project, based on the latest plan.

While Harbor Bay Isle Associates were determined to push ahead, the court began to lose patience with Oakland Airport's attempts to block all development for the sake of environmental protection. When airport spokesmen tried to have the court set even tougher conditions before the already approved first phase of development could get under way, the court's response was: "the Plaintiff's ultimate objective is to try to solve potential noise versus residents' problems before they are created; this Court believes that this is an honorable objective on behalf of Plaintiff, but on the other hand . . . there is no need for Plaintiff to have every pound of flesh."[8]

Finally, in July 1976 Oakland Airport, the city of Alameda, and Harbor Bay Isle Associates reached an agreement to drop their various lawsuits against one another. Within an area of about 100 acres under the flight path from the airport's main runway, Harbor Bay Isle Associates agreed to build no housing for two years. During that time the airport would have an option to buy a noise easement and release to protect itself against future lawsuits from people living there. The airport agreed not to oppose other development of the Harbor Bay Isle property, and Alameda and Harbor Bay Isle Associates agreed to withdraw their opposition to expansion of the airport. The mayor of Alameda declared the agreement would clear the way for continued friendly relationships among the parties, while Ronald H. Cowen, Chairman of Harbor Bay Isle Associates, said he was delighted to be able to begin development of the new community.[9] With an end to litigation that at one time included seven lawsuits going simultaneously, the San Francisco Bar Association might well have considered declaring a day of mourning.

The High Price of Regulation

Although this controversy promoted the welfare of the legal sector, it imposed once more substantial costs on the housing consumer. Under the May 1972 plan Bay Area families would have found more than 9,000 condominium units available at prices ranging from $21,000 to $37,000. The April 1976 plan cut the volume of housing down to little more than one-third of what was originally intended, while simultaneously raising the price to roughly three times the original level (see table 2).

Why did the regulatory system lead to these results? Many interest groups and governmental agencies were able to block, delay, or reshape the original housing proposal; yet none of the public agencies was concerned with meeting the area's housing needs or with protecting the interests of housing consumers. The city of Alameda was overwhelmingly concerned with protecting the interests of its already established residents, many of whom wanted to avoid the arrival of thousands of newcomers in their community. When the city government did not look after their interests aggressively enough, Alameda citizens took matters into their own hands by amending the city charter.

Similarly, the County Airport Land Use Commission was concerned with protecting the airport, and the Bay Conservation and Development Commission was

Table 2
Lower volume and higher prices: Harbor Bay Isle, Alameda

	Housing units		Price
May 1972 plan	9,055	mostly condominium apartments	$21,000–$37,000
September 1973 plan	4,385	single-family houses	$38,000–$57,500
	565	two-family houses (duplex)	$70,000
Total:	4,950	units	
April 1976 plan	3,170	mostly single-family houses	$55,000–$165,000 ($65,000 average)

concerned with protecting the bay. The bay commission staff, for example, argued against handling additional air traffic at existing airports because this policy might require some filling of the bay. It suggested instead dispersing the new flights to smaller airports in the region, such as a former military field in Marin County, even though it conceded that this would have to be done over the objections of nearby communities. Rather than permit any bay filling, it also suggested that since much of the traffic came from southern California, a better solution would be to build a high-speed rail transport line between the San Francisco area and the southern part of the state. In short, its position was to support any scheme, regardless of cost or political feasibility, that would leave the bay alone.[10]

The machinery of environmental regulation also made it possible for Oakland Airport to add greatly to the cost of the development. Airport officials came to court exercising rights that were established to encourage citizens acting on behalf of environmental protection; yet if any group in the controversy posed a threat to the environment, it was the airport officials themselves with their ambitious plans for expansion. Thanks to an environmental law, they were able to block housing that might be troublesome by going to court instead of by negotiating directly with the developer.

This experience also raises doubts about the quality of technical studies that public agencies use in order to influence regulatory decisions. Oakland Airport's studies, on close examination, turned out to be a good deal less scientific and objective than the public might have expected; yet airport officials were quick to characterize a study that disagreed with their own as "horseshit."

This controversy, as in the Mountain Village case, suggests that when compromises are made as a result of regulatory pressures, they are made at the expense of the person who is not there—the housing consumer. Once more, when the developer had to redesign his project to get regulatory approval, the revisions led to a steady reduction in the amount of housing and a steady escalation of housing prices.

Finally, the crowded field of adversaries and the ability of each one to contribute to a spreading development deadlock suggests the enormous difficulty of providing new housing by filling in remaining vacant sites within built-up communities. These sites are surrounded by a host of neighbors with a stake in preventing development and virtually none who have a reason to favor it. Further, the neighbors are not only people living nearby but also institutions such as Oakland Airport and the Bay Conservation and Development Commission, whose interests may be threatened by new construction. Under the circumstances infill development is more likely to generate controversy, political conflict, and litigation than it is to produce a sizable amount of housing at prices the average family can afford.[11]

Chapter 6
Environmental Merit Doesn't Win Votes

Will an environmentally sound development win the backing of environmental groups? Not if the alternative is no development at all.

This seems to be the lesson of a drawn-out battle over whether to build housing on the slopes of San Bruno Mountain, just south of San Francisco. No development was an alternative, though, only because other groups in addition to environmentalists were in the opposition. The results, therefore, also offer a few lessons about the power of alliances built around common interests in stopping development.

But why should environmentalists oppose environmentally sound development? In this case very few considered the broad environmental issues from a perspective of *where* and *how* a region should accommodate growth. Most looked narrowly at the local environmental impact, and many simply applied an ideology that rates open space as a good and housing as a bad.

The tangle of government regulations was once again a decisive factor shaping the outcome. In this case it not only took on the mine field character noted in Alameda but also led to exceptionally long delays before government officials were ready to make the key decisions. The developer began serious negotiations with county officials in 1967. In 1976 as the county supervisors were conducting long public hearings before taking a vote, one witness told them:

This show has been running longer than Abie's Irish Rose *on Broadway and I think it's time that you . . . make a decision. I'd like to find out if we're going to do anything with that hill before I die. I've spent nine years appearing before this board. . . . I have no animosity. I'm just tired.*[1]

Regulatory Routines

Crocker Land Company, which owned San Bruno Mountain and land around it in a site totaling 2,600 acres, drew up a proposal to build 12,500 housing units and began dealing with government officials in the moderately receptive political climate of 1967. A local service district made plans to provide sewage treatment facilities for the projected population, and the county built a major road through the Crocker property to serve the development.

Routine regulatory action required years of negotiations, studies, and hearings. The project was complicated, and the governmental machinery to deal with it was intricate. An important feature of the Crocker plan was a 1,250-acre regional park to be established within its property on top of San Bruno Mountain. The review sequence for the park began with months of informal discussion with county staff and public representatives. Then Crocker presented a formal proposal to the San Mateo County parks and recreation commission. The commission recommended the idea to the board of supervisors. The board of supervisors in turn asked the parks and recreation commission and the regional planning committee to study the park proposal further and to consider whether the county's general plan should be amended to add the park to its open space element. The parks and recreation commission and the regional planning committee conducted studies and held public hearings before recommending the park once more to the board of supervisors. Then the county planning commission conducted its studies and hearings and recommended the park, together with an appropriate amendment to the general plan, to the board of supervisors. The board of supervisors held another public hearing and then changed the county's general plan, as the planning commission had recommended.

Now that the plan was amended, the county government could proceed swiftly to the next steps. The parks and recreation commission held more hearings to consider the details of the park's size and location. Then the commission took a vote and recommended the park to the county supervisors. The board of supervisors approved the park and directed the parks and recreation commission to proceed with the preparation of a master plan for park acquisition and development. The parks and recreation commission made its plan, held a public hearing, and then adopted it. Then the board of supervisors authorized negotiations for the acquisition of the San Bruno Mountain regional park site. Crocker made its original presentation to the county parks and recreation commission in December 1971. The board of supervisors voted to begin negotiations for the site in January 1975.

Other regulatory routines were also time-consuming. County policy was to avoid having urban development in unincorporated areas such as the site around San Bruno Mountain. As various parts of the site were developed, they would have to be annexed to nearby municipalities in order to get public services. Under California procedures each county has a local agency formation commission which is set up to study and make recommendations on annexations or other changes in service districts. Crocker Land Company presented its plan to San Mateo County's local agency formation commission in November 1971. The process of holding hearings, drawing up specifications for a study of public service and annexation issues, contracting with a consultant to do the study, waiting for the results, holding public hearings on these, and recommending new governmental arrangements, took more than a year and a half.

Long reviews affect housing consumers in several ways. First, by stretching out the lead time prior to construction, they increase holding costs and overhead for the developer, and these in turn generate higher costs for the consumer. Second, the multiple reviews by separate agencies create repeated opportunities for opponents to bring political pressure against a development. This pressure, as we have seen, often translates into a message that the developer should build less housing.

Negotiation and Compromise

Citizen groups and public agencies both let the local agency formation commission know their objections to the proposed development. The consultants' study summarized the objections and complaints: "Development will increase the population of the Bay Area and add to all kinds of problems; San Bruno Mountain must be preserved; open space must be maintained . . .; views of the mountain must be preserved . . .; the trees, plants, and animals must be preserved." There were conflicting concerns about the housing itself. It would have to be "of good quality, certainly better than that recently built in surrounding areas"; yet "reasonable portion of the housing must be available for low- and moderate-income families." Other concerns were that development would increase the traffic on nearby streets, crowd the schools, add to air pollution of the Bay Area, increase the runoff in a local creek, use inadequate sewage disposal systems, and raise taxes in nearby cities.[2]

These concerns surfaced repeatedly during the next few years. They were the issues around which neighborhood and environmental groups organized opposition to the proposal. They also formed the agenda for negotiation between the developer and county staff over how the proposal might be made acceptable to county officials.

In December 1973 the developer filed a formal plan for county consideration. (By this time the developer was no longer Crocker Land Company, but Visitacion Associates, a joint venture of Foremost-McKesson, which had acquired Crocker in 1970 and AmFac, a Hawaii-based company.) The plan called for building 12,500 housing units—mostly apartments with some town houses—plus an industrial park and office and retail centers. More than half the site was to remain as open space.

During discussions soon after the plan was filed, environmentalists objected especially to ecological damage that might result from building in "biotically sensitive" Owl and Buckeye Canyons. In May 1974 Visitacion Associates agreed to eliminate these two canyons from the area to be developed.

The following month they brought in a revised plan that cut the number of housing units and increased the amount of open space. The new plan was for 9,690 units on land under county jurisdiction, plus another 960 on the part of the site lying within the boundaries of Daly City. Prices for the town houses were expected to range from $32,500 to $60,000, averaging $46,000. Rents for two-bedroom apartments were expected to range from $280 to $360. The proportion of the site to be kept as open space increased from 57 percent in the earlier plan to 66 percent in the revision.

As negotiations with the county planning staff continued, Visitacion Associates made further compromises. In September 1974 they drew up a third plan, cutting the volume of housing still further to 7,655 town house and apartment units. (Land in Daly City, and the 960 units planned for it, were by now excluded from proposals made to San Mateo County officials.) But reducing the density meant raising the prices. Thus the town houses were now expected to cost $39,500 to $69,500, averaging $55,000. Two-bedroom apartments were expected to rent in a range of $310 to $480, averaging $350. Visitacion Associates anticipated that most residents would be in the $15–$20,000 income bracket.

The extent of open space remained unchanged, amounting to two-thirds of the total site. This third plan, however, included the relocation of a community center in order to preserve a sensitive wetland area. The more than 800 acres of open space within the development, taken together with the proposal for an adjoining regional park of 1,250 acres, were over twice the size of San Francisco's renowned Golden Gate Park.

In addition to saving a large amount of open space, the plan met other important environmental criteria. Its location was ideal from the point of view of minimizing automobile commuting. It was close to the city of San Francisco and other job centers, close to major regional highways, and close to a subway terminal in Daly City. Further, Visitacion Associates promised to buy and operate buses between the new development and the transit station. Its central location meant that the new project could take full advantage of existing utilities and services. Its compact nature and efficient use of bypassed land near the center of the region were the very opposite of the scattered, sprawling suburban growth that environmentalists find objectionable. Moreover, it posed no threat to the coastline, the bay shore, or to farmland, while it held open the mountain-top and protected environmentally sensitive canyons and wetlands.

Despite these virtues the San Bruno Mountain proposal generated a storm of opposition as the county planning commission and board of supervisors moved close to their final decisions in 1975 and 1976.

The Organized Opposition

By the time the county planning commission and board of supervisors were ready to hold public hearings, the opponents were well organized and highly effective. Opposition came from two main quarters. First, and most important, were residents of nearby communities who had a direct stake in whatever happened to San Bruno Mountain. A second group of opponents were environmentalists from other parts of the county and other parts of the Bay Area. New developments around San Bruno Mountain would not affect them directly, but their commitment was to the protection of plants and wildlife, or simply to the preservation of open space.

Most local opponents joined together to form the Save San Bruno Mountain Committee. The active members were low-income people from Brisbane, South San Francisco, and Daly City. Although the turnout at typical meetings was no more than 25 or 30 people, the committee was able to recruit more than 100 people to work on special projects; and they could, on occasion, bring out 400 or 500 people for an important meeting. In addition, they increased their effectiveness in dealing with county officials by getting socially motivated young attorneys from the county legal aid society to represent them.

Interviews with members of the committee suggest several reasons for the local opposition. First, San Bruno Mountain was an important part of the communities of working people that encircled it. Many houses nestled against the mountainside, so that residents could go directly from their own backyards up to the mountain. They used it as a large playground. People went there to walk, picnic, and ride their motorcycles and jeeps across the fields. The new development threatened to take away their mountain; and the threat involved issues of class as well as space. The new development would bring in a large number of well-off people who would have no attachment to the close-knit, blue-collar neighborhoods nearby. In addition to taking control of the mountain, they might well dominate some of the neighboring communities. Earlier the county's local agency formation commission had proposed annexing most of the new development to the City of Brisbane. Brisbane's 3,000 residents had good reason to fear the takeover of their community by the 18,000 people who would eventually live in the new housing.

Dislike of big business prompted some local opposition. The Crocker Land

Company and the two conglomerates participating in the joint venture were symbols of outside wealth and power. Some opponents had more specific grievances against business: they resented what they believed to be the high-handed tactics of Visitacion Associates.

Others in the opposition were more concerned about tax increases than they were about mountain climbing. People in Brisbane, particularly, worried about the impact a large, new community would have on their small school system.

In May 1975 Richard DeLeon and David Tabb of San Francisco State University conducted a survey of some 400 Brisbane residents to discover what they thought about the San Bruno Mountain development plan. They discovered that two-thirds were either strongly, or somewhat, opposed to the plan. More than three-quarters of those interviewed thought the development would cause Brisbane to lose its small-town character, and they attached great importance to this. Other considerations that ranked high included higher taxes for Brisbane residents, an increase in traffic and air pollution, loss of political control to new residents, and environmental damage on and around the mountain.[3]

Environmentalists who opposed the project came mostly from the well-to-do suburbs in the southern part of the county. Their principal organizations, the Loma Prieta Chapter of the Sierra Club and the Committee for Green Foothills, both had their headquarters just across the county line in Palo Alto. Their main objections were that the housing development would destroy the last large open area in the northern part of the county, and that it posed a threat to endangered animals—the San Francisco garter snake and the red-legged frog—as well as a rare plant species, the coast rock cress.

North county neighborhood activists and south county environmental groups kept in touch with each other, but they operated independently in mobilizing political pressure. Tom Adams, legal counsel to the Save San Bruno Mountain Committee, minimized "bugs and flowers stuff" in the committee's public presentations because he was concerned not to identify it with environmental causes. Nevertheless, each group used the rhetoric of the other whenever it could advance their common purpose of stopping the development. In a bid to attract outside sympathy and contributions, the Save San Bruno Mountain Committee published "A Calendar of San Bruno Mountain Native Plants and Poems." And the Loma Prieta Chapter of the Sierra Club began its formal comment on the project's environmental impact report by emphasizing the need for "usable recreational open space" close to urban population as a top priority for the state of California.[4]

Real and Imaginary Problems

Were the objections well-founded? The fear of nearby residents that they would lose the use of the mountain for recreation certainly seems to have been exaggerated. Although some people may have envisioned the new development as one that would cover the mountainside with houses, the actual plan proposed to keep two-thirds of the site still in open space. The addition of a regional park adjoining the development meant that about four-fifths of the mountain and the land around it would remain open for recreation. Spokesmen for the Save San Bruno Mountain committee argued, however, that the land remaining open was too steep for most recreation and that Visitacion Associates was taking away the best land by concentrating its housing on the relatively flat "saddle" area of the mountainside.

Although the loss of open space was less serious than the local opposition contended, their fears that the development would change the social makeup of the area were more clearly justified. Tiny Brisbane, in particular, faced the likelihood that a new and more affluent population would eventually dominate its politics, unless the county government could be persuaded to annex the new development to much larger and less resistant Daly City.

The objections of the environmental groups were the most dubious of all. The environmental impact report supplied the basis for their anxiety with its findings that development of the saddle area threatened the "endangered San Francisco garter snake" and the "protected red-legged frog," and would reduce the range of the rare coast rock cress by up to 10 percent.[5] A staff report by the San Mateo County planning department repeated and confirmed the same conclusions.[6]

Both reports seem to have been based on shaky evidence and inadequate research. Thomas Schnetlage, a graduate student at the University of California in Berkeley, became interested in the San Bruno Mountain controversy and decided to check out the alleged ecological impacts of developing the saddle area. He discovered that concern for the San Francisco garter snake rested on only a single, unconfirmed observation of this snake around San Bruno Mountain. The reported sighting took place during an ecological reconnaissance conducted for the Crocker Land Company in 1971. Three subsequent survey teams failed to find the snake. Several experts pointed out that it is easy to confuse this rare subspecies with similar but nonendangered garter snakes that are found in the saddle area. Others who questioned the man who made the original sighting reported him as saying that *maybe* he saw the snake.

As for the red-legged frog, which both technical reports describe as "protected," Schnetlage found that neither the California Department of Fisheries and Game nor the U.S. Department of the Interior list this species as either "endangered" or "rare." To the contrary, he found that the frog lives in a wide range of locations in California and adjoining areas and is not endangered at all. Whether it is "protected" is unimportant because most wildlife in California is protected by statute in some way even if it is not rare or endangered.

The threat to the coast rock cress also seems to have been exaggerated. The environmental impact report concluded that development of the saddle area would reduce the range of this plant and noted that it was recently added to the rare and endangered species list of the California Native Plant Society. Schnetlage found that the Native Plant Society had described its status in more qualified terms, as rare but distributed widely enough so that the potential for extinction was low. While the plant was endangered in some locations, the society found it either stable or increasing in others. Crocker Land Company surveys had found the coast rock cress more prolific in parts of the mountain to be kept in open space than in the saddle area. Further, the company had reseeded the plant in different locations to increase its range and found it growing very well in the new places.

On closer inspection, the ecological objections to building housing in the saddle area amounted to protecting an endangered snake that probably wasn't there, preserving a frog that was distributed widely throughout California, and protecting the site of a plant that was rare, but that was growing as well, or better, in nearby locations.

In addition, Schnetlage's study found serious incompatibility between the environmentalists' pleas to preserve an ecological system based on a small freshwater marsh in the saddle area and the proposal of the Save San Bruno Mountain Committee to develop a park for active recreation in the same area. Construction for the park, as well as intense use of the area for recreation, would interfere with drainage patterns, remove wetland plants, and increase the pollutants carried into the marsh. As a result, stopping housing in the saddle area was likely to do very little to preserve its special environmental qualities.[7]

Planning Commission Hearings: Jobs vs. Open Space

In June 1975 the planning commission opened a series of eleven public hearings to consider the environmental impact report and Visitacion Associates' proposal for a general plan amendment to let them build their development on San Bruno Mountain. By this time the controversy had drawn in people and organizations from all over the Bay Area. The hearings became the focal point of a political conflict that magnified some issues and virtually ignored others.

People who came to speak in favor of the project were generally those with an economic interest in construction or business expansion within the county. The strongest support of this kind came from construction workers hungry for jobs in the midst of a severe building slump. As the first hearing got under way, they drove their trucks and heavy equipment around the meeting hall to stage a massive demonstration. Spokesmen for building trade locals came forward throughout the hearings. The business manager of the Building Construction Trades Council of San Mateo County summarized the situation as many of them saw it:

We have seen the present developer shrink his plans now down to where only 20 percent of the San Bruno Mountain area will be developed. The Save San Bruno environmentalists have done their job. They have saved for recreation and open space 80 percent of the land in this area, where only the most hardy recreationist would want to spend his outdoor time.

Now what do they want? . . . Ninety-five percent? Or do they want the whole thing? Well, I think they have gone too far already. Too bad we can't back up a few years and build on a little larger portion of the area, so the developer could spread the cost and build even more houses that all the people can afford.[8]

One construction worker, speaking as an individual, created a stir by breaking with the union leadership: "All construction workers do not want this development to go through. While maybe this development might mean a job for me, I think a park is more important for myself and the people around."[9]

A few citizen groups also came out in favor of the project. The representative of a Daly City women's organization said:

People need work. People need homes. People need recreation. But it has to be provided for man, not for the snake. If I hear one more word about the garter snake, I am going to drop on the spot. . . . The Good Lord gave us this world. True, we've got to take care of it. But at the same time he gave us the animal of the field for the use of man, not the other way around.[10]

The noisy and theatrical atmosphere, with foot-stomping, cheering, and jeering, stimulated speakers to dramatize their positions. One natural scientist issued sweeping prophecies about the project's environmental consequences:

If San Bruno Mountain is hidden behind a concrete screen of towering infernos, so much for the integrity of that southern bulwark of the basin's natural framework. . . .

Anyone with a lick of common sense knows where land destruction leads. Developers also know where the land destruction leads. It leads them to live in Hawaii, in Acapulco, in the Bahamas, or along the French Riviera. Few of them have any intention of living in land they have so thoroughly and relentlessly gutted. . . . But we think that natural land is more important to the county and the state than is the making of money. . . .

You will be choosing between life itself and the corporate American way of death.[11]

On another theatrical occasion an eight-year-old girl scout stood on a chair to reach the microphone and say: "There is lots of nature and trees and other animals on the mountain. If they build houses on it, they will just ruin the animals and everything else."[12]

Many speakers, however, directed their fire at "no-growthers" among the opponents, describing them as simple obstructionists or as people looking only for personal recognition. The main speaker for the Save San Bruno Mountain Committee was careful to separate herself from a no-growth position:

We are not no-growthers. The issue here is not growth vs. no growth. The issue here is what is the right location for needed growth and what is the right location for needed open space.

To deal with the fact that the proposed development brought with it a large amount of public open space, she attacked the quality of the land that would remain open:

The recurring theme of the landowners is to propose dedication of unusable land . . . such as we have seen with the billy-goat land of the original park, Owl and Buckeye Canyon, buffer zones, and open spaces proposed within the V.A. [Visitacion Associates] project and, in return, demand that the people of this county and the county staff and our representatives accept the V.A. plan for intensive development.[13]

To dramatize their claim that only billy goats would be able to use the land left open on San Bruno Mountain, opponents brought a goat to one of the hearings.

The need for additional housing in San Mateo County, and the contributions the development might make to that need, never emerged as important issues in the planning commission hearings. At the opening session the county's assistant planning director noted that the houses proposed for San Bruno Mountain would be priced lower than much other new construction in the county and would, therefore, reach a wider market. Later the lack of low-income housing within the San Bruno Mountain project was a recurring but minor theme. A number of speakers argued that there was a shortage of low-income housing in the county but said this proposal would do nothing to cope with it.

Though none of the witnesses recognized that a middle-income housing development would help families of more modest incomes by relieving the pressures of a very tight housing market, several members of the planning commission saw the connection and seemed prepared to give it some weight in their deliberations. During one of the last hearings commission member Wayne Thomas asked whether the high cost of housing in San Mateo County might not be a result of low vacancies and limited housing availability. The commission chairman replied, "I think you are referring to supply and demand. I mean, this is what dictates housing cost, or any other costs." Thomas added, "Exactly what I am getting at, what a fallacy it is to talk about low-cost housing in an area where you have no growth."[14] At the final meeting another commissioner observed that many young families who worked in San Mateo County were unable to live there because housing prices were too high. "Crocker Hills," he went on, "is going to take people from their older houses, as I see it, moving into these new units, and some of the older houses could be made available to some of the young people at a lower cost."[15]

During the lengthy hearings the issues put before the commission members amounted mostly to the importance of jobs versus the importance of open space. Very few witnesses suggested that the need for housing should also be weighed against the need for open space. Still some commissioners seemed to value new housing as a way of meeting the county's needs, and in November the commission voted three-to-two in favor of the general plan amendment for San Bruno Mountain. In accepting the Visitacion Associates proposal, the planning commission attached a series of conditions to it. These included requiring the developer to submit specific plans for each stage of the project to the planning commission and board of supervisors for final review of zoning prior to construction; requiring planning commission and board of supervisors review to determine that necessary facilities and services will be available as each stage goes into construction; and, most important, requiring the developer to make available 20 percent of all housing units for low- and moderate-income families to be subsidized under state or federal programs. With these and other conditions attached, the planning commission gave formal approval to the general plan amendment in December 1975 and forwarded the San Bruno Mountain proposal to the county supervisors for final action.

Deciding on the Saddle Area

The board of supervisors began their public hearings in January 1976 before big and noisy audiences. Witnesses covered the same ground and made most of the same arguments as before, but the earlier hearings had succeeded in narrowing the issues for decision.

The main point of contention between Visitacion Associates and their opponents was the relatively level saddle area part way up the mountainside. Visitacion's plan was to concentrate more than 70 percent of all the housing units and about half the total retail and office space in this one critical section. In contrast to the steep slopes and ravines around the rest of San Bruno Mountain, the saddle area had 264 acres of only moderately sloping land highly suitable for development. This same land, however, was ideal for picnic areas, riding and bicycle trails, and sports fields that would be hard to carve out of the steeper hillsides. Visitacion's plan for the saddle area itself set aside 83 acres of the best land for parks and open space but used the remaining 181 acres for high-density development.

Whether those 181 acres were to be used for development or kept as open space was the essential disagreement between Visitacion Associates and the Save San Bruno Mountain Committee. Although the Visitacion Associates proposal set aside more than 800 acres of public open space, in addition to the 1,250-acre regional park adjoining the development, most of this land had a slope of more than 30 percent. Of the land within the development that had less than a 30-percent slope, Visitacion proposed to keep about one-third as open space. This amounted to slightly more than 200 acres scattered among different parts of the site. To the opposition, stopping development in the saddle area offered a chance to get another 181 acres of highly usable recreational land all in one place.

The county planning staff suggested that the planning commission and the board of supervisors consider several alternatives to the Visitacion Associates plan. One alternative called for a 60-percent reduction in the development proposed for the saddle area while another alternative called for eliminating all development from the saddle area. Visitacion Associates warned that neither of these alternatives was economically feasible and that a county decision to make a substantial reduction in the development of the saddle area would have the effect of killing the entire project. Nevertheless, these options remained on the agenda as the board of supervisors considered whether or not to approve the San Bruno Mountain plan.

The proposal put before the board of supervisors differed in important ways from the one the planning commission had begun to consider six months earlier. Visitacion Associates had agreed to accept the series of conditions that the planning commission attached to its approval. The requirements for further review and approval of specific development plans for each stage, and for evidence that enough classroom space and other public facilities would be ready on time, offered new assurance that the project would not overburden the services of nearby communities. The agreement to make 20 percent of the housing available under federal or state subsidy programs meant that the development could provide a very large supply of housing for families of low and moderate income.

At an early hearing Visitacion Associates announced several other concessions that might generate additional support. Responding to concerns about school costs, they offered to provide one elementary school at their own expense. In response to objections that tall buildings in the saddle area (from 14 to 20 stories) would spoil the view of the mountain, they agreed to limit building height to a maximum of 12 stories. And they presented further details of the transit system they had earlier offered to provide, which would connect the new housing to the BART subway terminal in Daly City.

The developer's leading allies were still the construction workers. Many labor representatives came forward to argue for the project and made the job issue even more prominent than it was earlier. One speaker added a new dimension to the issue by describing a special program he directed that was bringing minority apprentices into the building trades. From the start of the program in 1968 through the summer of 1974, he reported a steady increase in the number of minority apprentices. Then the building slump began to destroy his program. In San Mateo County alone, between October 1974 and November 1975, the number of registered apprentices dropped by 235. With no new apprenticeships in sight, recent minority advances in the building trades were about to be lost for lack of work. He concluded: "Sure, let's preserve the environment, but not on the back of the working man."[16]

An unemployed construction worker testified bitterly: "... I am getting sick and tired of being out of work because a few people say 'Save the lilies and save the flowers.' I wish to hell they'd feed those lilies and those flowers to their children. Mine won't eat them." He drew mixed applause and jeers.[17]

Uncertain Tax Impacts

The effect of the development on local tax rates also emerged as an important issue; yet there were so many uncertainties that it was difficult to know what that effect would be. Fiscal impact analysis is a very inexact procedure, even under easier circumstances than the ones surrounding this project. Financial consultants who studied the situation for the county reported that if Visitacion were able to complete all construction within the 15 years they contemplated, the project would generate net fiscal benefits for all local governments except the Brisbane school district. Under "worst case" assumptions of a slower marketing of the project, most jurisdictions would still benefit although there would be problems during the development period.[18]

The county planning staff made use of data and methods from this study to rank the options they had proposed in terms of their local tax consequences. They found the Visitacion Associates plan more desirable in fiscal terms than either a lower density alternative for the saddle area or a plan that would keep the saddle area entirely open.[19]

One of the big uncertainties was how additional school costs would be financed. According to the consulting study the Brisbane school district would have to spend from 7.2 to 9 million dollars for new school construction, as well as increase its operating budget. By this time, however, the California Supreme Court in *Serrano vs. Priest* had found the existing method of financing schools out of local property taxes unconstitutional. Under a new system that substituted state revenues for local property taxes, Brisbane might not have to bear the costs of an increased school enrollment. The superintendent of the Brisbane school district testified about his frustration in trying to predict the school impact of a new development when the legislature had not yet put together a system of financing in line with the court's decision:

. . . If the legislators in Sacramento get off their asses, which they're going to have to, because they have been remanded by the Courts now to come up with a change that meets the Court's decision within four years, and there are things in the dockets now, but I hate to discuss those because they are all tentative.[20]

Similarly, the local tax consequences of stopping the development and turning all of San Bruno Mountain into a county park also depended on the unknown factor of how much aid the state might give. San Bruno Mountain was too expensive for the county to buy on its own, and several witnesses discussed the amount of state aid that might be forthcoming, but no one really knew how much it might be, or when it would come. As a result the hearings became a forum for raising anxieties about fiscal impact, but there was no way to put these anxieties to rest. Except for the special case of the Brisbane school district, however, Visitacion's proposal seemed generally advantageous in tax terms while the other options looked more costly to county and local governments.

Conflicting Environmental Positions
Environmentalist opponents stressed the need to save open space and the need to have recreation land in the northern part of the county, but without acknowledging the conflicts between active recreational use and preservation of the saddle's special ecology. Some speakers tried to highlight the environmental issues in original ways while others tried to broaden them. One voiced the familiar theme of profit-seeking men threatening to destroy nature's goodness: "I trust and hope and pray," he said, "that you will not yield to the pressure and sacrifice a beautiful natural resource for the financial benefit of a developer recently arrived on the scene," overlooking the fact that Crocker Land Company had owned the property since 1884. He went on to paraphrase William Jennings Byran—"You must not sacrifice the people upon a cross of gold"—to the usual mix of applause and jeers.[21]

The president of a prominent Bay Area environmental organization introduced a new argument that hillside housing would lead to wasteful use of energy:

There is this saddle area up on the mountain. It is way up high, hard, difficult to get to. It is going to be an energy-consuming development....
...Our concern about the energy-intensive development that a large number of new homes way up high, going up and down to get back and forth for all kinds of daily activities. ought to be considered by the board.[22]

In addition to these elaborations of familiar environmental themes, the supervisors also heard a new kind of environmental analysis—one that argued for support of the project because it would accommodate new growth in an environmentally sound way. They heard it first in the opening presentation by Visitacion Associates. Robert Follett described the transit system that Visitacion Associates would pay for and operate at its own expense. The equipment would consist of 18 large buses, three small ones, and two dial-a-ride vans costing about

$1.5 million in all. This system would carry residents between the new housing and the BART station nearby in Daly City, as well as between different parts of the development itself. Having public transit promised to cut down automobile use. In addition, Visitacion's traffic consultant pointed out that the project location, close to San Francisco and near two major freeways, meant that whatever automobile commuting it did generate would require only short-distance travel and would, therefore, keep air pollution and energy use to a minimum.

He contrasted this situation with what the same amount of population growth would do to traffic if the people bought typical new suburban homes in the southern part of the county:

They will be . . . scattered. They are going to be not next to a BART system like ours. But more insidious than that, they are never really noticed, and suddenly this growth in traffic comes about, but the guys [suburban homebuilders] are so small that you wouldn't dare ask them to put in a bus system, would you? But we are having a bus system. [23]

The supervisors heard an even clearer analysis of the project's advantages from a regionwide environmental perspective in a statement by Polly Roberts, an active environmentalist and a doctoral student in agricultural economics at the University of California. As an environmentalist, she said, she had learned that in ecology it is necessary to deal with systems as a whole. Later she had discovered that what applies in ecology also applies in economics and that the relevant whole system for considering a major development proposal is the housing market in the Bay Area. This housing market, she said, would accommodate the population growth in one location or another. The basic question was not whether there would be growth but where people would live:

So where should people live, according to environmental criteria? Well, the closer to the center that people live and the higher the density at which they live, the less resources it takes to house them and supply them. Town houses or apartments require less land, lumber, steel, copper . . . than suburban tract houses on one-acre lots. Town houses and apartments require less gas, less electricity, and less water. I mean, they have all those one-acre lots with all their little lawn-sprinklers going. That's a lot of water.
More central locations also save time, distance, and cost of travel. . . . a central location means more viable transit, less smog, and less distance for auto commuting, to the extent there is auto commuting. [24]

Other environmentalists who were active in the opposition were unwilling to concede any merit in these arguments. They were angry that Polly Roberts had mentioned her connection with the Sierra Club and informed her that people who disagree with official policy should either keep quiet or conceal their affiliation. In a follow-up letter to the board of supervisors, Roberts told them that she was a Life Member of the Sierra Club, as well as a member of Friends of the Earth and California Tomorrow, and she concluded that "San Bruno Mountain is an issue on which even convinced environmentalists may disagree."[25]

The technical staff of the county planning commission might also have been expected to analyze the San Bruno Mountain proposal in terms of a regional housing market and a countywide growth pattern. Instead, their report to the planning commissioners and the board of supervisors attacked the relevance of this broader perspective. While the staff agreed that large, well-planned development was "preferable to traditional patterns of uncoordinated fragmentation," they argued that the limited power of county government did not allow it to make a choice between these alternatives. They noted first that the county had no growth strategy (although they did not argue that it *should* have one). Second, they pointed out that county government could not control suburban development within incorporated cities where the typical small subdivisions were likely to be built.

They said nothing about whether the construction of nearly 8,000 housing units on San Bruno Mountain might absorb part of the demand for new housing that would otherwise generate homebuilding in the southern part of the county. Their argument was that suburbanization would continue "inexorably, in many remaining undeveloped and developing bayside areas." The issue, as they framed it, was "whether the impact of intense development on the mountain, in addition to the impact of continued suburbanization, can be tolerated. . . . "[26] The phrasing of that question suggested that the professional planners were unwilling to "tolerate" a desirable form of development as long as they were unable to control less desirable developments in other parts of the county.

Mistrust of Government
Although the notion of environmentally sound growth management failed to take hold during the hearings, the more familiar concern that a big development on San Bruno Mountain posed a threat to nearby working-class communities ran as strongly as ever. Even the very open and exceptionally long process of reviewing Visitacion Associates' proposal seemed to inspire little confidence that government would make fair decisions or that it would respect the interests of average citizens.

The thoroughness of the review process is worth recalling. It had taken nine years of reviews before the board of supervisors approached the point of making a final decision. Numerous technical studies supplied information and raised issues for debate at public hearings. The environmental impact report that was the subject of these hearings was a massive and thorough analysis that took into account even unlikely and minor consequences of the proposal. It was a heavy document: 1,500 pages, including technical appendices plus comments filed by six city governments, 17 other governmental agencies, and 16 private groups and individuals.

Moreover, the conditions the planning commission had imposed made it clear that detailed plans for each part of the project would be subject to the same painstaking, open review by both the planning commission and the board of supervisors that the entire proposal received in 1975 and 1976. Before approving each phase of the plan, the county government would consider every identifiable impact it might have on surrounding areas (such as noise, traffic, drainage, and appearance) and would also review evidence to determine that all necessary public and private facilities and services would be available as soon as they were needed.

Nevertheless, people living near San Bruno Mountain continued to worry about the project's impact on their neighborhoods, and to fear that government would not protect their interests when they conflicted with those of big corporations. A spokesman for the Daly City Protective Association, which had earlier fought off an unwelcome urban renewal project, was especially eloquent on this theme:

We have been threatened continually with development by the city. We know the city's plans for us, which is to take out our lower- and middle-income housing because it will help to service this coming big development. . . . We people know that a lot of promises have been made that nothing will be disturbed, that everything will be fine. But we have seen things turn otherwise in the past. We have seen the government agree to cost overruns in the Defense Department. The developers or the big interests involved will come to the Supervisors, will go to the authorities and say, "This has to be done now because we are in a fix. This will be enlarged. We will put in more housing. We will put in more roads. . . . " Once the process is started, it has a snowballing effect and it cannot stop. . . . We the people operate more by common sense than we operate by the results of EIR's [Environmental Impact Reports] and all the other accumulated data. Now our common sense tells us we are about to be destroyed.[27]

The Missing Issue

At the supervisors' hearings the arguments against the San Bruno Mountain project covered a wide range, from environmental issues to fiscal consequences, to impacts on nearby communities, and to the need for more recreation land in the northern part of the county. On the other side, the single issue of construction jobs was the only strong argument in favor of the project. Building housing to meet the needs of the growing number of families in the San Francisco region never came across as an important matter.

Only a few speakers gave even brief attention to the need for housing and the contribution the San Bruno Mountain development might make to it. Polly Roberts' presentation was exceptional in placing this proposal within a regional housing market. Picking up the theme that the most pressing housing needs were those of poor people, she argued that even new housing built for upper-middle-income groups would help expand the supply of housing available to the poor:

Even poor people do benefit from the [construction of new housing as better-off people vacate older housing to move to new.

I know it is very popular to deride what is called the "trickle-down theory," but the fact is, if you look at the housing that poorer people currently occupy, all of it was once upon a time high-income or moderate-income new housing.

Now, of course, the housing market by itself can't solve the income distribution problem, but it can provide cheaper housing if it is allowed to operate.[28]

Also, as a result of one of the new planning commission stipulations, Visitacion Associates was now committed to setting aside up to 20 percent of the new housing for use under federal or state subsidy programs for low- and moderate-income families. As of early 1975 the county housing authority had only about 800 subsidized housing units available, while the county planning commission estimated that at least 9,000 families in the county were inadequately housed.[29] The 1,500 new subsidized units potentially available in the San Bruno Mountain development would have doubled the county's previous efforts and made a substantial contribution toward meeting the overall need; yet neither the county supervisors nor most of the speakers paid much attention.

Two reasons may explain the low visibility of housing needs during the supervisors' hearings. One is that housing subsidy funds were very hard to get at the time. The major federal housing subsidy programs had been suspended early in 1973, and a new program enacted in 1974 had hardly made a start. There was great doubt about the availability of funds under state housing programs. As a result no one knew how many of the 1,500 low- and moderate-income units might ever be built.

The second reason is that San Mateo County simply did not give very high priority to housing issues. The very small volume of subsidized housing in the county was indicative of where housing ranked among the concerns of county government. So, too, was the fact that the planning commission and the board of supervisors were very slow to produce a housing element as part of the county's general plan. The board of supervisors adopted an "initial housing element" in January 1975, only after the county legal aid society brought a class action suit against them for not having acted sooner.[30]

The newly adopted housing element conceded that San Mateo County had one of the highest housing cost levels, and provided the smallest percentage of moderate-cost housing, among all Bay Area counties. "Production," according to the housing plan, "has approximately kept pace with population increase, but has not been great enough to allow for a normal rate of vacancies." As a result the plan report described the county's vacancy rate as lower than that of any other Bay Area county and noted that "the effects of San Mateo County's tight housing market are felt by most income groups."[31]

Despite this official recognition of widespread housing problems resulting in part from too little new construction, the board of supervisors gave no serious attention to questions of housing policy during the hearings and, unlike the planning commission, reached a final decision that gave great weight to open space and practically none to housing. In March 1976 the supervisors voted three-to-two to keep the critical saddle area in open space. Deleting the saddle area from the plan reduced the amount of housing that could be built from 7,655 units requested to 2,235 units approved. Although the supervisors' decision technically permitted development to go ahead as proposed elsewhere around San Bruno Mountain, this sweeping reduction was no longer a compromise. As Visitacion Associates spokesmen had made clear during the hearings, it was a vote to stop the development.

The Pattern of Conflict

The San Bruno Mountain controversy followed a familiar pattern. As in the case of Mountain Village in Oakland, people who lived near the proposed development and who found it objectionable organized themselves politically to try to stop it. They found allies among environmentalists who had no particular tie to the local community, but who were prepared to fight for the preservation of open space. The combination of neighborhood and environmental activists once again proved to be a powerful political force for blocking construction.

In this controversy, however, there were two conflicting environmental views. The organized environmental groups focused their attention on how the new housing would affect the place where it was built and the land immediately around it. Not surprisingly, they found these effects to be negative because they had to mean disturbing an existing state of nature.

Yet a different environmental analysis—representing a minority of one in this case—found that the planned development was a highly desirable way of accommodating inevitable growth. It would have made efficient use of land and other resources, and would have minimized pressures on the region's transportation systems and air quality. But the organized environmental groups refused to consider the proposal in a regional perspective and insisted on interpreting its impact locally and narrowly. This perspective and the political tactics that flowed from it both led to the usual pattern of environmental opposition. As one former county official with a good deal of experience in these controversies told the board of supervisors, "I have never heard of any EIR report that environmental groups have said was complete and adequate, or was the project in the proper place."[32] But the conflict between a regionwide view of environmental issues and the position that actually prevailed raises an important question: does opposition to compact developments on leftover land near the center of the region help or hurt the quality of the area's environment?

The elaborate nine-year ritual of decision-making brought many issues to the attention of the public and of county officials, but the need for more housing was not one of them. As a result all the technical studies, public hearings, and official deliberations never led to a balanced decision that weighed the region's need for housing against those impacts of the proposal that opposition groups found objectionable. The neglect of regional housing need as a factor in the final decision was not an accidental feature of the San Bruno Mountain controversy. It repeats the experience of other situations described in earlier chapters and comes directly out of the structure of the review process itself.

This process did give reasonably balanced consideration to issues that organized groups within the county considered important. Housing needs were left out because they did not have an organized local constituency. The people who would have lived in new housing were scattered throughout the entire region. Until houses were available for them, there was no way of even identifying who they were. People who wanted to buy or rent new houses had the greatest stake in the decision, but they were unorganized, probably unorganizable, and without local influence.

What then was the function of local development reviews? Their function was mainly to regulate new homebuilding according to the wishes of people who already lived in the community. While reviews delayed construction, established residents had plenty of time to consider how new housing might affect them, to organize themselves for political action, and to object to anything they considered damaging. The damage could range from minor inconvenience to serious disturbance. But since there were few costs attached to registering objections, and since local government gave no weight to the needs of widely dispersed families that wanted new housing, the final decision was very attentive to even minor drawbacks and unsubstantiated fears.

The review process also encouraged the pattern of compromise that we have seen before, in which the developer and his opponents struck bargains at the expense of housing consumers who were not represented in the proceedings. The compromises in other cases took the form of reducing the amount of housing to be built and raising the price for those houses that remained. This type of bargaining got under way in the San Bruno Mountain case when the proposal shrank from 12,500 units down to 7,655 while prices began to edge upward (see table 3). This time, however, the density reductions went well beyond the point of possible compromise. The board of supervisors' final decision cut the earlier

Table 3
Cutting beyond the point of compromise· Crocker Hills, San Mateo County

	Housing units	Price
December 1973 plan	12,500 town houses and apartments	
June 1974 plan	9,690 town houses and apartments	$32,500-$60,000 (for town houses) $280-$360 (for two-bedroom apartments)
September 1974 plan	7,655 town houses and apartments	$39,500-$69,500 (for town houses) $310-$480 (for two-bedroom apartments)
April 1976 county zoning approval	2,235 town houses and apartments	

compromise figure by another 70 percent, down to 2,235 housing units. At this level the developer could no longer build marketable houses, and the project was dead.[33]

Chapter 7
Abusing Technical Studies

Governmental reviews of housing development plans stack the cards against them. They give the opponents repeated chances to shoot down a proposal. They create so many delays and uncertainties that they wear down the developer and make him ready to compromise in order to get anything built. And they fail to represent housing consumers who have the biggest stake in new homebuilding. This much is clear enough from the controversies reported in earlier chapters.

These reviews also stack the cards by using unreliable technical studies to justify delay or opposition. Analyses of the environmental and fiscal impacts of new developments are usually well publicized, and often they become important weapons in a political controversy. Their declared purpose is to bring in the best information available so that local officials will have all the relevant facts before they make a decision. But how good are these technical studies? A brief look at Oakland Airport's traffic projections and the study of environmental impacts on San Bruno Mountain has shown that they were far less than the scientific, objective analyses that most people expect government to use in making decisions.

A closer look at development impact studies will show that they mix together facts, beliefs, and prejudices. Many staff members who work on these reports are sympathetic to environmental causes and to growth-restricting policies, and their sympathies affect their analyses. Also, in the stormy atmosphere of environmental politics, groups that oppose new housing have been quick to seize on studies favorable to their cause and to use them indiscriminately. Two recent controversies are outstanding examples of these abuses of technical studies. One, in Contra Costa County, is the subject of this chapter. The other, in Palo Alto, will be described in chapter 8.

Searching for Bald Eagles

A familiar landmark in the countryside east of San Francisco is 4,000-foot-high Mount Diablo, located on the outer edge of suburban development almost 30 miles from downtown San Francisco. New interstate highways have made the area more accessible to regional job centers and, therefore, more attractive to homebuilders. In July 1973 the Blackhawk Corporation filed a plan and requested rezoning that would permit it to build 4,500 housing units on its 4,800-acre ranch at the southern base of the mountain. The Contra Costa County planning department began to study the proposal and to prepare recommendations for the planning commission that would have to consider the zoning request. The planning department arranged for private consulting firms to prepare reports on the environmental and economic impacts of the Blackhawk Ranch proposal.

The Blackhawk Ranch proposal was a predictable target for environmental groups. Its large size made it highly visible. It was located next to an important scenic area. Although the top of Mount Diablo was well protected within a state park, this development near the base of the mountain threatened to disturb the view of open country from the mountaintop. Moreover, much of the ranch was in territory not yet intended for urban development, according to the county's general plan. Opponents began to organize early; thus the technical studies were prepared in the atmosphere of a gathering storm.

The consultants, however, submitted balanced technical reports indicating that the environmental and fiscal consequences of the Blackhawk Ranch development would pose few serious problems for the county. The planning department, which had final responsibility for the studies, promptly rewrote them in ways that would provoke much greater opposition.

Two separate consulting studies failed to find any rare or endangered plant species on the site. They did point out, however, that development of the land would change some of the vegetation. The county planning staff was unable to argue that new housing would threaten any scarce plants since they knew of none in the area. But they added a sentence to the final report warning of a more subtle danger: since development would inevitably change the existing vegetation on the site, "this would essentially preclude the discovery of any rare or endangered . . . plant species."[1]

Similarly, the county planning staff strained hard to argue that the development of the area might increase the hazards of grass fires. According to their analysis, with more people in the area the number of fires started would probably increase. But they conceded that so, too, would the likelihood of early detection, and with new fire equipment nearby, fires would probably be put out sooner. Furthermore, they also granted that the greenbelts and golf courses proposed as part of the development would reduce the total amount of flammable vegetation. However, they warned that after existing cattle grazing came to an end, the grass would develop more fully and grow thicker and "consequently, fires which are slower burning but harder to suppress may result."[2]

So, too, was the rationale with wildlife. The consulting reports concluded that the development would have only a minor impact on animals in the area since it would be concentrated almost entirely on the open grassland parts of the ranch and would leave intact the places where most wildlife lived—the streamside woodland habitat and the higher-elevation grasslands. At the lower elevations some animals would be displaced by development, but others would be attracted by it. The increased year-round water supply, the establishment of a golf course, and the new landscaping of trees and shrubs near the houses would establish a favorable habitat for deer and songbirds.[3]

Deer and songbirds, however, had no place in the gloomier vision foreseen by the county planning staff. They rewrote the text to argue that a residential development would "create habitats for noxious animals or even animals dangerous to man." As examples, they cited houseflies, mosquitoes, fleas, house mice, and Norwegian and roof rats. According to their report, "many of these organisms 'out-compete' native species and eventually displace them entirely." And the arrival of these pestilential animals might generate further threats to the ecology: "The result may be an attempt by man to control these noxious organisms, often by using dangerous chemicals."[4]

Although no rare or endangered animal species had been sighted on the ranch, a consulting report nevertheless mentioned two that *might* be present only in order to point out that even if they were, the development would have no more than a slight effect on them. The California tiger salamander, according to the report, "will not be significantly affected by development of the ranch, provided that the existing watering and irrigation ponds are retained and are provided with a nondeveloped periphery." And a rare snake, the Alameda striped racer, would suffer no loss of its preferred chaparral-covered habitat because no development was planned for those parts of the property; construction elsewhere on the ranch, however, would reduce the amount of grassland available to the snake as a secondary habitat.[5]

The county's new version once more dwelt on possible negative impacts. The California tiger salamander is not an endangered species, but the planning department's report noted that it "is being considered for placement on the depleted species list by the California Department of Fish and Game." The report did not claim that it is actually present on the site, but noted that it is found in Contra Costa County and that there are suitable habitats for it within Blackhawk Ranch. The conclusion: "Presuming the species is present, the project development could have a direct impact on it."[6]

As for the Alameda striped racer, the county report pointed out that it is not only rare but that even in areas where it is known to live its normal density is very low. "Therefore," the report went on, "actual verification of the existence of this species on the property is very unlikely, even if it is present." While its primary habitat in the chaparral would remain undisturbed, the county report still anticipated adverse impacts that could come from altering the habitat of its food sources—small rodents, frogs, lizards, birds, and other snakes.

The county's report also worried about the black-chinned sparrow, a small bird neither rare nor endangered that lives in nonthreatened chaparral but "is diminishing in numbers in Contra Costa County." It worried, too, about coyotes and contended that they have been maligned unjustly: "The coyote is not always considered a beneficial animal. Although this animal is implicated as being a serious predator upon livestock, this aspect of its behavior has not been clearly documented."[7]

The apocalyptic vision of the county planning staff even included a vague threat to the well-being of our national bird, the bald eagle. Here, the reasoning was particularly tortured. The bald eagle has forty known nesting sites in California, none of them in Contra Costa County. The eagles have feeding areas away from their nests, but apparently there are no feeding areas for them on the property, either. But the more northern populations of bald eagles do migrate to several large lakes in California during the winter season and "it's a possibility that they fly over the project area."[8]

Measuring Fiscal Impacts

Another set of technical studies tried to project how much local governments in Contra Costa County would have to spend to service people living in Blackhawk Ranch and how this amount would compare with the tax revenues the development would produce. Fiscal impact analyses of this kind have been in widespread use across the country since the 1940s, but despite their popularity they have many built-in limitations. They consider only service costs and tax revenues for local government and not the full range of costs and benefits that people derive from new developments, such as the value of improved living environments or better access to suburban jobs. They are far from scientific because they depend on a whole series of very crude assumptions.

Some of the most critical assumptions are also the most debatable: these include the number of children each family is likely to have in school at a given point in time and the proportion of school costs that will be financed out of local property taxes rather than state or federal aid. Despite the shakiness of many underlying estimates, these studies often carry great weight in local deliberations. In this case the highly judgmental nature of future cost and revenue projections left the analysis wide open to manipulations that could forecast huge governmental deficits if the project were ever built.

The first environmental impact report on Blackhawk included a memo estimating that, after the project was completed, it would generate a large revenue surplus for Contra Costa County and the local school and service districts responsible for it. This study projected tax income exceeding local government service outlays by some $3.3 million per year.[9] Since the memo was brief and the projection methods were unclear, the county planning department arranged for a more complete fiscal impact study by another consulting firm.

The new study was careful and thorough, subject only to the unavoidable hazards of picking reasonable assumptions to describe an uncertain future. It concluded that the cost of public services for Blackhawk Ranch would be very substantial but that the development would generate more than enough local tax revenue to cover it. Education costs accounted for more than 60 percent of the total. However, with school construction financed by bond issues and with state aid available to supplement local funds, the school district would still collect $400,000 more per year in taxes from Blackhawk than it would spend for operating and capital costs.

In total, this fiscal impact analysis forecast a net annual surplus of $1.2 million for the county and for all other local governments serving the proposed development. The final report went to the county in December 1973.[10] Four months later the Contra Costa County planning department released its own fiscal impact study. This time the bottom line showed that the Blackhawk Ranch development would result in an annual deficit of $104,418 for local governments.[11]

How could two fiscal impact studies reach such different conclusions? First, the county planning department assumed that there would be more pupils per household living in Blackhawk Ranch than had the consulting firm. It is impossible to say which of the two assumptions was more realistic. The planning department may well have taken a protective role toward local governments and on this basis could have justified more extreme assumptions about the future school load. The fact was, however, that both the consulting firm and the county planning staff built in a substantial margin of safety by using relatively high assumptions for school population and also by assuming that a higher proportion of children in the area would go to public schools than was currently true in the county at large. The county's assumptions on pupils per household had the effect of increasing projected school costs by more than $400,000 per year.

At the same time the county planning department study used a lower estimate of assessed valuation for the new office and retail buildings that were planned as part of the Blackhawk project, and it did not place any assessed value on land used for golf courses. The result was a lower projection of annual revenues than in the consultants' report.

Further, the county planning staff study covered only three public services: education, sewage treatment, and water supply. By omitting police, fire protection, and county general administration, it left out services for which the consultant's study had projected a combined fiscal surplus of $840,989—more than enough to offset the deficit that county staff had calculated for the three services they chose to include.

The planning staff report also raised new arguments against the Blackhawk Ranch proposal. The consultant's study, for example, pointed out that state loans used for school construction would not reduce the overall fiscal impact, but they would simply transfer part of the burden from the local school district to state government. The study concluded, however, that because the state loans would probably be made wherever the potential Blackhawk residents might live, this particular project should not be considered the cause of a special state outlay. The only way to avoid the state construction loans, it suggested, would be for families with school-age children to find housing in a school district with extra classroom space; but most districts with underused schools were built-up cities with no room for new housing that could substitute for construction at Blackhawk Ranch. The county planning department report turned this logic around to argue that people should stay put in the older cities:

It should be brought out, however, that according to a State Department of Education official, the State Aid would not have to be offered if students (and their families) were not migrating to areas like San Ramon [Blackhawk's school district] from areas like Oakland, Concord, and Hayward where decreasing enrollments have created excess classroom capacity. This migration has caused severe problems in many other areas throughout the state.[12]

The county planning staff then assembled its heaviest ammunition to use against the project by presenting the capital costs of all new public facilities as though they were paid for out of current revenue rather than financed by bond issues and amortized over time. In the case of $12 million needed for new schools, the report argues that, since school district voters had recently turned down a bond proposal, they might not approve bonds for Blackhawk's new schools. On the basis of this strange procedure, the report then identified close to $20 million needed for new capital facilities and contended that existing residents would have to bear these costs on behalf of the newcomers to Blackhawk Ranch. It then calculated the deficit per new dwelling unit by dividing the number of new units in each phase of the Blackhawk project into the total cost of all capital facilities required for that phase. Thus the county's analysis showed a capital deficit per dwelling unit running as high as $12,820 after the first two-year phase, and declining eventually to $4,340 per dwelling unit after the completion of the entire development.

Having presented a one-sided technical report grounded on doubtful assumptions, the planning staff summarized its conclusions :

A large public "subsidy" in the form of services and capital investmest is required at the onset of the project, and although the amount in per-housing unit terms is substantially reduced by project completion, the project still does not "pay for itself" at initial full development. In other words, even at full development revenues from taxes, fees, and utility charges must be supplemented by revenues from older development and other land uses to provide the funds for necessary roads, utilities, and schools.

This subsidy situation is hardly unique. . . .The question is how much of a financial burden the taxpayer (or service customer) can or should be obligated to take on for a privately initiated project?[13]

The closing summary used similarly loaded language: "The large capital investments presently required to actualize projects must be considered in the light of diminishing public economic resources and the need for additional residential services. . . .The issue with regard to new residential construction, particularly in areas not previously developed, thus concentrates on the amount of residential growth the general public can afford or should be obligated 'to buy.' "[14]

Grounds for Revision

Why did the planning department rewrite the consultants' technical reports to change positive conclusions into negative ones? The county's planning director offered several explanations. First, the planning staff objected to the proposal because it was not in conformity with the county's general plan, which they had prepared and which they believed it was their mission to protect. No compromise in the project's design could bring it into conformity with the general plan because it proposed to develop some land that the plan designated as open space. Another factor influencing the way the staff reworked the technical reports was that many staff members themselves placed a high value on protecting the land and the natural environment.

More important, planning director Anthony Dehaesus was well aware of pressures from environmental groups in the county that had already complained of insufficient attention to wildlife during reviews of earlier development proposals. He suspected that a project as large and important as Blackhawk Ranch might well lead to litigation, and he wanted to make the environmental impact review as complete and as lawsuit-proof as possible. As for the fiscal impact study, Dehaesus believed that his role was to marshall all the relevant facts and that it was important to highlight the large capital investment that public agencies would have to make in order to serve the Blackhawk Ranch development.[15]

What the planning department did to the fiscal impact analysis led the consultant who wrote the technical study to challenge their revised findings. Claude Gruen was especially disturbed that the county planning department report cited his study as a source for much of the data it published, since he believed these citations would suggest that his own analysis led to the same conclusions. He prepared a written critique of the planning staff report for the planning commission and the county supervisors and then went to one of the commission hearings to reiterate his own conclusion that the development would more than pay for the public services it would use. A few months later another consulting firm completed a fiscal impact study for the local school district that also contradicted the planning department's findings. This study assumed, as Gruen had earlier, that bond issues would finance new school construction. On this basis it concluded that the Blackhawk Ranch development would generate greater revenues than costs for the school district.[16]

The easy transformation of environmental and fiscal impact studies from positive to negative suggests a few things about the special character of these studies. First, they cannot be very scientific if different investigators applying established methods reach strikingly different conclusions. They are, in fact, highly judgmental.

Second, the political pressures surrounding a major development proposal actively discourage whatever objectivity may be possible within the uncertain state-of-the-art. The presence of organized environmental groups, their fondness for lawsuits, and the receptivity of the courts all create a reasonable expectation that the "adequacy" of the environmental impact analysis will eventually be decided in court. Under the circumstances prudent administrators will make sure that their reports err on the side of exaggerating any conceivable threat to the environment. Even the high-powered imagination of the Blackhawk Ranch environmental impact report, with its conjecture that the bald eagle might sometime fly overhead, was not enough to prevent environmentalists from bringing a lawsuit later, but it apparently helped to prevent them from winning.

Fiscal impact analyses are far less likely to be contested in court, but they, too, are shaped by the politics of the review process. Public agencies and the elected officials to whom they report have a natural sense of obligation to keep future public service outlays in line with tax revenues. Neither revenues nor outlays can be predicted with any precision. Prudent administrators, as a result, will choose their assumptions so as to overstate possible costs and understate possible revenues. Shading the fiscal impact studies to emphasize possible financial strains provides a degree of assurance in a world of uncertainty. For somewhat different reasons, therefore, both the environmental and the fiscal impact studies are likely to show the consequences of new development in a harsh and unfavorable light.

The rationale for conducting these studies is that they serve as useful informational supplements to an otherwise politically dominated process. But in reality many of them are not so much a supplement to the political process as they are an integral part of it. Their findings owe something to the natural sciences and to economic analysis, but they owe as much to the art of politics.

Environmental Oppositon

The Blackhawk Ranch controversy followed a generally familiar pattern, but there were several surprises in the story, not the least of them the final outcome.

An early surprise was Sierra Club support for the proposed development. A local branch of the Sierra Club negotiated directly with the Blackhawk Development Company in order to prevent their plans from damaging the environment. The negotiations were a success. They concluded with a written agreement in which the developer promised, among other things, to donate 2,700 acres of land to Mount Diablo State Park and also to allow public access to the large open space preserve that would be part of the Blackhawk Ranch project. In return the Sierra Club committed itself to endorse the plan.

At a planning commission meeting in March 1974, the chairman of the Sierra Club's Mount Diablo regional group spoke in favor of the Blackhawk Ranch proposal. He praised it as accomplishing "a first in the history of the county; namely the development of a parcel of land with a sensitive eye to avoiding to the greatest extent possible, every major environmental problem." Further, he cited the "unique level of cooperation, professionalism and environmental sensitivity demonstrated by Blackhawk."[17]

A month later the Sierra Club repudiated this agreement. The chairperson of the club's San Francisco Bay chapter went to the next planning commission hearing to announce that the chapter had reviewed the position taken by the Mount Diablo regional group and decided to reverse it. Once again, as in the San Bruno Mountain controversy, environmentalists preferred to fight for no development at all rather than press for environmentally reasonable development. And once again resolving problems through direct negotiation proved unworkable.

Environmental opponents within Contra Costa County had other objections that left no room for compromise. Their organization, Amigos de Diablo, was not concerned with specific features of the development but opposed any development at all in that location: "There are certain places—our national treasures—where housing developments simply do not belong. These include the slopes of Mount Diablo. . . .Blackhawk would destroy the serenity and majesty of views from the Valley toward the Mountain, and from the Mountain toward the rolling hills and valleys below."[18]

Other opposition was less than total. A public meeting of nearby residents, for example, focused on specific problems—flood control and traffic—for which solutions might conceivably be found if the development went ahead. The objections of the planning staff also seemed to allow some room for compromise. Only part of the property was in an area designated for open space on the county plan, while the other part was in a planned unit development zone. And the first phase of the proposed development was located entirely within this zone, where it would conform to the county's general plan.

Further, the planning staff's objection that development of Blackhawk Ranch would trigger premature development of the valley around it had more to do with the rate of development than it did with the decision to have any development at all. The San Ramon Valley, in fact, had already been growing quickly— from a population of 13,000 in 1960 to 34,000 by 1974. Other housing developments already approved could be expected to raise the valley's population to about 60,000 by 1990. Blackhawk Ranch would have added another 15,000 to the total.

Environmental groups dominated the opposition, however, and gave it the character of total rejection rather than a willingness to compromise. In Contra

Costa County, however, the opponents had to operate in a political climate that was relatively favorable to development. As a result their tactics were different from those used so successfully in San Mateo County.

Despite considerable opposition at the public hearings, and the negative recommendations of the planning department staff, all the county governmental bodies that were required to approve the Blackhawk Ranch proposal did approve it. The planning commission attached a number of conditions to its approval, the most important of which required the developer to donate the park land as he had promised the local Sierra Club branch even though the club had withdrawn from its part of the agreement. The Blackhawk Ranch plan, therefore, came to include a donation of 2,700 acres of land to expand Mount Diablo State Park.

Lawsuits and Referenda

Before the board of supervisors could act on the planning commission's favorable recommendation, the Amigos de Diablo tried to take it out of their hands. They asked the supervisors to place the Blackhawk rezoning issue before the voters as a referendum item on the November 1974 ballot. The supervisors turned them down by a vote of 5 to 0.

In September 1974 the county supervisors approved the necessary rezoning and filed a statement giving some of the reasons for their action. The supervisors cited Claude Gruen's memo disputing the findings of the county's fiscal impact study and also cited the San Ramon Valley school study as evidence that the Blackhawk Ranch development would bring economic benefits to the county. They also considered the chance to expand Mount Diablo State Park, as well as the high quality of the housing plan, as other factors in favor of the development. And they went further to say: "This Board is not against growth so long as that growth is adequately planned."[19]

A month later the Sierra Club, the Amigos de Diablo, People for Open Space, and three local residents brought a lawsuit against the county government, charging that it acted illegally by rezoning the land in a way that violated the general plan. Just as the planning director had anticipated, the suit charged also that the environmental impact report was not adequate or sufficiently detailed and that it failed "to discuss adequately the impact of the project on . . . rare and endangered plant and animal species."

The Blackhawk Corporation also had to arrange for a number of utility and public service districts to redraw their boundaries so that they could provide ser-

vices for the new development. In May 1975 the county's local agency formation commission approved a single reorganization plan covering all the service
districts at once. A month later the board of supervisors gave its formal approval
to the plan.

The Amigos de Diablo immediately organized a referendum campaign. Within
30 days they collected 34,000 signatures, far more than the number needed for
the purpose. Their petition called on the board of supervisors either to rescind
the service boundary reorganization plan or to put the plan to a public vote.
The county's own counsel advised that the reorganization plan could not legally
be decided by a referendum. The supervisors refused to put it on the ballot, nor
were they willing to rescind their own decision. The Amigos de Diablo and the
Sierra Club then started another lawsuit to try to compel the county to have a
referendum on the service plan.

Since the county's elected officials were unsympathetic to the views of environmentalists, the most promising way to stop the development was through
the courts. The opponents pursued their litigation with dogged enthusiasm. In
September 1975 the trial court considering the zoning and environmental impact
report (EIR) challenge took note of the thoroughness of the EIR—it had more
than 1,500 pages and weighed sixteen pounds—and ruled in favor of the county.
Commenting on the EIR, the court said:

*It need not be exhaustive, include all potential comments, nor be perfect, but is
adequate if it provides the decisionmakers with information which enables them
to make a decision which intelligently takes account of the environmental consequences and is adequate and complete. The EIR at bench is all that, and more, it
is exhaustive.* [20]

The opponents promptly appealed the decision.

In early 1976 the trial court hearing the service reorganization case also ruled
in favor of the county. The environmental groups appealed this decision as well.
Further litigation flowered when the developer discovered that he, too, had
resource to legal channels. He brought defamation and libel actions against two
of the leaders of Amigos de Diablo. The opponents considered these to be
nuisance suits but not serious problems since good legal help was available both
to defend the leaders and to pursue the appeals. [21]

The lawsuits delayed the project, and the possibility of adverse decisions on
appeal compounded the risks of getting started. In addition, the fact that the
county had approved rezoning and public service provision for Blackhawk Ranch

did not mean that the specific plans for each phase of the project would have smooth sailing. When the planning department staff reviewed the subdivision plans for the first phase, they raised many objections to it. As a result Blackhawk Corporation revised it to eliminate features that posed traffic and drainage problems and—most predictably—they made a big cut in the number of housing units to be built.

In the Blackhawk Ranch controversy the opposition was strong enough to pose a serious threat to the development but not strong enough to stop it. The review process, as usual, was one-sided. Instead of presenting a balanced view of how the Blackhawk Ranch development would affect the county, it offered an exaggerated set of worst-case assumptions. The county's elected officials, however, found reasons to doubt the accuracy of governmental staff studies. As a result they reached their decisions without much help from the cumbersome and costly review process that was intended to generate information for their use.[22]

Chapter 8
Finding Profit in Open Space

The abuses of technical studies include not only slanting the findings but also looking at the issues too narrowly. Palo Alto made an important decision on community growth and local housing almost entirely on the basis of a narrow calculation of the fiscal impact of new development. A technical study found that the least expensive form of development from the point of view of city taxpayers was no development at all, even if the city had to buy a large amount of land at market prices in order to block homebuilding.

Local growth opponents were delighted with these results. They meant that a no-growth policy was not only meritorious as an expression of ethical values but also that it made sense in cold cash—at least in the special circumstances of Palo Alto. Since the new land ethic also appeared to pay well financially, the city moved quickly to keep the foothills open. When the cost of preserving open space proved to be higher than anticipated, Palo Alto continued to cite high-minded environmental goals in support of its policy while resorting to growth-control tactics that would have embarrassed a nineteenth-century political machine. A U.S. District Court eventually struck down the city's action. But even the court decision failed to get any housing built.

Studying Development Options

Palo Alto is a wealthy suburb of 55,000, located 25 miles south of San Francisco in Santa Clara County. It is the home of Stanford University and of modern industrial parks where electronics and pharmaceutical firms like Hewlett-Packard and Syntex employ a work force as large as the city's resident population. Most of Palo Alto's fine neighborhoods are in the flat, eastern half of the city, which is now almost completely built up. To the west lie 7,500 acres of scenic, rolling foothills that are almost entirely open. In the mid-1960s some of the foothill land was used for a private golf course, a public park, and a sprinkling of expensive homes, but most of it was in private ownership and potentially available for development.

As landowners began to draw up plans for their property, the city commissioned an "environmental design study" to help it decide what kind of development would be best in the foothills. The scope of the study was ambitious and the city assembled top consultants to carry it out. The city planning firm of Livingston and Blayney was in overall charge. Their team included Lawrence Halprin and Associates, the designers of Ghirardelli Square, who were responsible for ecological, visual, and recreation studies, as well as specialized consultants in urban economics, civil engineering, and geological and soil analysis.

When the study got under way in 1969, the consultants projected potential demand for housing, office space, and industrial development in the foothills. They investigated the area's ecology, geology, and visual appearance. These early studies turned up no reason to withhold most of the foothill land from development: the consultants suggested keeping only certain sites of special topographical character for permanent open space. Their report recommended that market-priced housing would be "a logical use for much of the foothills area" and that many different types of housing would be well suited to the various parts of the foothills.[1] Even on aesthetic grounds, they saw no reason to exclude housing:

A number of differing aesthetic judgments can be made about development of the foothills, and none can fairly claim exclusive validity. In the eyes of some observers, the beauty of the area will be destroyed if there is any significant amount of development. Others would prefer to see the rolling foothills made greener by development of relatively small lot subdivisions . . . with ornamental tree plantings and well-tended gardens covering almost every square foot. . . . even steeper slopes have been developed with aesthetically satsifying results. Night views of developed hillsides studded with sparkling lights are pleasing to most people.[2]

The consulting team also found no need for additional recreational open space in the foothills. Palo Alto was already well endowed with recreational areas, including a 1,400-acre park in the study area. Still it was easy to find other reasons for preserving more open space. If new housing were built near the established foothills park, that park would lose some of its wilderness character, the consultants pointed out. Furthermore, even though it was hard to justify additional acreage for Palo Alto's recreational needs, more open space might meet a need for people from nearby communities with less parkland of their own. If more open space were justified on this basis, however, it would raise a question about Palo Alto's established policy of keeping nonresidents out of its foothills park.[3]

As the study progressed, the consultants turned their attention to the fiscal impact of different development possibilities in the foothills. Palo Alto's residents enjoyed an exceptionally favorable tax arrangement. Over the years the city had managed to attract high tax-paying development—light industry and office buildings—while blocking population growth that might have led to increased demands for public services. As a result the city and its school district were able to provide high-quality services at very low cost to local homeowners. Palo Alto's property tax rate was only half as high as the average rate for cities in Santa Clara County; yet its expenditures per capita were twice the countywide average.[4] The reason was simple: business and industry paid two-thirds of all the property taxes collected in Palo Alto. Because the tax rates were so low, hardly any housing developments in the city paid enough in taxes to cover school costs for children who lived there. There was no need for housing to "pay its own way" since business firms were footing most of the bill for educating Palo Alto's children and supplying its public services.

Under these conditions the consultants were not surprised to discover that most new housing that might be built in the foothills would not produce enough tax revenue to pay for the additional school costs it would generate. Working in 1970, they anticipated that average market prices for new homes in the lower foothills would range from $45,000 to $80,000. At the low prevailing tax rates in Palo Alto, only far more expensive housing, ranging from $62,500 to $116,500 in value, would pay for its own school costs.[5]

Another discovery was more surprising. Because of the low tax rate in Palo Alto, new housing priced from $45,000 to $80,000 would yield very little local revenue in comparison with the new school costs it would bring. Other taxpayers would have to make up the difference between new costs and new revenues. The study concluded that it would be cheaper for them, instead, to have the city buy the land outright and to finance the purchase through 30-year bonds.[6]

Was this finding so compelling that it alone should have decided the future of Palo Alto's foothill land? Tax advantages might be critical in a heavily burdened or low-income community, but Palo Alto's residents were well-to-do and lightly taxed. Business and industry paid most of its tax bills and would continue to do so. The consultants, in fact, projected further substantial increases in industrial development in the future. These would surely cover any tax deficit resulting from new housing. Yet the consultants decided to give overwhelming weight to the fiscal outcomes of land use decisions. Although they conceded that business and industry paid two-thirds of every property tax dollar, they still took note of "widespread concern among residential property owners over mounting school costs," and argued that "the most important consideration in the minds of the majority will be the effects of developmental alternatives on property taxes."[7]

But they hesitated to base their recommendations entirely on narrow fiscal grounds. Instead they turned also to an unfailing source of support for open space preservation: environmental issues. Their report praised the Sierra Club, the Committee for Green Foothills, and other conservation organizations for having created ecological awareness in Palo Alto and for challenging the belief that growth is good. Earlier, when the issue was what kind of development to have, the consultants interpreted their own ecological, visual, and geological studies in a balanced way that showed how land development could be reconciled with environmental goals. Now they took a different position, arguing that in at least some ways their studies confirmed the fears of environmentalists. "Development," they said, "unquestionably would radically alter the ecology and the visual aspect of the foothills." Furthermore, they warned, "Extreme caution will be necessary if landslides and floods are to be avoided."[8]

On the basis of fiscal and environmental considerations, the consultants drew up their recommendations. They proposed blocking all development throughout the foothills, except for one section set aside for industrial growth. Although Palo Alto had no special need for more parkland, they urged it to join with nearby cities and county governments to buy the upper foothills for regional open space. Since "preservation of the Skyline Ridge properly is a regional rather than a local responsibility,"[9] Palo Alto should contribute only a part of the costs. For the lower foothills, they proposed that Palo Alto buy all the undeveloped land and hold it open as a site for possible park expansion or for whatever future development proposal might seem advantageous to the community. The consultants described their recommendations as "bold and precedent-making," said they would "serve the public interest," and suggested that preserving the foothills would be an "innovative, farsighted" action.[10]

They had, in fact, taken a broad look at questions involving open space. Where parkland was concerned, they were willing to consider not only Palo Alto's needs but also the needs of a much larger region. As far as housing was concerned, however, they had tunnel vision. Palo Alto had serious housing problems and the city government was well aware of them. Yet the consulting study gave only narrow and inadequate attention to the impact their proposals would have on the local housing market.

Pressure for More Housing

The housing problem on the public agenda in Palo Alto had to do with the growing shortage of houses that families with low and moderate incomes could afford. At the request of the city council, the Palo Alto planning department wrote a report on the subject at about the same time that Livingston and

Blayney were preparing their recommendations. The planning department offered a persuasive diagnosis of why low-cost housing was disappearing. First, the demand for housing in Palo Alto was very great, partly because the community itself was a very attractive place to live and partly because it was a major job center. Palo Alto, the report noted, had approximately 50,000 jobs and only 20,000 resident households.

Despite the tremendous pressure for more housing in Palo Alto, there was very little vacant land suitably zoned for new housing. As a result people who wanted to live in Palo Alto had to compete with each other for a fixed supply of housing. Those with high incomes were outbidding those with low incomes. The consequences were clear: "Palo Alto's already short supply of low-cost housing is being diminished . . . as a result of clearance, demolition and remodeling activity."[11]

Spokesmen for low-income groups were loud and insistent in presenting their complaints to the city. At a wild meeting of the city council in July 1970, they threatened violence if the city did not act to improve the housing situation. A speaker for the Stanford Labor Action Group described what was happening: "Poor people are eliminated to make more room for high-income people, making Palo Alto a canyon of finance. . . .a united front is developing in Palo Alto of the black, brown and street people who are being evicted from their premises. . . . the hospital has been stopped, traffic has been stopped, and you people will be stopped."[12]

A representative of the East Palo Alto Tenants' Union went further. As reported in the minutes, he "stated there are hundreds of people on waiting lists to get into homes in East Palo Alto and if Palo Alto's plans continue, the housing shortage in East Palo Alto will be even more serious. . . .The people in East Palo Alto are very concerned with the housing shortage in Palo Alto and stand united for a moratorium on the superblock, demolition on existing houses, and no evictions until the housing needs are met. . . .He commented that if the people of Palo Alto are so proud of their city, they had better do something about low-income housing, because if they don't, they won't have a city to be proud of much longer."[13]

The housing problems facing low-income people were relevant to the future of the foothills in several ways. First, any substantial amount of housing construction, even for high-income groups, would meet part of the demand for more housing in Palo Alto, and would therefore relieve some pressure to convert existing low-income units into housing for the better-off. Second, the city could have coped with low-income housing needs more directly by encouraging developments in the foothills that included subsidizing housing.

In addition, homebuilding in the foothills would have helped meet a region-wide need for housing to keep up with population growth. Palo Alto's growth strategy of maintaining its privileged tax status as a major job center, while imposing on other communities the costs of housing its workers, had important implications in a regionwide housing market. Yet the same consultants who looked at regional open space needs were unwilling to look at regional housing needs or even to look adequately at local ones.

Having discovered that there were tax advantages in stopping all development, the consultants then dismissed the possibility that any development alternative might offer social advantages: "Proposed park expansion aside, none of the alternates studied would have any great social utility except those that include low-moderate income housing . . ., and these would have significant disadvantages in other respects."[14] As disadvantages they cited street widenings, ecological and visual damage, and potential landslide and flood problems. They noted only a single factor in favor of development: urbanization would reduce fire hazards in the foothills. The failure of this study to give more than passing attention to housing needs may well have been a good reflection of the political climate in Palo Alto. If so, this ambitious, comprehensive study did not broaden the perspective of decision makers but instead reinforced a narrow political concern with getting the most tax advantages out of future development while also preserving the environment at a clear profit.

Blocking Homebuilding in the Foothills

The new open space policies of the environmental design study were put to an early test when Palo Alto had to handle a large-scale housing proposal for the lower foothills. A development group, Arastra Limited Partnership, bought a 530-acre tract in the foothills and submitted its plans to the city in August 1969. Arastra proposed keeping about half the site as open space and building 1,776 housing units on the rest—a mix of apartments, town houses, and single-family homes, with most of the apartments to rent for less than $200 a month and most of the homes to sell at prices of $50,000 or more. Three months later Livingston and Blayney issued their first report, which concluded that housing would be appropriate for many parts of the foothills and that Arastra's land was especially well suited for development. Livingston and Blayney then did a special study of the Arastra plan. They raised some aesthetic objections to it but concluded that on the whole it was a reasonable development proposal.

Other studies looked at the fiscal consequences. An economic consultant to the developer found that the completed project would yield the city of Palo Alto an annual tax surplus of $450,000, but that with current low tax rates it would generate an annual deficit of $475,000 for the local school district. Still the foothills community would come much closer to covering its school costs than the other residential areas of Palo Alto. Residential property taxes from the entire city contributed only 35 percent of the school district's budget. By contrast homeowners in this new development would pay three-fourths of their own school costs. Taxes on industrial land paid for most of Palo Alto's school budget, and future industrial development would continue to cover school costs without increasing the property tax rate. Less than one year's typical industrial growth would be enough to cover the remaining educational deficit for the Arastra development.[15] These findings showed that housing in the foothills would not create new tax burdens for other Palo Alto residents as long as Palo Alto kept attracting new industry. They also showed, however, that Palo Alto's taxpayers could improve their already good situation still further by getting new industry *without* allowing any new homebuilding.

In early 1970 the planning commission held a hearing on Arastra's plan and invited the developer to reduce the number of units and include some moderate-income housing priced below current market levels. Two weeks later the developer returned with a new plan, reducing the housing he would build from 1,776 units to about 1,500. He now proposed to set aside 45 acres for the Palo Alto Housing Corporation, a private, nonprofit housing sponsor that would build and manage some 200 low- and moderate-cost units. Although this plan was responsive to the earlier request for some lower-priced housing, the overall size of the project remained about the same. The commission voted to turn down the new plan but also stated its willingness to consider another plan with less housing.

Within a month, however, the city council voted to delay consideration of Arastra's plan until after Livingston and Blayney completed their third report. In June they filed their report recommending that the city buy all the land in the lower foothills, including Arastra's site. In November the city council held a public hearing on this proposal. A long parade of speakers gave enthusiastic support, including representatives of the Committee for Green Foothills, League of Women Voters, Palo Alto Branch of the American Association of University

Women, Palo Alto Civic League, and the Loma Prieta Chapter of the Sierra Club. There were no speakers in opposition. The council then voted to accept the recommendations in the Livingston and Blayney report, and they commissioned their consultants to recommend specific next steps to acquire the land.

Arastra promptly shelved its development plans and prepared to sell its land to the city. City officials meanwhile began to explore possibilities for state and federal aid to help pay for the foothill land, and they arranged for appraisals of the property. To make sure the land remained open, the city council established a six-month development moratorium for the lower foothills, beginning in July 1971.

By late August the city staff became convinced that their chances of getting federal open space funds were very slim. In October the city council decided to give up its search for federal aid and to try instead for a combination of gifts and city purchases. When the six-month development moratorium expired, the council extended it for another six months.

Buying the land began to look less and less attractive. Not only were federal funds unavailable, but the appraisals turned out to be high. Several major tax-payers wrote to city officials to register their concern about major land purchases that would raise the tax rate.

In the spring of 1972 the Palo Alto planning department began to suggest another, less expensive, way to proceed. They proposed using zoning rather than city purchase as the way to preserve open space in the foothills. In May the council quickly gave preliminary approval to highly restrictive zoning regulations that applied precisely to the parcels of the land the city had earlier intended to buy. Immediately afterward Arastra notified the city that it was prepared either to sell the land to the city or develop it, but that unless the city acted promptly Arastra would bring a lawsuit charging Palo Alto with taking its property without compensation.

In June 1972 the city council gave final approval to an open space zoning district that included Arastra's property. The new regulations permitted the land to be used only for several improbable activities that would all have the effect of preserving open space. These included agriculture, botanical conservatories, outdoor nature laboratories, wildlife sanctuaries, guest ranches, riding academies, clubs, stables, golf courses, and educational and philanthropic institutions. Single-family residences would be allowed, provided that each had a minimum lot size of 10 acres; that no more than 3.5 percent of the site had structures, roads, or pavement on it; that all houses on adjacent lots were clustered near each other; and that all buildings were located in inconspicuous places. The city then refused to make an offer to buy Arastra's land.

Blowing the Whistle

Arastra brought a lawsuit against Palo Alto, as it had threatened, charging that the city's actions amounted to an unconstitutional taking of its land. After three years of legal proceedings, Arastra won its case. The U.S. District Court for northern California, in addition to deciding in Arastra's favor, wrote a scathing analysis of Palo Alto's tactics. Although the judgment is on the particulars of the Palo Alto case, much of the analysis behind it could apply as well to the devious growth-control policies of other California communities.

First, the court dissected Palo Alto's purposes in enacting the open space zoning regulation. The main purposes cited in the ordinance itself included protecting the public health, safety, and welfare; and protecting life and property in the community from the hazards of fire, flood, and seismic activity.

In the court's interpretation this ordinance had a different purpose: to preserve open space at minimum cost to the local taxpayers. The court described it as follows:

By 1972, it began to appear that the costs of acquisition were going to be substantially higher than had originally been hoped. Federal funds were not available, no gifts of land had been generated, the land's values . . . would have required expenditures of substantial public funds and some of the larger taxpayers were expressing objections.

While the costs were high, the City remained anxious to prevent development and to preserve open space. All development had been foreclosed during the period, but the time was running out within which it could continue to be prevented without some definitive action. . . .While acquisition now seemed less attractive, the intent to preserve the open space continued. . . .

When the open space ordinance is examined in this context, it compels the conclusion that the City had the purpose, by way of zoning regulation, to accomplish without expense to the taxpayers all of the benefits it could have received from the acquisition.

The City Council purported to find a series of health and safety factors, that were recited as little more than a formality, in order to justify the open space ordinance. They had no adequate information before them to support any such findings. They found, for example, that the open space ordinance was compelled by the fire hazards of the Foothills. The only information they had before them was information from their own fire chief to the effect that a fire hazard existed in the Foothills only if the Foothills were to remain in their natural condition and that any hazard from fire would be materially reduced by development. While ordinarily, the factual determination made by a city council to justify passage of an ordinance is final and not subject to judicial review, the recitation of imaginary or non-existent hazards can be considered with the other evidence to determine the purpose and effect of the enactment. [16]

Among the other purposes Palo Alto cited to justify its new zoning were the protection of agricultural land, the conservation of valuable natural resources, and the prevention of harm resulting from seismic activity. But the court noted that the only information available to the city council made it clear that the land in question could serve none of these purposes. Because of its soil and slope characteristics, it was not suitable for agriculture. The city conceded that it contained no valuable natural resources. And the council had no information about seismic hazards on the site. Further, the court added, the city itself did not consider this land to be valuable as a watershed, as an area for flood control, or as an important place for the preservation of wildlife. (Indeed, the open space element of the city's general plan, prepared in April 1972, had a hard time justifying the preservation of land in the foothills without resorting to such meaningless generalities as the following: "the need to conserve, and return the area's biotic communities to the indigenous environment of the Foothills without further altering the ecological balance there.")[17]

Behind the screen of new zoning regulations, the court recognized Palo Alto's strategy for blocking all development:

While the regulations purport to permit residential development on ten-acre sites, an analysis of the limitation makes it plain that no such development could ever have taken place. Minimum development costs would have required [the lots] to be marketed for at least $100,000 each. . . .

It seems obvious that the purchaser of a building site at a cost of $100,000 might plan to construct some rather elaborate structures on his ten acres, but the ordinance would prohibit that.   Only 3½ percent of the site could be covered with impervious construction, so roads, tennis courts, barns, outhouses, swimming pools, etc., would be subject to severe limitations. Nor would the prospective purchaser be allowed to select the most attractive location for his property. The regulations require both clustering of structures, as well as a minimum ten-acre lot size, so even though parcels of land are very large, the houses would be required to be grouped together in sight of one another. Nor could a desirable knoll be used as a building site, because, to protect the view from the park and the roads, sites were required to be unobtrusive. It was certainly totally unrealistic to expect any purchaser to spend such an amount of money to acquire so little freedom to use his property. It must be concluded that the framers of the *ordinance had just that in mind. They designed a purported permitted use but surrounded it with so many limitations in order to make it, as far as they were able, a use that could never be made of the property.*

The facts as found indicate that the other uses, purportedly permitted, were equally unrealistic. It is plain that the objective and the effect of the open space regulations was not to control development, but to prevent it.[18]

The court, of course, did not question the desirability of preserving open space but rather the way Palo Alto went about its business: "However laudable the motive to preserve scenic beauties, the City must act, not by subterfuge, but by law."[19]

A summary of Palo Alto's complicated maneuvers was sufficient to resolve the case in favor of the developer:

The basic question of the law, then is this: If a city with power to do so, decides to acquire property to preserve scenic beauty, open space and the view from a public park and city roads, takes substantially all steps toward doing so, short of payment, leads the public and property owners to believe that the acquisition is inevitable, delays all development of the property while preparing for acquisition, and then, when it has determined that the cost is higher than hoped, on the pretense of protecting against non-existent hazards found to exist without substantial evidence, enacts a zoning ordinance, accomplishing all of the purposes of the acquisitions, which purports to allow uses of property which are not economically realistic, with no inquiry as to the economic feasibility of the purported uses, is the resulting loss of value to the property affected compensable? The answer must be "yes."[20]

Following the decision, Palo Alto agreed in an out-of-court settlement to buy the land for $7.5 million. Although the developer eventually collected fair compensation, the outcome still generated no homebuilding that might have relieved Palo Alto's housing shortage or helped to meet a regionwide housing need. It may, however, have suggested to other communities that there are limits to what the courts will tolerate from local government even in the name of environmental protection.

Two phrases, particularly, stand out in this decision. One, "the recitation of imaginary or non-existent hazards," is an apt description of the way many communities justify measures to stop growth. The other phrase, equally apt, describes the way local governments use tightly drawn regulations as a subterfuge for blocking development: "They designed a purported permitted use but surrounded it with so many limitations in order to make it, as far as they were able, a use that could never be made of the property."

The Palo Alto story also reveals something else about growth-control politics. A respected professional study set Palo Alto off on its dubious course of action by reducing complex issues about community development to a simple notion that public policy should be based on the twin principles of saving property tax dollars and preserving open space. Each of these purposes had a very special meaning in the Palo Alto context and could have been given a critical investigation. Instead when joined together they became irresistibly alluring, so much so that public-spirited and idealistic organizations helped commit the city to growth control through opportunistic tactics. The outcome not only calls into question the contribution of technical studies but it also suggests that strange alliances emerge in support of environmental goals.[21]

Chapter 9
Why Do Environmentalists Attack Homebuilding?

In the growth controversies of northern California, environmental groups and other opponents of homebuilding have struck close alliances. The other opponents have been active for a long time, resisting new housing because they were afraid of what it would do to their property taxes or to the social makeup of their neighborhoods. But they never enjoyed as much success before as they have since they learned how to team up with environmentalists.

Environmental issues have given new respectability to defenders of the suburban status quo, spreading a cover of the public interest over what would otherwise be a narrow case of self-interest. In addition, the environmental movement has created new channels for housing opponents to use, such as environmental review procedures and court challenges of their adequacy. At the same time the environmental movement has directed public attention to new problems, such as the protection of wildlife, that are useful for blocking development.

In short, local environmental groups are not only trying to stop homebuilding themselves but they are also generating issues that help other groups stop homebuilding. But why should environmentalists oppose new housing? Adverse environmental impacts, such as water pollution, are exceptional and can usually be controlled without blocking entire developments. There is almost no connection between housing and the big environmental issues of our times—use of toxic substances, nuclear radiation hazards, conservation of natural resources. The attack on homebuilding does not follow from the central concerns of the environmental movement. Instead it represents a stretching of the environmental agenda to issues that are marginal. Under these circumstances the attack on homebuilding is able to inflict damage on housing consumers without making any important improvement in the quality of the public environment.

Reasons Environmentalists Give

One way to discover why environmental groups oppose homebuilding is to look at the arguments they have advanced in actual controversies. In northern California, a look at the record only deepens the puzzle, however.

Many housing controversies do not focus directly on homebuilding but have to do with public services such as roads and water lines needed for new development. In one such case the San Francisco chapter of the Sierra Club opposed plans to replace an existing bridge across southern San Francisco Bay with a newer one that could handle more traffic. It argued that a new bridge would encourage more homebuilding in East Bay communities for people who would then commute long distances to jobs on the opposite side of the bay. This increased traffic, the club contended, would degrade air quality and make the fuel shortage worse.[1]

Opposition to new housing where it leads to avoidable long-distance commuting is entirely consistent with environmentalists' concerns about both air pollution and energy use. But if new housing is objectionable where it leads to unnecessary commuting, then it should not be objectionable where it would let people live close to job centers. Yet earlier, when the voters were asked to approve a bond issue to bring more water to southern peninsula suburbs where a large number of jobs are located, the Sierra Club's San Francisco chapter came out in opposition. The club's reason at that time was that the water facilities would encourage "unplanned" growth in the suburbs "at a time when San Francisco was actually losing population."[2]

Apparently, the Sierra Club was opposed to housing in the suburbs because it could have been located instead in the central cities, in spite of the advantages of reducing commuting distances by building housing near suburban job centers. When new housing is built in the central cities, however, it normally involves either rebuilding existing neighborhoods at higher densities or filling in the remaining open areas of the cities. But when some San Francisco citizens mounted a campaign to discourage new high-density construction by limiting building heights to 160 feet in the downtown area and 40 feet in the rest of the city, the Sierra Club's San Francisco chapter supported this proposal.[3] And when the San Bruno Mountain development was proposed on open land just south of San Francisco, under a plan that would have kept about three-quarters of the land still open after the development was complete, the Sierra Club's Loma Prieta chapter found that objectionable, too. Their reason was that "the energy crisis and rising fuel costs make the provision of adequate public open space and park facilities close to urban concentrations of people the highest of needs." As a result they objected to a plan that would fill in any part of the scarce remaining open space close to San Francisco.

A look at the positions taken by another prominent California environmental group, People for Open Space, shows the same pattern of argument. This group objected to housing in the fertile valleys of northern California because it would destroy farmland and pave over the rich black soil.[5] But if the valleys are poor locations because their soil is too good, People for Open Space has found the hillsides objectionable for other reasons: construction on hilly sites is more expensive than on flatland; extra miles of roads and utility lines must wind their way uphill to reach scattered houses; and hill developments increase the chances of landslides, floods, and brushfires.[6] This group has said it favors accommodating population growth in new towns rather than in suburban tracts, but it attacked the only recent proposal for a new town in the San Francisco area on the grounds that it would increase air pollution.[7] Elsewhere, it objected to new development because of its location in a "corridor of outstanding scenic beauty" —although very little land in the San Francisco Bay Area does not have scenic beauty.[8]

What can we make of these many arguments? They shift back and forth from issues of regional growth management—such as holding down commuting distances—to very local impacts such as the loss of a scenic site. There are many grounds for objection, with no clear sense of priorities among them. As a result any proposed housing is sure to be attacked for some reason. One possible interpretation is that environmental groups are simply no-growthers who will not come out of the closet and admit it. They use different arguments strategically to suit each controversy, but their underlying aim is to stop land development wherever it can be stopped.

A more charitable interpretation is that environmental activists are not fully aware of the contradictions in their own positions and have not yet figured out how to handle growth in an environmentally sound way. If this view is correct, it means that environmentalists attack homebuilding because their own priorities are unsettled and because some are bound to conflict with almost any housing proposal. New construction makes waves. Its local impacts always include creating *some* extra traffic and (unless it replaces existing developments) consuming *some* open land. It may also change the regional environment in some important way, such as crowding a major highway or building over an outstanding landscape. Further, it may violate some general principle environmentalists believe in, such as preserving prime agricultural land or minimizing energy and resource consumption for urban development.

Environmental groups, however, seem unwilling to compromise some objectives in order to achieve others. They may, for example, oppose homebuilding located where it will minimize local and regional impacts, on the basis that this location makes construction unnecessarily costly in resource or energy requirements. Yet if another proposal is more efficient in terms of resource use, but adds moderately to air pollution or commuting flows, they may oppose that, too. In short, environmentalists may find it easier to attack homebuilding than to straighten out their own priorities.

Environmental Policy Studies

Several groups concerned with environmental quality have prepared detailed, systematic statements of their positions on urban growth issues. Their statements show still other connections between environmental thinking and opposition to new housing.

The Rockefeller Task Force Report.

One of the best known recent works on environmental policy is *The Use of Land,* prepared by a task force sponsored by the Rockefeller Brothers Fund. This report criticizes past urban growth for producing "too many dreary, environmentally destructive suburbs of a single life-style; too many bland, indistinct city centers."[9] In defining the problems of urban growth, the task force returns to a twenty-year-old critique of postwar suburbia as an ugly, monotonous, and wasteful environment. "Suburban sprawl" was a favorite phrase of urban critics in the 1950s. And it lives again today in the age of environmentalism.[10]

The authors of *The Use of Land* are not opposed to all new housing, but they are against poorly planned or uncontrolled development. As an alternative they propose large planned developments (each with at least 500 housing units), with a full range of services and facilities, a variety of housing types, and imaginative, unified site designs. Although the task force tries hard to reconcile environmental goals with the need for a high volume of new housing, and although they offer a solution in the form of the large planned development, their argument still helps explain why environmentalists attack homebuilding.

First, selective opposition to poorly planned, uncontrolled development may not be very selective at all. Environmental groups are quick to characterize most new homebuilding as "poorly planned." Very little new housing is in developments as large as those the authors consider necessary to achieve good planning. Much of it is in planned unit developments, but at a smaller scale. The task force never explains why smaller planned unit developments cannot also offer satisfactory environments, nor has it taken a critical look at the "suburban sprawl" indictment of the 1950s. Although postwar suburbia certainly had its faults, several studies since then, as well as the evidence of the market place, have shown that a very large number of people find the typical suburban environment highly acceptable and desirable.[11] A Gallup poll taken in 1974, for example, reported that 75 percent of the people wanted to see future housing take the form of single-family homes spread more or less evenly through the region, instead of clustered multifamily buildings with open space between them. And two-thirds of the people surveyed regarded "a sizable piece of land up to one acre" as an important criterion for choosing a new home.[12]

The task force itself recognizes that in reality many people who share its environmental concerns will be less than discriminating in their opposition to housing: "Those fearful of large-scale projects and increasingly aware of what a continuation of piecemeal low-density development entails in destruction of open space and other environmental assets often select the simplest course: fight development wherever it rears its head."[13]

Further, the task force recognizes that people concerned about environmental quality are establishing so many regulatory obstacles that direct government help may well be needed to get an adequate volume of homebuilding.[14] Elaborate discretionary reviews proposed in *The Use of Land* would create fresh opportunities for opponents to block large planned developments. The report's proposal to exempt small projects from discretionary reviews[15] would encourage developers to operate at a small scale, which the task force finds objectionable, while the review process would be so risky and time-consuming that developers would be unable to build the large communities favored by the task force—without special government help. The search for environmental quality, as conceived by the task force, would lead either to deadlocks and underbuilding, or would require still unknown government innovations in order to keep housing markets working.

The Use of Land also reveals a more direct source of conflict between environmentalists and homebuilders in its proposals to protect large tracts of urban land from development. Although the task force urges "a balanced framework that is respectful both of conservation and development priorities,"[16] it also lays the groundwork for a less moderate approach. On the question of how much open land government should acquire, the answer is "buy as much as we can, as soon as we can."[17] Where states determine that privately owned land lies "in critical agricultural and environmental areas" the task force suggests that they encourage low-density zoning on the order of a minimum lot size of 50 acres per house.[18] The task force also proposes federal funding for an extensive green-space land acquisition program in urbanizing areas.[19]

Attempts to keep homebuilding out of very large areas of land around major cities, whether through 50-acre zoning or through public purchase, will disrupt land markets by restricting the sites available for new development. The task force concedes that its proposals might lead to increases in land cost, but brushes the point aside by describing them as "short run" and claiming that higher economic and environmental values will offset them "in the long run."[20] In reality, ambitious programs to protect open space may also require direct government intervention in order to keep homebuilding at a socially desirable level.

The California Coastal Plan

Another detailed statement of environmental policy, the California Coastal Plan, gives further evidence of how environmental objectives lead to conflicts with homebuilding. The California Coastal Zone Conservation Commission claims that its plan does not aim at stopping development but instead at channelling it in an orderly way to reduce the costs of urban sprawl:[21] "New . . . development shall not be permitted to sprawl, project by project, into open areas."[22]

Once more the enemy is sprawl, but finding workable alternatives to it is very hard within the framework of the coastal plan. One alternative might be compact development at the edge of existing built-up areas. The plan rules out this possibility by declaring "expansions of existing developed areas . . . shall not be allowed until the land resources within the existing developed areas are effectively used."[23] This policy calls for locating new growth on whatever open sites are still available in built-up communities, plus sites that can be cleared for rebuilding. Both infill development and clearance projects, however, generate strong political opposition that makes them very difficult to carry out, especially at a time when public control over land use decisions is increasing.

The coastal plan attaches still further conditions that make difficult types of development close to impossible. First, in certain coastal communities and neighborhoods with "unique cultural, historical, architectural, and aesthetic qualities," even infill development is not to be permitted if it might detract from their special qualities.[24] Second, major housing developments away from shopping and job centers are permissible only if they will have adequate transit service, and only if they will not generate traffic that reduces air quality significantly or leads to unnecessary fuel consumption.[25] Third, *all* new development must be planned to provide transit service, nearby shopping, and nonautomobile circulation such as bike paths and walkways.[26]

The environmental thinking reflected in the California Coastal Plan leaves open very few possibilities for housing development. After forcing new construction into already existing communities, it then restricts the number of communities that can take anything other than development of a very special character, and further imposes demanding requirements that new housing not generate much automobile traffic. This restricted notion of what constitutes acceptable environmental quality would surely not permit very much homebuilding in the coastal zone. It illustrates the way in which a declared concern for sound growth management amounts in reality to hostility to new housing. One of the court's conclusions in the Palo Alto case applies here: "They designed a purported permitted use but surrounded it with so many limitations in order to make it, as far as they were able, a use that could never be made."

The California Coastal Plan also lays the basis for land use conflicts between housing and agriculture, and between housing and open space. It establishes a policy of preserving all prime agricultural land for farming as well as preserving other nonprime land if it is currently used for crops or grazing or even if it only has the potential for such use.[27] The plan cites several reasons for this policy— including world food shortages, rising prices, and the economic value of agriculture—but presents no supporting information or argument on these points. Many of the crops that flourish in the coastal climate are specialty items, such as artichokes, asparagus, and avocados, that will not do very much for the hungry overseas. The plan establishes no connection between coastal agriculture and food price levels, and despite claims of great economic value for farming, the authors find it necessary to recommend state financial help to keep farmers in business.[28]

In addition to removing farmland and potential farmland from the supply that might be available for development, the plan also calls for more public acquisition of coastal land. With about half the coastline already in public ownership, the case for acquiring still more is not self-evident. However, the claims of the plan are that public ownership figures are misleading since about one-sixth of the public land consists of military reservations and that only 38 percent of the prime sandy swimming beaches are actually open to the public.

Setting aside places suitable for housing and community development is a low-priority item in the California Coastal Plan, ranking far behind such considerations as preserving farmland, open space, and air quality. Future population growth will somehow have to fit into the areas that were already urbanized by the early 1970s. If that fit is difficult to make, housing developers will have to figure out solutions or else move to another part of the state.

The California Tomorrow Plan
Another California plan, prepared by a notable group of private citizens, also illustrates why the environmental mind-set gives short shrift to housing. The

California Tomorrow Plan would zone most of the state for conservation. Its conservation zone includes "lands for protection of ecologic, scenic, historic, and archeologic values; the preserves of threatened or unique animal or plant species; lands for conservation of water, forest, rangeland and desert resources, and game; open water, shoreline, and aquifer-recharge zones; and fire, flood, erosion, or earthquake hazard areas."[29] The second largest zone is for farmland and potential farmland. The zone for urban development consists of "lands which do not fall in either of the first two categories and which have already been urbanized."[30]

Once more housing ranks below other, more urgent considerations. And a growing population will have to find room somewhere within already established communities. This plan has certain features of the California Coastal Plan. Both suggest that part of the environmental attack on homebuilding is simply an expression of a value system that gives top priority to activities that keep the land open and scenic. There is no reasoned attack on housing in either plan, but simply a neglect of housing in pursuit of other objectives. Both plans treat housing as an encroachment on valuable open space and a spoiler of clean air.

Conventional land use plans start with forecasts of population and economic growth and then propose ways of handling this growth and the needs it creates for housing, industrial land, shopping, transportation, and public services. By contrast environmentally based land use plans begin with surveys of natural resources and pay little or no attention to projections of population increase and economic change. The California Coastal Plan contains no forecast of either population or jobs for the coastal zone. The California Tomorrow Plan covers anticipated population increase in two sentences. These plans have no housing goals, and they place no positive value on future homebuilding. They view housing mainly as a source of potential trouble for the environment. If they cannot avoid having some, they shunt it into existing communities rather than let it bring inevitable degradation to natural areas not yet spoiled by urban growth.

Other Sources of Environmental Opposition to Housing

The statements and writings of environmental groups have suggested some sources of their conflict with homebuilding. But there is more to the story. To understand why the political agenda of environmentalists has come to include stopping homebuilding, it is useful to look first at the values and attitudes that come out of the background of the conservation movement, then at the relationship between environmentalism and more narrowly based pressures to protect the suburbs against change, and finally at the personal stake that many environmentalists have in blocking suburban growth.

Historical Background

The notion of environmentalism that considers housing just a polluter of nature is no true descendant of the mainstream conservation movement in the United States. That movement, which led to the creation of national parks and forests, to comprehensive water resource development, and to many innovations in public land management, had as its guiding principle the wise, efficient use of resources. The purpose of national forests, for example, was to promote scientific timber management. According to Gifford Pinchot, chief forester during the Theodore Roosevelt administration and a leading figure of the conservation movement, "The object of our forest policy is not to preserve the forests because they are beautiful . . . or because they are refuges for the wild creatures of the wilderness . . . but [because they are essential for] . . . the making of prosperous homes. . . . Every other consideration comes as secondary."[31] The national forests have, in fact, been managed with economic development purposes in mind and have been open to both grazing and lumbering under controlled conditions.

Environmentalists who take a dim view of urban development inherit much of their perspective from another movement that emerged late in the progressive era, that of the preservationists. In 1908 and 1909, when the Theodore Roosevelt administration tried to broaden the base of political support for its conservation policies, new interest groups came forward that disagreed with the prevailing emphasis on economic growth. Their members were mainly well-to-do people from the eastern cities who deplored the changes industrialism was bringing to American society: urban growth, materialistic values, and the decline of the traditional virtues. They believed in promoting rural life as an alternative to the growing cities with their social disorder. For them conservation was a moral crusade. Protecting nature had a spiritual, not a material, purpose. "National Parks," according to one spokesman, "represent opportunities for worship through which one comes to understand more fully certain of the attributes of nature and its Creator."[32]

The different perspectives of the conservationists and the preservationists came to a head in a controversy over the Hetch-Hetchy Valley in Yosemite National Park. The city of San Francisco asked the federal government for permission to use a reservoir in the valley for its water supply. Gifford Pinchot supported this request, arguing that water supply was a more important public use than recreation, and he persuaded Theodore Roosevelt to support it as well. John Muir and his Sierra Club, who were instrumental in persuading Congress to include the valley within Yosemite National Park, were thoroughly outraged. The controversy went on for half a dozen years before Congress finally authorized the reservoir. Meanwhile the political alliance of conservationists and preservationists split apart. Conservation leaders characterized their former allies as "misinformed nature lovers." John Muir in turn wrote bitterly of the "triumphant growth of the wealthy wicked. . . . We may lose this particular fight, but truth and right must prevail at last."[33]

The current attack on homebuilding comes essentially out of the preservationist tradition. By contrast the major recent environmental literature, such as Commoner's *The Closing Circle,* still reflects mainstream conservationist concern with the wise use of resources and of technology to provide for society's needs. In the preservationist view, however, nature is to be protected from change. Where the material wants of society threaten to disturb nature, preservationists are likely to call for society to reform itself by reducing its material wants.

In this spirit, when the California Coastal Zone Conservation Commission had to develop standards for siting energy plants along the coast, it tried to solve a large part of the problem by calling on Californians to use less energy: "Nonessential consumption of energy shall be reduced statewide, thereby reducing the adverse environmental impact of energy supply facilities on the coast."[34] Further, the commission puts the burden on any company proposing an energy plant to show that "energy conservation efforts, including concerted efforts by the applicant within its service area, cannot reasonably . . . eliminate the need for the proposed facility."[35]

Similarly, when preservation-minded groups turn their attention to housing, they propose policies that call for society to change itself rather than change the environment. Thus they argue that consumers should do without new housing in open areas and should instead settle for locations in existing communities; that homebuilders should find ways of coping with high land prices and other obstacles to infill development; and that government should subject new housing to elaborate discretionary reviews, regardless of whether these reviews limit the amount of homebuilding or increase costs to consumers.

Nor are environmentalists always very discriminating in deciding what in nature is worth preserving. When a rare or endangered animal lives on a site proposed for housing, opponents have a logical preservationist reason for trying to block it. But when there are no rare or endangered species involved, the case is harder to make. Harder, but not impossible: "The coyote is not always considered a beneficial animal," conceded the Blackhawk Ranch environmental impact report as it opened a discussion of how new housing might affect the number of coyotes living in the area.[36]

Stretching the Concept of Environment

Another reason for environmentalists' opposition to homebuilding is that the concept of the environment is a loose one easily stretched to include many values and purposes. In suburban America, preserving the environment usually means preserving the social status quo as well. If no open land is to be developed, then newcomers cannot move into a town except through the gradual turnover of older housing.

In political controversies the new concept of the environment has been able to absorb an earlier and more selfish agenda concerned with preserving the status quo against newcomers. During the suburban build-up of the 1950s, suburbs were already using their land development controls to keep out undesirables.[37] The main fiscal undesirables then were families living in modest homes with young children whose education would use up property tax dollars. Other undesirables were people whose arrival in a community would lower its social tone— that is, people whose occupation, income level, life-style, religion, or skin color might threaten the prestige levels established by earlier residents. Concern for the environment, as such, was not an important political factor in the 1950s. When this concern emerged later, it reinforced and provided cover for local groups more concerned with fiscal and social undesirables than with protection of wildlife.

The environmental view was easy to reconcile with the earlier opposition to suburban change because neither outlook considered the welfare of people not already living in the community. In the 1950s suburban pressure groups asked, "How can we avoid property tax increases in this town?" or "How can we maintain a desirable social status here?" The later environmental groups asked, "How can we maintain the territory of this town as an attractive environment?" Neither group cared much about the impact of local policies on the well-being of people living outside the community who might have wanted to move in.

Environmentalists have found powerful allies in groups that oppose suburban development for reasons other than their own. Often they have cultivated this support deliberately. A guidebook for local environmental activists gives this advice: "if the key vote on rezoning a parcel for more intensive use is held by a councilman who has no interest in conserving open space but who opposes development which will increase the local property tax load, he, ideally, should be approached with tax-related arguments."[38] One problem with this new political alliance is that it lends the legitimacy of an environmental crusade in the public interest to what is otherwise a selfish and provincial concern with the local tax rate. A second problem is that in trying to recruit others, environmentalists sometimes find themselves marching in somebody else's demonstration.

Thus while taxpayer groups put on the mantle of environmental protection, environmentalists sometimes lose sight of their own objectives and oppose growth carelessly for economic reasons that they have not looked at critically. In the San Francisco area, People for Open Space seems to condemn almost all growth and not just environmentally destructive growth, on the grounds that housing developments require public services that cost the taxpayer money: "Grapes and cows need no schools, nor do they pollute the air . . . Compare these advantages to what the whole community must pay for sprawl and tract housing."[39] "Growth continues accompanied by smog and skyrocketing taxes. Citizens now know,—alas!—that there is a community price to pay for growth in the form of new streets, new schools, new water supplies and sewers."[40] This ready exchange of rhetoric between environmentalists and suburban status quo groups helps explain why opposition to new housing sometimes seems like an integral part of environmental doctrine.

The Private Interests of Environmentalists
Still another reason why environmentalists oppose homebuilding is that this opposition also serves their own private interests. Environmental groups active in local growth politics have an upper-middle-class membership with strong representation of professionals, executives, scientists, and engineers. A recent survey of the Sierra Club membership showed that fully two-thirds of the main wage earners in members' housholds came from the following occupational groups: lawyers, doctors, dentists, other professionals, college teachers and other teachers, managers and executives, and engineers. More than half the members have had some postgraduate education, with 18 percent having a Ph.D., law, or medical degree, and 21 percent a master's degree.[41]

This is not a typical cross section of people who buy homes in new tract developments. Highly educated professionals and executives can usually afford the high cost of a house in an established, desirable suburb with an attractive environment. Their opposition to homebuilding is usually opposition to someone else's opportunity to buy a moderate-cost house. And the environment they protect is an environment they can afford to enjoy. The Sierra Club membership survey spoke clearly about whether its members were concerned with everyone's environment or only with their own. When asked, "Should the Club concern itself with the conservation problems of such special groups as the urban poor and ethnic minorities?", 58 percent of the members answered that they either strongly or "somewhat" opposed such involvement.[42]

Protecting Farmland—for Whom?

To uncover the sources of environmentalists' opposition to homebuilding, it is also useful to investigate why environmental groups support other policies that put them in conflict with new housing proposals. The clearest example is the case they make in favor of protecting farmland against urban development. They argue that protecting farmland serves important national and even international interests. Yet a close look at their position shows that the public interest rhetoric is deceptive and that the most likely underlying purpose is simply to protect certain local qualities of life that environmentalists enjoy.

The Sierra Club has given strong support to California legislation designed to block the use of farmland for urban debelopment. The club's public statements emphasize world food shortages as the main reason for preserving productive agricultural land. In 1975 the California legislature considered a bill to prevent local governments from allowing almost any construction on prime agricultural land. The Sierra Club's Sacramento lobbyist, John Zierold, explained his support for it in these terms:

Population has finally overtaken food. . . .
During the next decade 250 million will doubtless die of starvation. World hunger is no longer remote, no longer the abstract privation of faraway lands, lamented by the affluent only when they say grace over sumptuous holiday provender. It is a moral concern that clings to all humankind, with us to stay because we have not husbanded resources with the providence necessary to bring into balance land, water, fertilizer and energy in a manner essential to a small, overcrowded planet. . . .
The need for AB15 [the proposed bill] is inarguable; clearly evident to conservationists, consumer groups and, indeed, the thoughtful and compassionate

everywhere. As energy, transportation and food costs continue to spiral, condoning the spendthrift conversion of productive farmland to urban sprawl is perilous folly. . . .[43]

To drive home the connection between California's urban development policies and world hunger, the Sierra Club illustrated Zierold's column with a cartoon showing a starving woman and child crumpled on the streets of a foreign city.

But does the urbanization of California farmland threaten either the nation's or the world's food supply? It clearly does not, according to evidence of the recent past. During the 1950s and 1960s California gained three times as much farmland through irrigation as it lost to urban development. On the average, from 15,000 to 20,000 acres per year went from agricultural to urban uses while irrigation produced a *net* gain of 56,000 acres each year.[44] Some environmentalists argue that the land lost to urban development was of higher quality than the new farmland resulting from irrigation. Little information is available on the quality of the land that was lost, but most of the new farmland returns a high yield per acre and falls within the established state definition of prime agricultural land.[45]

If urban development results in no net loss of productive farmland, it is hard to understand how it can add to the problem of hunger in the world. Furthermore, most of the California farms that are sold to subdividers grow specialty crops and not the basic foodstuffs that could relieve hunger overseas. The much-lamented farmland absorbed by the rapid growth of San Jose, for example, had earlier been used to produce prunes, apricots, and walnuts.

Since environmentalists argue for preserving farmland as a national policy, a look at some national numbers is also in order. Urban development uses only a tiny portion of the country's land supply—2.7 percent as of 1969, including land used for all roads, railroads, and airports. By contrast nearly 60 percent of the country's land is used for agriculture.[46] The amount of farmland taken over for urban development every decade comes to less than eight-tenths of 1 percent of the total land used for agriculture. Normal fluctuations in farming from year to year shift much greater amounts of land into and out of crop production as prices rise and fall. In 1973 when food prices increased and the federal government cut back soil bank subsidies, farmers increased their cultivated cropland by 28 million acres—enough to accomodate a full century of urban growth at current land conversion rates.[47]

Even in rapidly urbanizing parts of the country, recent losses of cropland to urban development have been small. The U.S. Department of Agriculture studied 53 counties that had rapid urban population increases between 1960 and 1970; together, these counties accounted for 20 percent of the entire country's population growth during this period. Cropland in these counties declined slightly from 32.9 percent of their total area in 1961 to 30.4 percent in 1970, but even here only 49 percent of the decline resulted from land lost to urban development. A greater amount of cropland was simply withdrawn from production and left open and idle as a result of economic factors and changing farm technology. Significantly, these counties added more new acreage to their cropland than what they lost solely as a result of urban expansion.[48]

Urban development is no more than a minor factor influencing the country's supply of farmland. The authors of a recent study conclude: "On the basis of existing data, it would appear that the conversion of farmland to urban uses does not constitute a serious threat to the nation's capacity to provide agricultural products."[49]

Perhaps the Sierra Club's argument that saving farmland near California cities will alleviate world hunger results from a belief that the United States should greatly expand its food shipments to poor countries and will need to use even farmland near cities for this purpose. If so, the club hasn't looked very carefully at the problem. First, whether massive exports are a promising solution to food shortages in poor countries is debatable. Many experts in this field argue that sending surplus food from North America to developing countries is counterproductive in that it discourages their governments from making reasonable use of their own agricultural resources.[50] Second, even if the United States decided on a big increase in food production for shipments overseas, the country already has a very large reserve of land that could be planted. If cropland already existing but now unused were brought into production and if available technologies were fully adopted, by 1985 the United States could increase its grain exports by nearly 200 percent over 1972–1974 levels and still meet all domestic demand.[51]

Even more to the point, Is the Sierra Club itself in favor of increasing food production in the United States for the benefit of third world countries? By no means, according to the club's statement of agricultural policy:

Within environmental constraints, we must develop stand-by food reserves. However, efforts to expand drastically North American food production, at potentially great environmental cost, must be viewed with caution.[52]

The Sierra Club then argues that preventing California cities from expanding onto nearby farmland, most of which is used only for specialty crops, will somehow alleviate hunger in the world; yet the club itself does not favor expansion of American food production. Despite its claims of moral concern and compassion for the poor, the Sierra Club clearly is not conducting its campaign to preserve farmland for the benefit of hungry people in foreign countries. For whose benefit do environmentalists want to preserve farmland? Is it possible that behind the facade of concern for the public interest environmentalists have mainly their own interests in mind?

Costs to Consumers
Sierra Club statements on farmland preservation suggest at least one more purpose that goes beyond the private interests of their own members. They speak of "spiralling food costs" as one of the outcomes of urban sprawl in California, and they offer to help the American consumer by limiting urban development.[53] But this concern for the consumer is too limited. It considers only the size of his food bill but not the additional costs that a program of farmland preservation would impose on him. One of these is the extra amount he will have to pay for housing if the supply of land for new homebuilding is restricted by stopping the conversion of all farmland. Another important item is the consumer's tax bill. Preserving farmland almost always means giving preferential tax treatment to the owners of farm property. When their assessments are reduced, other taxpayers pay more to make up for the lost revenue. This situation is especially familiar to Californians because, as noted earlier, the current state program to preserve farmland (the Williamson Act) cost California taxpayers some $60 million a year in revenue losses and compensatory payments to local governments by the early 1970s. The Williamson Act has become a boondoggle by giving tax reductions mainly for nonprime land located far from urban growth, with the biggest subsidies going to agribusiness corporations that have no intention of developing their property.[54] Even environmentalists no longer defend it, but the new measures supported by the Sierra Club and its allies would offer reduced assessments to even more landowners than are now covered, at correspondingly higher costs to the public.

The Sierra Club's very partial look at consumer welfare makes its interest in consumers about as convincing as its interest in poor countries that suffer from food shortages. This is not to say, however, that there are no legitimate farmland issues affecting a large part of the American public. The present system does involve major costs for irrigating and fertilizing new cropland to make up for other land lost to urban development, but neither the Sierra Club nor anyone else has done a thorough study of all the costs and all the benefits in the present system compared with some feasible alternative.

Costs to Environmentalists

Environmentalists have more personal concerns at stake in their campaign to save farmland. Murray Rosenthal, chairman of the club's California legislative committee, identified one of them: "... we can expect severe pressures within the foreseeable future to pay for today's mistakes by converting our forests, or our grasslands or our wilderness into the food production we lost by the urbanization of prime land."[55] The development of new cropland, in short, threatens to reduce the amount of open, nonagricultural land in the country, which environmentalists consider part of their own recreational turf. The trade-off here is between making a small reduction in wilderness areas prized by outdoor recreationists versus blocking a comparably small loss of farmland that could provide enough living space for the country's growing urban population. There is no question how environmentalists view that trade-off.

Environmental groups also support measures to keep farmland because of the reasons noted earlier in Marin and Napa Counties. Keeping agriculture alive is a cheap way for local governments to preserve open space—certainly much cheaper than having to buy the land. The attractiveness of local farms to tax-conscious residents who want open space has certainly not been lost on the farmers themselves. People for Open Space quotes with approval this ad that turned up on milk cartons in the San Francisco area:

We need green-belts surrounding our cities and towns. Clover Dairy Farms provide more than 72,000 acres of green-belt land in the north bay counties ... at no expense to taxpayers.[56]

Keeping some farming in suburban areas adds to the scenery, shuts out unwanted population growth, and satisfies the tastes of many environmentalists as well as other citizens. As environmental writer Harold Gilliam has interpreted agricultural preservation in Marin and Napa counties, "The objective was ... to preserve scenic, agricultural, and recreational values against the bulldozer, ... in short to enhance the quality of life in a superlative environment."[57]

"To enhance the quality of life" in communities where environmentalists live is a far more accurate account of why environmental groups want to protect farmland than their professed concern about world hunger or spiralling food prices. A local food supply, incidentally, can also contribute to the quality of life. T. J. Kent, Jr., president of People for Open Space, has written:

No one in the Bay Area needs to be told that there is a life-enhancing difference between fresh blackberries, artichokes, and apples and their usual supermarket counterparts, . . . between fresh tomatoes and supermarket tomatoes. Thus with open space systems . . . we will be able to retain not only unique and highly-valued agricultural land such as the Napa Valley Vineyards, we will also be able to greatly increase our production, use, and appreciation of local agricultural produce.[58]

To the minor extent that food supply explains environmentalists' interest in protecting farmland from urban development, the food involved seems to be mainly treats for their own tables. Their manipulation of serious environmental issues, such as the availability of cropland resources and the production of food for the third world, calls to mind a phrase quoted earlier from the court decision in the Palo Alto case. These statements amount to "the recitation of imaginary and non-existent hazards" useful for persuading government to do what environmentalists want, while charging the costs to other people.

Why is the Environmental Opposition Effective?

The haphazard, almost incidental, origins of the environmental attack on home-building, plus the elite character of its advocates, would not seem to provide a strong base for political success. Yet environmentalists and their friends have succeeded, in many parts of the country, in putting tough new growth regulations into place and in defeating homebuilders in political confrontations. How have they done it?

First, and most important, a large body of public opinion cares about the environment. Environmental issues do well at the polls—both the ballot boxes and the public opinion polls. In recent congressional elections, for example, most of the candidates endorsed by the League of Conservation Voters have won while most of the "dirty dozen" congressmen singled out by Environmental Action for their objectionable records have been replaced.[59] Environmental causes have also done well in state and local bond issues and in statewide referenda such as the one that established the California Coastal Commission. The growth of environmental organizations is itself a testimony to widespread public interest. There are now about 5,000 organizations active in environmental affairs, of which more than half were established after 1968.[60]

Environmental concerns rate high in the public opinion polls as well. Pollution/conservation ranked sixth in the public's top priorities for federal spending as reported in a Gallup poll in 1976.[61] Young people and the highly educated consistently give higher priority to pollution and environmental issues than the population at large. In a Gallup poll of 1973, for example, when the population at large ranked pollution sixth among the most important problems facing the nation, people under 30 and people with a college education ranked it second.[62] Education intensifies people's awareness of environmental problems, and right now 5,000 environmental groups, many public agencies, and the mass media are all educating the public to be concerned.

Also contributing to a favorable political climate is the high visibility of suburban growth problems and the near invisibility of the costs of stopping growth. Everyone who enjoys a drive in the country knows of places where uninspiring new homes have replaced charming scenery. Although the new homes have helped many families improve their lives, they still clutter the view for the passer-by. The spread of ticky-tacky houses has become an acknowledged image in American folklore, and the benefits of stopping new developments are almost as visible. Fields and hillsides remain open and scenic. Nearby residents avoid the inconveniences of construction work, new neighbors crowding the roads, and new children crowding the classrooms. The costs of stopping homebuilding are hidden. Although most people are aware of the recent escalation in home prices, very few connect price increases to local growth restrictions.

In politics at the local level, where most growth controls are made and enforced, greater awareness of the costs of stopping homebuilding would probably make very little difference in any event as long as these costs are imposed only on outsiders and do not affect the voters. The arena of local politics is ideal for environmental and other opponents of homebuilding. Present residents who elect representatives to make the decisions almost always benefit. Nonvoters who live elsewhere pay the cost, but they are not represented when the decisions are made.

In actual controversies the interests of nonresidents who may want to buy homes in a community get little or no attention. The issue generally emerges as community residents versus a homebuilder. Environmental opponents of housing almost never concede that the homebuilder is in business to supply a product that many families want. As People for Open Space describes the situation, "The developer makes his substantial profit in subdivisions, shopping centers, industrial parks ... True. But the whole community pays in constantly escalating county taxes for new highways, new water supply, new schools, new social services."[63] Or, as the planning director of a well-known California suburb put it to me, "The developer's function is simple and straightforward: he is here to rape the community for a profit."

So the availability of a popular scapegoat—the homebuilder, also known as the rapist of the landscape—makes the politics of stopping growth even easier. The benefits of growth control are spread widely in the community, but the only conspicuous person who pays a cost is the homebuilder, the new villain of housing mythology.

In short, environmental opposition to homebuilding is more easily explainable in political terms than as part of a reform agenda for improving the quality of American communities. It has descended historically from the preservation rather than the conservation movement. Although it draws on several themes of current environmental thinking, its underlying rationale has little to do with mainstream environmental issues. Housing is in fact a residual item on the environmental agenda, easily neglected in the pursuit of other goals. Opposing homebuilding, however, serves the private interests of many environmentalists and of other defenders of the suburban status quo. It offers an attractive political position, particularly at the local level. As a result it has become an important force shaping urban development and limiting the nation's ability to supply new housing at a time when the number of families who need housing is growing faster than ever.

Chapter 10
The Costs of No-Growth Politics

What have the turbulent politics of environmental and growth controls done to housing consumers? This basic question can have no simple answer. The housing market of a large metropolitan area such as San Francisco responds to many influences at once. There is no sure way of knowing to what extent housing shortages or high prices result from the state of the national economy, the availability of mortgage money, the impact of local growth regulations, or other factors. Still it is possible to trace some of the likely effects of the housing controversies reviewed in earlier chapters and to make informed judgments about what is happening as a result of the tough regulatory climate around San Francisco.

Several results are clear. The amount of housing blocked by controversies and either built after a long delay or not built at all is very large—large enough to make a difference in the price and availability of housing in the region. Second, the cumulative effect of successful efforts to stop housing developments must be to increase prices and to restrict the number of places where middle-income families can afford to buy new homes. Third, the effect of stopping or reducing the size of infill developments near the built-up parts of the region must be to increase the number of homebuyers who will live far from established job centers and will have to commute long distances at high personal and environmental costs. Finally, it is very likely that the pattern of growth controversies in the San Francisco area has discouraged the construction of carefully planned large developments and has encouraged in their place new homebuilding of lower quality.

How Much Housing is Caught in the No-Growth Squeeze?

Four of the controversies reported in earlier chapters led directly to the elimination of 22,069 housing units that developers originally intended to build in the San Francisco region (see table 4). Construction plans for San Bruno Mountain and the Palo Alto foothills were stopped entirely. The Mountain Village development in Oakland and Harbor Bay Isle in Alameda were not stopped, but the developers were able to keep them alive only by cutting their size.

One way to put this amount of unbuilt housing in perspective is to compare it with the normal volume of homebuilding in the San Francisco region. In this nine-county area, the number of new housing units built from 1970 through 1977 averaged 45,000 per year. Thus the amount of housing eliminated from these four developments alone totaled about half a year's production for the

Table 4
Adding up the losses

Development	Units lost
Mountain Village	
1972 plan	2,183 housing units proposed
1976 plan	− 275 approved (est.)
	1,908
Harbor Bay Isle	
1972 plan	9,055 housing units proposed
	− 3,170 approved
	5,885
Crocker Hills	12,500 housing units proposed plan shelved
Palo Alto foothills	1,776 housing units proposed plan shelved
Total:	22,069

entire region. It is true that only a part of this housing would have been built in any single year, with much of it scheduled to be built in later phases of each development. Still half a year's supply is obviously a significant amount of housing. If the losses from these projects were not made up by additional construction elsewhere, the result would be a drastic reduction in the availability of new homes.

Many other proposed developments around San Francisco have also become embroiled in controversies that either stopped them or cut their size. How much construction has been aborted in this way is unknown, but a reasonable guess is that other controversies affected at least as much housing as the ones reported in this study. As a result between 1970 and 1977 local regulations may have stopped the equivalent of as much as a year's normal volume of homebuilding.

In the two cases where substantial amounts of housing survived, growth politics forced it into much higher price brackets than were originally proposed. In Mountain Village the 1972 plan was to build houses at an average price below $30,000. The revised plan of 1976 not only provided for only one-eighth as much housing but jacked up the prices almost beyond recognition. Of the 275 units that survived, 100 were to be "estate lots" selling for $35,000 to $75,000 for the land only, which the buyers would probably use for custom-built houses costing on the order of $100,000 to $200,000 each. The other 175 houses remaining were intended for a price range of $40,000 to $60,000. At Harbor Bay Isle the 1972 plan was to build condominium units priced between $21,000 and $37,000. By 1976 the plan called for a third as much housing priced from $55,000 to $165,000, and averaging $65,000 per house.

What Replaced Lost Housing?

Many real estate ventures go sour for reasons having nothing to do with local regulation. If the demand for housing is still there, in time some other developer normally finds a way to build it. Undoubtedly most housing that was eliminated as the result of environmental controversies will also be built later and elsewhere. But building later and elsewhere means building something different from what was originally proposed. From the point of view of the housing consumer —especially the middle-income family—it probably means building something less desirable on several counts.

Because of rapid changes in the housing economy, what was feasible in 1972 was no longer feasible in 1977. In California as in the rest of the country, steady increases in construction costs together with other increases in homeownership expenses—mortgage interest rates, fuel and utility bills, and property taxes—have priced new homes beyond the reach of more and more middle-income families each year. Developers confronted with the new costs have had to build increasingly in high-price brackets.

In short, by blocking developers who were prepared to build in 1972 and 1973, the region lost an opportunity to make big additions to its supply of moderate-cost homes.

The lost opportunity is clear from a look at changing price trends for single-family tract housing, which is the major source of new homes for families in middle-income brackets. In 1972, 57 percent of the new tract homes in the San Francisco area sold for less than $30,000. A year later only 27 percent were in this price range, and by 1974 only 9 percent. For families able to afford a slightly more expensive home, the supply disappeared almost as fast. In 1972 more than three-quarters of all the new tract homes were priced below $35,000. By 1974 fewer than a fourth were available at this price.[1]

Official Denials

Growth policies around San Francisco have blocked a large amount of home-building and have shifted at least some construction from middle-income to high-income price levels. These conclusions seem clear enough from the analysis of a handful of housing controversies; yet official studies of what has been happening obscure and deny even these obvious conclusions. One study minimizes the importance of environmental litigation while another study minimizes the costs of delay resulting from regulatory reviews.

The controversies reported in earlier chapters show that lawsuits are a very important tactic used to delay or defeat housing proposals. Most of the lawsuits in these controversies involved charges that the environmental impact report prepared for the development proposal failed to meet the requirements of the California Environmental Quality Act. The State Office of Planning and Research undertook a study prompted by public expressions of concern that litigation under this act "has been excessive and frivolous, resulting in unnecessary legal costs and costs of project delay."[2] To see whether this concern was justified, staff members of the state agency prepared an inventory of all lawsuits filed between 1971 and 1975 that involved alleged violations of the California Environmental Quality Act. They found a total of 244 lawsuits filed during this period.

The case studies reported in this book involved four different lawsuits alleging violations of the California Environmental Quality Act (CEQA). It is not reassuring to discover that only two of the four appear in the state's inventory. One wonders how many other environmental lawsuits the researchers also missed.

The way the Office of Planning and Research appraises the volume of litigation is also interesting. The researchers compare the number of lawsuits filed to the number of public and private projects that could theoretically have given rise to court cases. This number includes not only projects for which environmental impact reports were prepared but also the much larger number of projects too small to require an impact report—on the grounds that some lawsuits challenge governmental decisions that no environmental impact report is necessary. For the year of 1974 the study uses a state legislative committee estimate that 4,000 environmental impact reports were prepared. It then multiplies this number by five on the basis of a different state agency estimate that the number of projects not requiring environmental impact reports exceeds the number requiring them by a factor of between five and ten. So the number of projects undertaken in

1974 may be some 20,000, while the actual number of cases filed that year was only 62. The study then concludes that environmental lawsuits challenged only a tiny fraction of all development proposals.[3]

Yet a closer look at the state's inventory tells a different story: First, very few people bring lawsuits against projects involving five or ten houses. Second, lawsuits are used to stop big developments. The state's inventory identifies seven lawsuits involving developments that proposed to build 21,537 housing units in the San Francisco area alone.[4] The Mountain Village and Harbor Bay Isle lawsuits missing from this list involved an additional 7,133 units. In all, environmental lawsuits challenged a total 28,670 housing units in the San Francisco region, or roughly two-thirds of a year's normal housing production. The large amount of housing at stake shows the highly misleading nature of the state's reassuring conclusion that "the incidence of CEQA litigation affects less than one percent of the total number of projects that are subject to litigation."[5]

The state legislature's Committee on Local Government commissioned another study to evaluate the effects of the California Environmental Quality Act at about the same time. The consulting team that carried out this study tried to estimate the public and private costs attributable to environmental reviews under the California act. Making these estimates is difficult. But the assumptions that the consultants used to simplify their job have little to do with the real world. Predictably, their effect is to minimize the cost estimates, especially those connected with housing.

This study defines the cost of delay so narrowly that it excludes the major price increases resulting from housing cost escalation over time. It counts as delay costs only carrying charges for incomplete projects plus losses resulting from a stretchout of the time before projects begin to yield income. The higher prices that consumers pay as a result of inflation during the course of delay are simply omitted: "It has been assumed that inflation effects are not a 'cost' because the user's ability to pay increases with the cost of inflation."[6] The report concedes that during recent years construction costs have been rising faster than consumer income but argues that at times in the future, income might conceivably increase faster than construction costs, so that project delays might then generate cost savings for consumers.[7]

The authors recognize that environmental reviews often lead developers to revise their plans. The case studies in this book show that these revisions go far beyond eliminating specific environmental problems. Developers often agree to set aside substantial open space and to make big reductions in the amount of housing they will build in order to placate environmental groups that oppose them. While many of these changes cannot strictly be attributed to the California Environmental Quality Act, the procedures mandated by that act certainly build up the pressure on developers to make such concessions. Contrary to the experience at Mountain Village, Harbor Bay Isle, and San Bruno Mountain, this study estimates the average cost of project revisions as no more than $2,000 per project and further assumes that only half of all private projects make any changes at all.[8]

Proceeding on the basis of unrealistic assumptions about inflation, a low estimate of the cost of project revisions, and an admittedly rough estimate that the average project delay resulting from environmental reviews is only about three months, this study then concludes that implementation of the California Environmental Quality Act raises the cost of an average new housing unit by only $150.[9] Although the authors are careful to qualify their findings and to acknowledge the limited scope of their research, the figures they offer can only mislead the public by concealing most of the costs that housing consumers pay as a result of regulatory policies in California.

Housing Availability in the San Francisco Area

The cumulative effects of delays, project revisions, and tight growth controls show up in the housing market of metropolitan San Francisco. There they reinforce a housing inflation that has its origins in the national economy. Increases in construction costs, mortgage interest rates, and fuel and utility prices would have generated big increases in housing costs regardless of local growth controls. But growth policies appear to be important secondary contributors pushing housing costs up much faster in San Francisco than in the rest of the country.

One of the few sources of current information on housing prices in individual markets across the country is the Federal Home Loan Bank Board, which tracked sales prices in sixteen of the largest metropolitan areas from 1970 through 1977. San Francisco had the highest price increase for new homes of all sixteen areas. Its average sales price of $75,400 in 1977 was almost twice as high as its average price in 1970 ($39,600), and almost one and one-half times the national average for 1977 ($54,300).[10]

In 1977 the Federal Home Loan Bank Board expanded its survey to cover 32 major metropolitan areas. San Francisco had the highest new home prices of all 32 areas, followed closely by Los Angeles ($72,600) and outranking by a wide margin such traditionally high-cost places as New York ($69,300), Honolulu ($67,200), and Washington, D.C. ($66,600). By contrast, in 1970 San Francisco ranked sixth of eighteen areas surveyed that year.

Sharp increases in new home prices in San Francisco led many families to buy existing homes as an alternative. The increasing demand for older houses has pulled their prices up close behind the levels for new homes. From 1970 through 1977 average sales prices for existing homes in San Francisco increased by 92 percent, from $37,000 to $71,000. Among the 32 areas for which comparable information was available in 1977, San Francisco and Los Angeles were tied for second place in the price of existing homes. Their price level, like San Francisco's price for new homes, was one and one-half times the national average of $47,500.

As the average figures climbed steadily higher, most inexpensive homes disappeared from the San Francisco market. The rapid decline of new homes priced below $35,000 in Bay Area tract developments—from 76 percent in 1972 down to 24 percent in 1974—has already been noted. Another annual survey of 40,000 existing home sales showed a similar pattern. In 1972, 59 percent of these homes sold for less than $35,000. By 1974 only 32 percent of them sold at this level.[11]

This price surge to levels far above those in other parts of the country has put severe strains on the budgets of most families trying to buy homes, new or old. Much of the cost squeeze resulted from factors beyond California's control, but a large part of it was avoidable. The combined effects of water moratoria and other utility restrictions, of 60-acre agricultural zoning, exorbitant development charges, tight regulation of the coastal zone, building moratoria, permit ceilings, drawn-out regulatory processes, and development controversies surely go a long way toward explaining why housing cost increases have hit San Francisco much harder than the rest of the country.

Fewer Locational Choices

Growth restrictions and rising prices have not only cut back the amount of housing available to middle-income families, but they have also reduced the number of places within the region where they can afford to live. Large parts of the region such as Marin County and southern San Mateo County have had very little moderate-income housing for many years, and since 1970 other parts of the region have also closed the gates to families with average incomes.

One recent study charted the location of new homes priced for middle-income families in 1970 and then in 1975. (Following the conventional rule-of-thumb, the study assumed that families earning the median income could afford to spend roughly twice that income to buy a home. The upper limits for "affordable" homes, figured on this basis, were $23,500 in 1970, and $32,000 in 1975.) In 1970 there were about 100 separate developments offering homes for sale at the defined price level. They were spread throughout most of the Bay Area, excluding, however, Marin and Napa Counties, and southern San Mateo County.

In 1975 a field survey was able to turn up only ten developments selling moderate-priced homes, according to this definition. As of December 1975 the total number of homes available in these developments was 82. Little was left of the earlier locational choices. Virtually all the new middle-income housing was in the eastern part of the region: in Solano County and northern Contra Costa County, in Union City on the East Bay, and in San Jose to the south. Several places that offered middle-income housing in 1970 no longer did in 1975: the Sonoma Valley, central Contra Costa County, the San Mateo County coastal area, and the Livermore Valley.[12] Both the Livermore Valley and the San Mateo County coastal area had put tight growth restrictions into effect after 1970.

The development controversies reported in earlier chapters also reduced locational choices. Four of the five developments were infill projects located on open land adjoining built-up communities and close to regional job centers. Three of these four were located near the center of the region, while the fourth—the Palo Alto foothills—was in the heart of a major suburban industrial belt. The blocking and reduction of these projects took away options that would have allowed more than 20,000 families to buy new homes in central locations within short commuting distances of a wide variety of jobs. The land where these developments would have been located is no longer available for housing, and the region offers few building sites with comparable advantages. As a result whatever houses may eventually be built to meet the same demand are sure to be located in more outlying places farther from the main job centers. In comparison with what might have been built, these alternative homes will force people to commute longer distances at higher costs to themselves in time and money. Longer commuting will also impose unnecessarily high environmental costs by adding more automobile emissions to the region's atmosphere, and by burning gas that might have been saved.

Lowering the Quality of Housing Development

The homebuilding controversies around San Francisco have sent signals to developers to build differently in the future if they want to avoid long delays and high risks. These signals will lead developers to avoid projects like the ones that have generated so much controversy. They will probably build housing less likely to arouse local opposition but also less likely to offer homebuyers the advantages of the plans that proved controversial.

The development proposals of the early 1970s were a big improvement over homebuilding practices of the recent past. In the 1950s most developers built nothing but small subdivisions of free-standing, single-family houses on individual lots with no provision for community open space or recreation areas. This was the building pattern that led critics to attack suburbia as monotonous, wasteful of land, offering little choice to consumers, and providing nothing that would encourage an active community life. In time both builders and homebuyers came to accept many of these criticisms, and by the 1960s developers were successfully marketing very different suburban projects. The newer style involved a larger scale of development, often several hundred units per project with a mix of different housing types, and with site planning that grouped the homes in clusters surrounded by community open space, and often with recreation buildings and small shopping centers as well.

These large planned-unit developments are precisely the kind that now draw the fire of growth opponents. Their size makes possible a diversity of housing types as well as common open space and community facilities. But at the same time their size makes them conspicuous and threatening to nearby residents. And even a very generous provision of open space, as on San Bruno Mountain, fails to win points in a political controversy.

The hard lessons of the recent past are clear enough to the homebuilders. William Leonard, executive director of the main homebuilding trade association in the Bay Area, connects the size of a development to its chances of getting a permit. Anything with less than fifty units is in the clear, according to Leonard, while anything with more than five hundred units is sure to come under heavy attack. In between there are gradations of risk. Furthermore, he points out, higher-priced housing is less controversial than moderate-cost housing.[13]

What the future holds for San Francisco is fewer planned-unit developments and a general return to building practices of the 1950s: expensive, free-standing, single-family homes, each on its own lot in scattered small developments of less than a hundred houses. Few developers will provide anything more.

This retreat has already begun. Builders who specialize in planned-unit developments are deciding not to build anything more in northern California. Some are deciding to do no more housing at all.

Political harassment affects developers as people and shapes their future decisions. The experience of San Francisco developer Gerson Bakar is instructive. Bakar's misfortunes attracted national attention when a boy scout succeeded in bringing his Lake Merced development to a halt on a regulatory technicality, as noted in chapter 2. He is an experienced developer who takes justifiable pride in his career and in his projects. He began by building very small developments, and it took him fifteen years to learn how to handle big ones. The big ones represented to him a higher level of accomplishment in terms of design quality as well as management skill.

In a series of recent and well-known developments, Bakar worked with some of the most distinguished designers in the country: Wurster, Bernardi and Emmons were the architects and Lawrence Halprin and Associates were the landscape architects with him on North Point Apartments near the San Francisco waterfront, on Woodlake in San Mateo, and on Oak Creek Apartments in Palo Alto.

Yet when Bakar describes his current experience, he uses the language of warfare, not of architecture. When I interviewed him, he offered to take off his shirt to show me five hundred battle scars on his back. He said a neighbor of one of his projects had dug a trench and filled it with mortars, artillery, and ammunition. He agreed that builders working with smaller projects might have advantages in guerrilla warfare with their enemies: "they can get in and out fast, without getting hit." [14]

Bakar himself will not build small projects. They would mark a return to what he did when he was a newcomer to the field, and would give him little professional satisfaction. He intends to continue working in real estate, but as an investor rather than a developer. "You're not a developer unless you have a site for your next development," according to Bakar. As of mid-1976, he had no sites since he believed it was no longer possible to build the type of development that would meet his own standards. He also doubted whether the public would be well served by a return to small-scale development.

The environmental politics and local growth controls that emerged in the San Francisco region in the early 1970s have already raised prices and reduced locational choices for homebuyers. In time they are likely to add to this damage by also lowering the quality and restricting the variety of new housing developments.

The Rest of California

Southern California also turned increasingly hostile to development in the early 1970s. Development controversies, building moratoria, and tough new growth controls have spread through the state. They have not been as numerous or as concentrated in southern California as in the San Francisco area, but there have been enough of them to make serious trouble for homebuyers.

The state-mandated environmental reviews, plus many new wrinkles in local regulations, have combined to stretch out the time it takes to complete a development. A suburban Los Angeles developer reports:

One of our technicians pulled out a copy of the Los Angeles Subdivision Regulations for the development of a subdivision in the Santa Monica Mountains; there were 98 administrative steps that had to be taken. If everything went well, it took from 10 to 14 months to get approval. . . . After we worked on this project for two years, we were the first to have a subdivision approved in the Santa Monica Mountains. [15]

According to Sanford Goodkin, a real estate consultant based in Del Mar, getting approval for a housing tract after buying the land was likely to take two years in 1976. Two or three years earlier the same process took only nine months. [16]

Building moratoria also took their toll. Los Angeles County put a freeze on building permits for 1.8 million acres of land, granting exceptions only for certain plans involving no more than one housing unit per acre. [17] San Diego also went into growth management in a big way. In the early 1970s it moved to restrict growth by rezoning more than 40,000 acres of land for lower development densities. [18] Later it put building moratoria into effect. By 1977 a survey of building lot availability found that about half the developable land there was under some kind of moratorium. [19]

Elsewhere growth controversies pushed developers to reduce project densities and make other compromises like the ones around San Francisco and with similar impacts on prices. A Santa Barbara home builder, Michael Towbes, reports that after three years of negotiation with the city of Thousand Oaks, successive changes in a project he proposed to build there raised house prices from $30,000 to $70,000. [20]

Other controversies succeeded in blocking or reducing several big developments in the southern California coastal zone. Michael Towbes also got involved in a long series of disputes with the coastal commission over a project he proposed near Santa Barbara. His experience there gets to the heart of another important way the new regulatory systems operate to raise housing prices. When I asked why he tried to build anything in a place as closely regulated as the coastal zone, he acknowledged that the risk of having his project rejected was very great. "But," he said, "anyone who can survive the reviews will have a near-monopoly on new housing near the shore and can market his homes at very high prices." The fact is that regulation is making homebuilding much less competitive than it used to be. Formerly, developers had to compete against each other for the consumer's dollar, and competition kept prices down. Now developers compete against each other for building permits. But once a developer has his permit in a place where local housing demand is strong, there is so little competition in the market-place that he can earn enough profit to make the risk worth taking.

In Santa Cruz County, south of the San Francisco region, the board of supervisors put into effect a series of housing regulations so unusual that they are unlikely to be imitated or even believed anywhere else in the country. New housing was beginning to encroach on territory near the home of the Santa Cruz long-toed salamander, an endangered species. The salamanders live in the hills, but once a year they walk down the hillsides to a nearby pond where they breed. Under the new regulations homes built on the hillsides near the pond must be on columns so that the salamanders can pass safely underneath; and all retaining walls must have built-in ramps for the salamanders to use in crossing them. How much these special regulations cost homebuyers in the area is unknown, but in 1976 a World Wildlife Fund conference applauded the county supervisors for their action.[21]

From Building Slump to Speculative Boom

As California and the nation emerged from the severe building slump in 1974-75, the new growth restrictions and time-consuming permit processes helped set the stage for a homebuyer's disaster and a speculator's bonanza. When the economy began to recover from the depths of the recession in 1975, savings deposits began to pour into California savings and loan associations. January 1976, in fact, was a record month for savings inflows. The savings and loan associations promptly paid off debts they had accumulated during the recession and found themselves flushed with funds they could use for new mortgage loans.[22]

By late 1975 consumer confidence was returning and many families that had put off home purchases during the past two years began to look eagerly for houses they could buy. The California homebuilding industry was in a weakened condition after the severe two-year slump. Even those builders who were organized and who recognized the turn of the market, however, were unable to start construction fast enough to meet the demand. They found little land available that was already zoned for single-family houses. In most areas they faced tough growth restrictions and long delays before they could get permission to build.

By the fall of 1976 people who wanted to buy new homes had to wait in long lines or bribe real estate agents for a chance to bid on the few that were available. In Irvine, south of Los Angeles, more than two thousand families gathered for a lottery that would determine who could buy 82 new town houses. Nearby at Sunwood, 65 families camped out for as long as five days during a tropical storm to have first crack at 29 new homes. Speculators began to buy houses for quick resale at a big markup. The Rossmoor Corporation tried to discourage speculation by requiring homebuyers to sign a pledge to live in the house. The Irvine Company, selling by lottery, tried to discourage speculation by dealing only with people in income brackets appropriate to the prices of the houses.[23]

With supply lagging so far behind demand, prices shot upward from week to week and speculators entered the market in large numbers, especially in Orange County and parts of the San Francisco area. Speculative homebuying increased the demand even more and pushed prices even higher. Maurice Mann, president of the Federal Home Loan Bank of San Francisco, explained how the speculators operated:

When a home is not yet constructed, a buyer typically makes a $500 or $1,000 deposit, which holds the home until it is completed. . . . During that time, the speculator reaps the gains from inflation on the total price of the house, not just his initial investment. To illustrate, let us say that a $1,000 deposit is made on a house costing $80,000 at the time of purchase. If construction requires six months, which is not unusual, and the annual appreciation rate on the house is 20 percent (which, again, is not unusual in some areas), the speculator will realize an annual yield of roughly 1,600 percent on his $1,000 investment in less than a year, excluding commissions and fees.[24]

By the spring of 1977 staff members of the Federal Home Loan Bank of San Francisco estimated that 15 to 20 percent of new home sales in California's metropolitan areas went to speculators. Other analysts thought the figure was as high as 40 percent in some places.[25] To slow the speculative boom, the Federal Home Loan Bank of San Francisco urged its members to reduce their lending, particularly to people who were not buying homes for their own use, and they underscored the point by increasing interest rates on their own advances to member savings and loan associations.

You Can't Go Home Again (You Can't Afford It)

The speculative fever cooled down afterward, and by 1977 California's 270,000 housing starts approached the 1972 pre-recession level. But the damage inflicted on the state's housing consumers will remain for a long time. In the Los Angeles metropolitan area, which includes Orange County, the average sales price of a new home jumped by 28 percent in a single year, from 1975 to 1976. The 1976 average price of $65,900 was the highest among 18 metropolitan areas surveyed that year by the Federal Home Loan Bank Board, with San Francisco's average price of $64,800 following close behind. In 1977 San Francisco led the nation in new home prices, as noted earlier, and Los Angeles was in second place. The price inflation spread to older homes as well. Average sales prices for existing homes increased by more than a third in both Los Angeles and San Francisco between 1975 and 1977. The 1977 average was $71,000 in both metropolitan areas. By 1977 San Diego was also one of the most expensive housing markets in the country, with average prices for both new and existing homes above $65,000.[26]

These tremendous price increases affected hundreds of thousands of California families. Many who were able to buy homes did so only by making great sacrifices elsewhere in their budgets. And the price explosion undoubtedly echoed throughout California's housing markets, putting pressure on rents as well as sales prices and affecting families at many income levels.

Major beneficiaries of the price inflation, in theory, should be families who are already homeowners and have now seen the value of their property rise dramatically. Even for this group, however, the price increase brought unexpected trouble. Tax officials were diligent about raising property assessments to reflect the new sales prices, and many homeowners had to pay tax increases of 50 percent or more after a new assessment. Local governments and school districts benefited from the revenue windfall, but taxpayers with limited incomes were afraid they could no longer afford to live in their own homes. Property tax opponents, who had failed three times since 1968 to get voter approval for plans to set tax ceilings, moved quickly to organize support for a new proposal. "Save the American Dream" was the slogan on their bumper stickers. This time they collected twice as many signatures as they needed to put a tax-limiting constitutional amendment on the ballot in June 1978. Proposition 13 swept the state by a 2-1 vote. Its main provisions returned assessed valuations to their 1975–76 level and limited property taxes to 1 percent of valuations. The initiative allows assessments to increase when properties change hands, but otherwise limits upward revisions to 2 percent a year.

As the measure went into effect, it was expected to cut $7 billion, or 60 percent, from city, county, and school district property tax collections.[27] Although a surplus in the state treasury was available to cushion the revenue loss for the first year, officials promptly began to trim staff and services to stay within a shrinking budget. Mayors and legislators elsewhere interpreted the California vote as the start of a taxpayer revolt and hurried to align themselves with it. A White House spokesman said the dissatisfaction of California voters with high taxes and the increased cost of government were the same concerns on which President Carter "campaigned and on which he bases his Presidency."[28] Lost in the scramble to join the tax revolution was any recognition that public policy in suburbia had a hand in creating it by accelerating housing inflation. For growth opponents in California, however, the new amendment meant that they could continue to restrict new homebuilding in their communities, enjoy the benefits of higher values when they sell their own homes, and pay no property tax penalty in the meantime. From a narrowly self-interested point of view, it was the best of all possible worlds.

State Policy

The bottleneck of land availability, resulting in large part from local growth policies, threatens to keep raising the price of new housing in California in the near future. One recent survey found lot shortages so severe in seven metropolitan areas across the country that they were expected to force cutbacks in the level of homebuilding. The three major California markets head the list: San Diego, San Francisco–Oakland, and Los Angeles–Orange County. In San Diego, only 8,000–12,000 lots a year are now being developed even though current single-family construction is at a rate of 20,000 units per year. In both the San Francisco and Los Angeles–Orange County areas, the survey found a great deal of suitable land tied up by moratoria or special growth restrictions. And its authors estimated that lot shortages would force a 25 to 30 percent decline in single-family homebuilding by the second half of 1978.[29]

State and local government policies have obviously contributed to the recent cost escalation in California. Although no new policies have yet emerged that will help contain future cost increases, the major state initiative on the horizon offers just a glimmer of hope for improvement.

While housing prices were breaking records, the State Office of Planning and Research was working on a new urban development strategy for California. Its first report, made public in May 1977, threatened to make the situation even worse. This draft report gave explicit recognition to the state's sizable housing needs, but its policy recommendations were concerned much more with environmental protection than they were with housing. Where the report focused on specific housing problems such as the recent cost increase, its analysis of the causes was highly selective and its proposals clearly inadequate. The report noted that housing expenses in California were rising much faster than family incomes. It failed, however, to attribute any part of the housing cost increase to local growth restrictions or regulatory reviews. Instead it explained that "in some areas of California, the price of housing appears to be artificially high due to speculation."[30] So it proposed a simple solution: a new tax on profits made from the quick turnover of real estate.

The report offered no proposal that would have stepped up the pace of needed homebuilding. Instead it cited the 1975 creation of a California Housing Finance Agency as a partial solution to the impact of rising housing costs. This agency was intended to supply below-market financing for housing intended to reach low-and moderate-income families. Because of various delays, however, its program was not yet in operation. The urban development report proposed a constitutional amendment to remove one procedural block to financing these projects, but even if all roadblocks were removed, the California Housing Finance Agency would be able to help only a very limited number of families cope with a cost squeeze that affects most of the state's population.[31]

Having acknowledged that California would need a high level of housing production to take care of its future growth, the report could not ignore the question of where this housing should be located. Its answer, however, did not come from a realistic look at the alternatives but rather from established environmental doctrine. Taking a leaf from the California Coastal Plan, the urban development strategy proposed to redirect growth to land "within or contiguous to existing urban areas." The order of priority was: "conserve what we have; infill where we can; expand onto new land *only* where it is demonstrated to be necessary."[32]

If recent San Francisco experience is any guide, favoring infill development for housing is almost the same as saying no housing should be built. Four of the five development controversies reported in earlier chapters involved filling in open land near established cities and suburbs. Two of the four were blocked, and the other two were cut to a fraction of their original size. The only development proposal of all those described that emerged relatively unscathed was Blackhawk Ranch, which went beyond the outer edge of urban development.

It is worth recalling why infill projects were blocked. Remaining open sites near built-up communities have neighbors who are affected by new homebuilding. They will object for many reasons: tax impact, traffic generation, destruction of remaining open space, interruption of a pleasant view, and the inconvenience of having construction and then new people nearby. Also, the sites that have been passed over have usually been passed over for a reason, such as steep slopes, poor drainage, or congested road connections. But developers who propose earth-moving operations to improve these sites will be attacked as "rapists of the landscape."

Did the policies in the draft report mean that the state would take a stand in support of future projects on San Bruno Mountain or in the Palo Alto foothills over the objections of nearby residents and environmental critics? Certainly not. The report proposed mainly to discourage outlying developments by making it hard for them to get water and sewer service. (The specific proposals were to give preference in water allocation and in sewage treatment grants to projects within or contiguous to existing urban areas.)[33] This would be equivalent to the state government standing by quietly while infill projects go down to political defeat, and then using its leverage to block public services to the only housing developments that are politically feasible, the ones on outlying land. This policy proposal is similar to the position of environmental groups that favor infill development only in general but never for specific projects.

After eight months of discussions with interested citizens, public meetings throughout the state, and a review of critical comments and suggestions, the Office of Planning and Research published a revised report in February 1978. Although the new version still fails to give open acknowledgment to the strong political pressures that limit homebuilding, and still draws most of its ideas from environmental doctrine, it gives at least implicit and belated recognition to environmental politics as a force adding to the state's housing problems. More important, for the first time it proposes a constructive measure to reduce environmental reviews.

The revised urban strategy continues to give top priority to compact development that will channel growth into existing cities and suburbs, and it argues that "with good design, density can be increased without sacrificing comfortable living."[34] Like the draft report, it contemplates using water supply and sewage treatment funds to favor compact and infill developments. But the report does state that in following the development priorities, "care must be taken to avoid driving up the cost of housing."[35]

One of the proposals to encourage infill development implies that reviews mandated by the California Environmental Quality Act discourage homebuilding and increase its cost. To promote more development in already built-up areas, the state government suggests skipping environmental impact reviews for some housing in these areas. Exempting a project from this requirement, according to the report, "will speed construction and thereby help reduce housing costs."[36] This is a startling admission in a report that is otherwise heavily slanted toward the views of environmentalists. It suggests the dawning of a new awareness of the cost of local environmental controversies and a willingness to take the first step toward deregulation.

The step proposed here, however, is a very small one that is unlikely to have much practical effect. Governor Brown's administration promises to sponsor legislation that would allow but not require local governments to waive environmental impact report requirements, and would allow them to do so only for developments that passed other forms of environmental review. To be eligible, a development would have to be consistent with a local plan for which an environmental impact report had been prepared and would have to cause no significant air or water pollution. It is easy to imagine the pressure that opposition groups will put on local governments not to grant such waivers, and the lawsuits they will mount to challenge any findings that developments are consistent with approved plans and cause no significant pollution.

Still the new urban strategy may mark a turning point. In it the state recognizes a need for new policies to encourage reasonable development and to simplify environmental reviews. But until that recognition produces effective action, Californians will continue to live with the consequences of construction delays, restricted choices, and high housing prices.

Chapter 11
National Patterns

Is California's turnabout on suburban growth just another westcoast fad, or is it a leading indicator for the rest of the country? While California was learning how to shackle homebuilding, new tactics for blocking growth were also spreading among state and local governments from coast to coast. Most were not as extreme as the ones in California, but they belonged to the same family.

Suburbs across the country reached the same conclusions as those in California: they wanted to avoid the strains of growth and change. Their earlier attempts to limit homebuilding, mainly through zoning, had won only limited victories. Because new regulatory tactics promised more striking results, they welcomed them with open arms.

Until recently, suburbs knew how to price only low-income families out of local housing markets. Thanks to the new growth controls, they have raised their sights higher. Now they aim not only at keeping out the poor but also at blocking homebuilding for middle-income Americans. As exclusionary policies have shifted upward, so too have the nation's housing problems. Housing costs have begun to lay heavy and growing burdens not only on the poor but on the middle class as well.

Local growth policies of the California variety promise still more cost increases in the future, unless the millions of families who will pay for them can somehow bring their weight to bear on the housing regulators. But the new no-growth politics, and the ideology behind it, have attracted enough support to make the prospects for change very uncertain.

Increasing Growth Regulation

The best evidence that California is not a national aberration, is the large amount of growth-control machinery that other states have also put in place during the past ten years. By 1975, 25 states required environmental impact statements for private housing developments in some or all areas.[1] Also by 1975, 22 states had established special development controls for wetlands areas and 26 states for flood plains. Federal grants for coastal zone management, which began in 1972, prompted all 30 states with Atlantic, Pacific, Gulf Coast, or Great Lakes shorelines to mount growth management programs for their coastal areas in the next three years. And as many as 42 states gave special property tax reductions to owners of agricultural or open space land by 1975.[2] This new burst of state activity had a clear purpose: to protect the environment by limiting new development.[3]

State actions to limit housing development are relatively new, but for local government they are part of an old tradition. Long before California began to try new ways of stopping growth, suburbs in the rest of the country were using traditional zoning and subdivision regulations for the same purpose. When these controls came into widespread use in the 1920s, their declared purposes were to protect the public health, safety, and welfare. Most recent students of the subject, however, agree with Richard Babcock, one of the country's leading zoning attorneys, when he dismisses these justifications as "the early legal fictions." The real purpose behind most zoning, according to Babcock, is "the protection of the single-family-house neighborhood."[4] President Johnson's National Commission on Urban Problems also concluded that "the primary demand behind zoning in thousands of communities was to protect established neighborhoods."[5] The commission went a step further in figuring out what local officials wanted to accomplish through land use regulation: "Many officials would prefer to have as little development as possible of any kind—to keep the community as it is."[6]

By the 1960s suburbs applying these land use controls were having reasonable success in protecting themselves, which meant that they were also succeeding in restricting housing opportunities for other people. Reporting in 1968, the President's Committee on Urban Housing observed that "the net effect of public land policy is to reduce the supply of land available for modest-cost housing and thus to increase its cost."[7] The committee pointed especially to zoning that required larger lot sizes and wider frontages than consumers wanted; to increasingly strict development standards for streets and community services; and to laws that specified minimum floor areas for new houses. "These restrictive zoning and subdivision requirements," its report concluded, "clearly raise housing costs for average American families."[8]

How the system worked in practice became evident from a 1970 study of four suburban counties in northern New Jersey. These counties contain most of the vacant land available for future suburban development around the western edge of the New York–New Jersey metropolitan area. Their land use regulations will affect the housing prospects of millions of families, and by 1970 these regulations added up to a policy of keeping out almost all inexpensive housing. Local ordinances prohibited all mobile homes and allowed apartment buildings on only one-half of 1 percent of all the land zoned for housing. Single-family zones were also drawn to keep out moderately priced houses. Only 5 percent of the land zoned for housing allowed single-family homes on lots of 20,000 square feet or less, while more than three-quarters of the land required minimum lot sizes of an

acre or more. In addition, more than three-quarters of the land zoned for housing required minimum floor areas of 1,200 square feet or more per house.

Two legal scholars pondered these severe restrictions and concluded:

*Zoning is above all supposed to promote the general welfare; clearly something
has gone very wrong. When minimum building size restrictions were first upheld
in New Jersey, it seemed likely that if one town could practice exclusion, all the
others could, and that they probably would. The facts are now available: almost
all the others did, with a vengeance.*[9]

Enactment of increasingly demanding zoning and subdivision standards, as a
national pattern, set the stage for the style of growth-control politics that flourished in California and elsewhere by the early 1970s. When local regulations
called for more expensive housing than the market would bear, homebuilders
who wanted to operate in a community had to apply for a change of zoning.
Having to decide on a change of zoning gave local officials a chance to review
each proposal carefully and to bargain with the developer over features that
might make it more acceptable to them. Local land use regulation then became
less a matter of establishing fixed rules for all players and more a process of
negotiation in which the developer was subject to political pressures. Behind-the-
scenes bargaining made it possible for local governments to regulate who would
be admitted to the community. As Richard Babcock put it, zoning became "a
technique to keep out all but the elect." After imposing regulations so strict that
they made development prohibitively expensive, local officials would agree to re-
lax them "only for those developers who . . . will be properly selective in deter-
mining future residents."[10]

Changing the Targets

Although many suburban governments wanted to limit their growth, neither the
political climate nor the regulatory methods available in the 1960s allowed them
to block very much homebuilding. They were effective at zoning out inexpensive
housing and the poor people and minority groups who needed it, but most
middle Americans were still able to afford new suburban homes even though
local restrictions raised their cost. Despite regulatory obstacles, developers managed to build enough housing to handle a huge increase in the suburban population during the 1950s and 1960s.

By the late 1960s a new mood of resistance to growth, and the invention of
new tactics to prevent it, lifted the hopes of suburban governments to more
ambitious goals. Instead of keeping out only the poor, they might even be able

to keep out the middle class. Besides, zoning out low-cost housing had become a dead issue by the late 1960s. Steady increases in construction costs by then made it impossible for developers to build new housing that poor people could afford, no matter how permissive local regulations were. The only exception was new housing built under federal or state programs that offered big enough subsidies to bring the prices within reach of poor people. Most suburbs continued to block subsidized housing developments except for a few token projects.

By the early 1970s innovative suburbs were working hard to stop as much growth as they could, including developments intended for a middle-income market. Many communities just applied the tested tools of zoning with more determination than before. Some raised the standards while others took a tougher position against requests for zoning changes. Montgomery County, Maryland, for example, set up a special "rural" zone requiring five-acre minimum lot sizes.[11] In 1971 Loudoun County in northern Virginia simply refused a rezoning request for a new community of 13,000 people proposed by Levitt and Sons. The county supervisors justified their decision on the grounds that the new community would not bring in enough tax revenue to cover the cost of providing the additional public facilities it would need. Levitt then offered to build all the needed facilities, including new schools, at no cost to the local government; but the county still denied the rezoning and won a court case challenging its action.[12]

Fairfax County, Virginia, just outside Washington, D.C., started turning down most requests for zoning changes. In 1971 the county supervisors had approved 78 percent of the rezoning proposals put before them. By 1972 they cut their approvals to only 37 percent.[13] The supervisors refused even to consider rezoning proposals from some parts of the county. Two property owners who had been unable to get a hearing took their case to court and won a lawsuit directing the supervisors to hold hearings on their requests. The board then began to work through its backlog of some 300 pending cases. Even after the court order, however, county officials put off action on the properties in question, on the ground that the court had failed to require them to both "hear" and "decide" the applications. The property owners returned to court to start contempt proceedings. Eventually, they got both their hearing and their decision. The decision was a negative one, of course.[14]

Other communities tried new tactics. In 1969 Ramapo, New York, set up a review procedure that withheld building permits unless a development could meet an elaborate set of criteria having to do with the availability of public facilities and services. The town itself controls the availability of these services through its plans for utility and street extensions over an eighteen-year period. The review procedure and public facility plans together govern both the timing and the volume of new development.[15] Several other places set up similar procedures to stop homebuilding until the local government provides necessary public facilities. These include Prince Georges County and Montgomery County in Maryland, as well as a handful of communities in Minnesota.[16]

A similar approach involves limiting development to a defined urban service zone within which public facilities either are or will soon be made available. Local governments then rule out both homebuilding and utility extensions beyond the urban service boundary. Places using this approach include Manatee County, Florida; Salem, Oregon; Boulder, Colorado; and Lexington-Fayette County, Kentucky.[17]

Some communities have legislated ceilings on their own future growth. In 1971 Boca Raton, Florida, made national news by amending its city charter to limit the total amount of housing that could ever be built there to 40,000 units. The city promptly tightened its zoning requirements to implement the new law.[18] Also in 1971 Boulder, Colorado, rejected a charter amendment to set a population ceiling of 100,000 but approved a resolution directing the city government to "take all steps necessary to hold the rate of growth in the Boulder Valley to a level substantially below that experienced in the 1960s."[19] Then in 1976 Boulder voted to cut its population increase to no more than 2 percent a year or 450 housing units, about half the recent rate of growth. The Boulder plan set up a merit system to allocate the 450 units.[20]

Of all the new devices for stopping homebuilding, by far the most popular is simply to impose a temporary moratorium on requests for rezoning, building permits, or water or sewer connections. The legal justification for a moratorium is to give local government time to cope with a short-term but severe problem, such as a lack of sewage treatment capacity. Many communities, however, are in no rush to resolve the problem that gives rise to a moratorium. A national survey in 1973 found that 19 percent of the local governments responding had recently initiated some type of development moratorium. The average one lasted for eleven months, but some lasted for years.[21]

Dade County, Florida, pioneered in the systematic use of building moratoria. In 1970 the county made provisions to stop new sewer connections wherever sewage treatment facilities were inadequate. A 1972 ordinance set up a three-stage process for declaring moratoria on building permits, and the county commission established parallel procedures for suspending zoning applications. By March 1973 the county had imposed seventeen building moratoria affecting some 5,500 acres plus zoning moratoria affecting 310 square miles.[22]

Although the full extent of development moratoria in the country is unknown, the Department of Housing and Urban Development compiled a careful tabulation of sewer moratoria from 1968 through 1976. It identified as many as 815 communities located in 35 states and in 132 of the country's 272 metropolitan areas that had sewer connection moratoria during this period.[23] In some areas a combination of sewer moratoria in different communities blanketed large parts of metropolitan housing markets. In 1974, for example, sewer moratoria were in effect in most of suburban Washington, D.C.[24]

Further evidence of the nationwide spread of growth controls comes from the people who feel their impact first—the homebuilders. When members of the National Association of Home Builders were surveyed in 1964 and 1969, very few of them identified government regulation as an important problem of doing business. In 1969 only 1 percent mentioned building codes and another 2 percent mentioned zoning as their most significant problems. By 1976 government regulations headed the list by a wide margin, with 38 percent of the builders citing them as their single most significant problem. Moreover, they stood out as the major problem in all regions of the country. The range of responses went from 34 percent of builders in the South, who considered them the most important problem, to 47 percent in the West.[25]

The Results

There are enough examples of anti-growth tactics to show that what happened in California was part of a national movement. Although it is hard to measure direct effects of this movement on the cost of new homes, there are signs that it has raised land costs, led to density reductions within developments, required homebuilders to pay a greater share of public service costs, and added several months of delay to the average time for completing a construction project. All these results would raise the cost of new homes. The information at hand, both from California and elsewhere, suggests that local growth policies are important contributors to the housing problems of families with average incomes.

Recent increases in land costs for new single-family homes are one sign that consumers are paying a price for anti-growth policies. Land costs are especially sensitive to local development controls. These controls increase land prices by limiting the total supply of land available for development. They further increase the price of land per home when they mandate large minimum lot sizes. They also increase the cost of converting raw land to finished house lots when they jack up required standards for streets, sidewalks, landscaping, and utility systems. Increases in hook-up fees for water and sewer connections also raise the cost of site development. Local governments have been putting all these measures into effect in the 1970s. It is not surprising then that land costs have been increasing much faster than labor or materials costs for new single-family homes.

Land costs were climbing fast even before the no-growth movement took hold. The National Commission on Urban Problems, writing in 1968, found that "the single most dramatic increase in the cost of a major [housing] component has occurred in site costs."[26] The growth controls of the 1960s, such as large lot zoning, undoubtedly had an effect at that time, but local restrictions and cost increases have both been on the increase since then.

The best source of data on land costs for typical new homes comes from membership surveys of the National Association of Home Builders. These show big increases in the cost of buying and developing land during the 1970s. From 1950 through 1969 the builders reported average annual increases of less than 8 percent in the price per square foot of finished lots, and from 1960 to 1969 average annual increases of only 5 percent. By contrast from 1969 to 1975 the cost per square foot shot up by an average of about 15 percent per year.[27]

A survey of eighteen of the largest metropolitan areas in 1977 provides more evidence of especially fast inflation in land costs for new homes. The Advance Mortgage Corporation found that in half the markets it surveyed finished lot prices had increased an average of 30 percent in the past year and in some cases 50 percent or more. In half the major markets—New York, Philadelphia, Chicago, Detroit, Baltimore, Washington, Los Angeles, San Diego and San Francisco—it estimated the minimum price for a subdivision lot in a good white-collar area as $20,000. This study specifically identified many familiar growth control tactics as contributors to the high land prices. These included processing times up to three or four years for land development, moratoria, special environmental restrictions, service area boundaries that shrink the available land supply, and high inspection and hook-up fees.[28]

Land costs continue to climb faster than any other component of new home construction, thanks in part to local growth policies. As a result, they now account for as much as 25 percent of the cost of a typical new single-family house.[29]

The increasingly harsh regulatory climate also generates other changes in homebuilding that are sure to raise prices. Environmental politics in California encourages developers to build for a luxury market. Opposition demands for low density and open space rule out moderate-cost housing and lead developers to build what they think will sell to high-income families. Besides, opponents who are concerned to protect either their tax rates or their social prestige want their new neighbors to be wealthy if they must have any new neighbors at all.

Environmental regulations seem to be pushing developers throughout the country to cut the number of houses they build to less than what they had originally planned. A national survey of 400 developers in 1976 asked those working in states with required environmental impact reviews what kinds of changes they made in their construction plans because of these reviews. The most common change, mentioned by 60 percent of the developers, was a reduction in housing density.[30] Research on environmental impact reviews in both California and Florida also found density reductions among the conditions imposed most often by regulatory agencies. According to the environmental impact studies, the main reasons for reducing the density were to relieve traffic congestion or improve air quality. But interviews with local officials revealed a different motivation: established residents were concerned that newcomers living in higher-density housing might be socially undesirable. Beneath the environmental arguments the underlying objections were social or sometimes fiscal.[31]

Reducing the amount of housing in a development almost always means raising the price per unit since the developer will have to divide his land costs and other fixed expenses among fewer houses. And if the local motivation is to eliminate inexpensive housing that might attract social undesirables, political pressure will reinforce economics in persuading developers to build more expensive homes. the evidence suggests that the California tactic of whittling away at project densities, and thereby raising housing costs, is part of a national pattern.

Experience in Florida illustrates still another consumer cost of environmental regulation. An analysis of the conditions attached to development approvals found that their main effect was to shift public service costs from local governments to the developer and future residents.[32] This finding is entirely consistent with the long tradition of using land use regulations for fiscal protection, and it is also consistent with the high priority given to tax impact questions in the California controversies. Like the high hook-up fees noted earlier, it is basically a way of imposing special taxes on newcomers—taxes that raise the price of new homes.

The stretch-out of development time noted in California appears to hold true in much of the country. On this point, a nationwide homebuilder survey tells a clear story. In 1976 some 2,500 homebuilders estimated the length of time it took them in 1970 and in 1975 to go from their decision to develop a project to the day when a building permit was issued. More than three-fourths reported development times of six months or less in 1970 while half the builders reported development times of more than a year in 1975. The average periods were 5 months in 1970 and 13.3 months in 1975.[33] Extra development time adds extra carrying charges to the sales price. It also prevents builders from responding quickly to market changes, as in California when construction delays led to major price inflation because the volume of homebuilding lagged too far behind current demand.

Evidence at hand also means that the new regulation has raised housing costs without doing very much to improve the public environment. The major trend in project design is a reduction in housing density, which runs exactly counter to the environmentalists' rhetorical commitment to compact, efficient land development. And the shift of public service costs from local governments to new residents does not change the quality of the environment; it only changes who pays the bill. Both these outcomes are consistent with long-term suburban efforts to protect social and fiscal advantages—efforts that continue to turn development reviews to distinctly nonenvironmental purposes.

Finally, a predictable result of the new regulatory climate is that it encourages developers to build on the outer fringes of urban regions, where communities not yet hit by growth have not yet set up the proper machinery for harassing homebuilders. This result produces inconvenience and high travel costs for the homebuyer, together with the environmental costs of dispersed development, extra energy use, and more air pollution from long-distance commuting. A study of sewer moratoria found evidence of exactly this result:

The moratoria were encouraging sprawl by sending builders to jurisdictions that were not so strict on service provision and where land was cheap. People were getting houses, but at the expense of even longer driving times and an even more inefficient pattern of urban growth—hardly what the environmental advocates of moratoria anticipated.[34]

Losers and Winners

The new suburban attempts to stop growth have not stopped it in the nation at large. Near-record levels of single-family homebuilding—1.2 million new home starts in 1976, and 1.5 million in 1977—suggest that although individual communities may have succeeded in blocking homebuilding on their own turf, developers found other sites where they could build. But the new regulatory climate does seem to have reduced the options available to homebuyers and to have made new houses more expensive than they had to be. These outcomes hurt above all the average family that did not already own a home and wanted to buy one, and they hurt these families more than comparable policies in the 1960s. Suburban growth regulations at that time also reduced choices and raised prices but much less so than in the 1970s. During the 1960s the average family enjoyed steady increases in real income so that it could afford to buy a typical new home even if large-lot zoning raised the price. By contrast in the 1970s real income grew more slowly, and families whose incomes were near or below the national average were hard-pressed to find the money to pay for a first home.

For most Americans homeownership remains a centerpiece of the good life, and a source of economic security as well as personal satisfaction. It is especially important to working people with moderate incomes. A survey of AFL-CIO members taken in 1975 illustrates who is hurt by the high cost of homeownership. The members surveyed had incomes just above the median for all U.S. households at that time, and their attachment to homeownership was especially strong. Seventy-seven percent of the union members were already homeowners in 1975. Of those who were renters more than 60 percent wanted to move in the next few years, and the reason most of them gave was that they wanted to buy a home. Further, over 97 percent of the people surveyed believed that most Americans want to own their homes.

Owning a home offered clear economic advantages, particularly for old people. Median housing expenses for homeowners who were 65 or older amounted to only 15 percent of their income, while renters in the same age-group had to commit nearly twice as much (28 percent). The survey made it clear that continued increases in home prices would in time pose a serious threat to the economic well-being of union members:

The result of continued inability of young family households to become homeowners will be increasing numbers of workers with unduly high housing expense burdens in later years when they must live on reduced incomes. Not only will individual elderly households be placed in financial hardship, but there will also be an increased need for housing assistance for the elderly. On the other hand, ... workers who assumed ownership in earlier years accumulated equity through mortgage payments. They also had protection against inflation in housing prices and rents. Many households had paid off their mortgage by the time they were in their fifties and sixties and could meet their housing expenses with a reasonable proportion of their income.[35]

In the 1960s the victims of suburban exclusion were mainly poor people, a small and powerless minority. They are still victims of it in the 1970s. But now there are many more victims than before. Middle-income America, in addition to the poor, is now bearing the costs of suburban growth policies.

Why have suburbanites, who are overwhelmingly middle-class themselves, turned against other middle-class people who want to move into their communities? If California's experience is a guide, the fight is usually between families who have already made use of homeownership to improve their situation in life and other families trying to advance themselves by becoming suburban homeowners. Those who already moved up the status ladder are enjoying a new life-style in comfortable suburbs, but they worry about how secure their gains are. Their fears seem to run as follows. First, growth might bring property tax increases that could threaten their ability to pay for the good life-style. Also more homebuilding might crowd their schools and destroy the scenic qualities that give their property prestige and value. No matter that there is strong evidence against these fears, or that there are ways to manage growth while still keeping the desirable qualities of suburbia. People fight homebuilding even in the least threatened places, such as affluent Marin County with close to 500 square miles of open space. By joining local homeowner and environmental organizations, suburbanites can use political action to protect what they have. Although they themselves took full advantage of government policies that promoted homeownership for families of average income, they justify denying the same opportunities to others by calling it environmental protection.

The change from keeping out the poor to keeping out the average family comes from a change of purpose. Earlier the goal was exclusion—keeping out people of lower status. Now the goal is freezing growth—keeping out everybody in order to hold on to what you have. Policies that freeze growth are a threat to families outside the suburbs who want to get in, but outsiders can do very little about these policies. They have no vote in the suburbs that exclude them, no organizations to join that will fight for their interests, and no persuasive rhetoric to use in local growth controversies.

The established suburbanites are coming out ahead in all ways. Growth restrictions have added to the value of the homes they bought a few years ago. Many are selling these homes at high prices and using the proceeds to buy even better ones. A large number are refinancing their houses at the new price levels in order to raise cash for other expenses. They are managing to protect their personal environments and their suburban life-styles while passing the costs to other people. And thanks to the policies that succeeded in spreading homeownership in the past, these beneficiaries of no-growth policies greatly outnumber their victims.

Prospects for Change

When the impact of earlier suburban growth policies became clear in the 1960s, many people tried to figure out strategies for opening up the suburbs to the poor and racial minorities. Some organized lawsuits to try to get the courts to strike down exclusionary zoning. Others worked at persuading metropolitan councils of government to parcel out subsidized housing developments among the suburbs according to "fair share" plans that would keep the burden light for each community. A few activists managed to set up state programs to promote subsidized housing in the suburbs. Most important, congress set up and funded large new federal subsidy programs that homebuilders could use in the suburbs without getting any special clearance from local officials. George Romney, as Secretary of Housing and Urban Development from 1969 to 1973, used all the leverage he could find to try to open the suburbs to the new housing programs.

None of these strategies worked. The courts overruled only the most blatant zoning abuses, and the suburbs used their rapidly growing political influence to resist fair share plans and to block state and federal attempts to build subsidized housing wherever the neighbors objected to it. Michael Danielson's analysis of the politics of exclusion summarizes the dismal results:

HUD's initiatives were checked by suburban political pressures, concern for suburban constituencies in the White House and Congress, and a lack of commitment to subsidized housing and social change in a conservative national administration. Courts, in fact, did not strike down local zoning. . . . Quite the contrary, the nation's top court strongly endorsed local zoning designed to preserve community character, upheld the use of local referendums for public housing, denied the existence of a fundamental right to housing, constrained the grounds for challenging local housing actions to explicit instances of racial discrimination, and severely limited access to federal courts by those excluded from suburbia. Few state courts have imposed significant restrictions on suburban land use controls. . . .

Clearly, policy change on an issue as controversial as suburban exclusion requires substantial political support. Almost everywhere, such support has been lacking.[36]

The suburbs then prevailed against the poor and their advocates. The question now is whether they can also prevail against the millions of middle-income families who are coming of age and searching for suburban homes they can afford.

A first possibility to consider is whether changed circumstances may weaken the suburban opposition from within. There may be a slight weakening for two reasons. Fearful suburbanites who feel threatened by poor people or minority groups have less cause for worry when the housing at stake is for middle-income people very much like themselves. Similarly, those concerned with social prestige have less reason to mobilize opposition against market-priced homes than against subsidized developments. But protection-minded suburbanites, as noted earlier, want to keep out everybody and not just the poor.

Suburbanites who rivet their attention on the tax rate also have some grounds for relaxing their opposition to new housing. School costs are by far the dominant local expense resulting from new development. In the past new subdivisions brought with them many youngsters who needed new schools. Families today are having fewer children. In many suburbs the main school problem now is a shortage of children to fill the new schools that were built in the fifties and sixties. In Palo Alto, for example, soon after the city cited the high cost of new school construction as an important reason to block homebuilding in its foothills, the school superintendent proposed closing 5 out of 20 elementary schools immediately and 3 or 4 more within a few years.[37] School officials are finding that it is unpopular to close neighborhood schools and hard to reduce education budgets when enrollment dwindles. Under the circumstances, a moderate supply of new school-age children whose parents pay reasonable property taxes could begin to look like a very good thing.

For other reasons as well, school finances should generate less opposition to new housing in the future than they did in the past. As a result of increased state and federal aid, local taxes pay for a smaller share of school costs than they used to: for the country at large, the local share of education outlays was down from 56 percent in 1955–56 to 44 percent in 1975–76.[38] In addition, state courts have begun to find school financing arrangements based on local property taxes unconstitutional. The state supreme courts in California, Connecticut, New Jersey, New York, and Texas have already ruled against the present system because of the great local disparities resulting from property tax financing. Similar cases are working their way through the courts in more than a dozen other states. What the legislatures will do to replace the present system is unknown, but almost any reform in line with the court decisions will reduce the impact of new growth on local property taxes.

So there may be some weakening of suburban opposition, but the change is likely to be small. Many opposition groups appear to operate more on the basis of some notion about what is desirable and proper for their communities than on careful calculations of fiscal consequences. The fiscal impact studies that encourage so much opposition to homebuilding are, in fact, notoriously unreliable. Few people have taken the trouble to learn what actually happens as a result of community decisions to grow or not to grow. One recent study is an exception. A review of experience in 175 municipalities in rapidly growing parts of New Jersey found that property tax rates on the average were no higher in fast-growing communities than they were in those with little recent growth. Further, per pupil school costs and per capita outlays for municipal services were actually lower in high-growth municipalities.[39] Since fiscal opposition to homebuilding has only a weak connection with reality to begin with, whatever happens in the world of public finance is not likely to affect it very much.

Latching onto New Causes
Redirecting suburban growth policies will require political muscle. Suburban opponents of homebuilding have enjoyed great political success, partly because they have packaged their self-interested purposes together with causes that attract a wide and uncritical following, such as protecting the environment or saving farmland. The confusion of purposes and slogans is so thorough that many victims of suburban growth policies hardly know what is victimizing them.

What are the prospects that the public-interest veneer will wear thin enough to help the public recognize and act on the underlying issues? They are probably not very good. For one thing, the slogans and arguments that growth opponents have been using all along seem to have plenty of mileage left in them. Even the worn-out charge that growth means ticky-tacky developments still has fresh potential in political controversies. Recently, Nelson Rockefeller made plans to sell his 25-acre estate in the most fashionable part of Washington, D.C. to developers who proposed to build about a hundred houses on it, each selling for some $300,000. His well-to-do neighbors, including several other millionaire estate owners, promptly organized a protest rally and denounced the $300,000 houses as "ticky-tacky."[40]

If the present arguments ever do wear out, others are waiting in the wings and some have already had their first tryouts. Each one claims that stopping suburban growth serves some broad and important public purpose. When energy conservation became an important item on the national agenda, environmentalists and other growth opponents were quick to claim that suburban homebuilding would lead to wasteful energy use because of the low-density living pattern it creates. When a new study, The Costs of Sprawl, agreed with this position, they picked it up and used it uncritically. A close analysis of The Costs of Sprawl has shown that it greatly exaggerated the energy savings that might be achieved through compact development, even on the assumption that most people would live in apartments rather than in single-family homes. After correcting for several factors that biased the results, Alan Altshuler calculated that a shift from low-density residential sprawl to highly compact apartment development would reduce total urban energy consumption by no more than 1 to 3 percent.[41] The energy conservation argument then is more an expression of doctrine than a result of analysis.

The latest argument to appear is that stopping suburban growth can serve another national interest by forcing new development into the deteriorating central cities that would benefit from it. California's draft proposal for an urban development strategy, for example, proposed helping the run-down older cities "by giving priority to rehabilitation and new construction in older areas over new development in new areas."[42] It is well known that new housing development and renovation of existing homes almost always push poor people out of old neighborhoods. Advocates of forced redevelopment of the cities cannot explain how it will help the city's residents, particularly since the prior step of slowing suburban growth is likely to send housing costs higher for everyone.

Nor have they acknowledged the fact that most cities are as opposed to large housing developments as the suburbs are. The best illustration of this point comes from a now-forgotten federal program known as "New Towns In-Town." In 1967 President Johnson decided to help meet the need for urban housing by making surplus federal land in seven cities available for big new developments that would include housing for poor people. The program offered vacant land by the acre, at low prices, with no prior residents to be displaced, plus federal subsidies and support from Washington officials. Yet local controversy blocked or delayed every development. There were objections from nearby residents, demands for different projects that would generate more tax revenue, and—in San Francisco—pressures from conservationists to leave the land open. Four years later, three of the projects were dead, and the others were stalled indefinitely by local opposition.[43]

Even without any help from public policy, there probably will be increasing demand for central-city housing in the next ten years. Changes in family life are making central-city neighborhoods more attractive than the suburbs to large numbers of people who can afford good homes in either place. Young people are staying single longer, having children later, and having fewer children than their counterparts of ten or twenty years ago. For a large part of their adult lives, many may value the convenience of in-city living more than the schools and open spaces of child-oriented suburbia. As an increasing number of families manage two careers at once, more may decide to pass up the suburban chores of carpooling children and looking after lawns and gardens. And the increase in suburban home prices will soon make renovating a Victorian town house look like a bargain in comparison.

But the unprecedented increase in young families will inevitably generate a huge demand for additional housing somewhere, and there are limits to how much of it the cities can absorb. From 1970 through 1976 only a third of all new metropolitan housing construction went into central cities. Even if the cities capture more of the market in the future, there is no realistic alternative to suburban locations for most new housing. And if opinion surveys tell us anything, it is that for most Americans there is still no good substitute for a single-family home in the green suburbs. So even a generation pioneering in new lifestyles will want housing in both suburbs and central cities. Still, slogans such as "Save the cities by stopping suburban growth" will serve the interests of people who want to protect established suburban neighborhoods, when the real issue is who shall have access to the suburbs and on what terms.

Regulatory Reform

Will suburban growth regulations become less hostile to homebuilding in the future? Some business groups mauled by the new review processes have been searching for changes to simplify them in the hope of giving development proposals a fighting chance. Regulatory procedures in this field certainly need managerial attention, and they probably will get it; however, administrative reform can offer only minor help in opening the suburbs to middle-income housing. To reduce the complexity of development reviews and the repeated veto opportunities they offer to the opposition, one popular proposal has been to consolidate permit procedures into a single operation. But the best study so far of what has become known as "the permit explosion" concludes realistically:

"One-stop shopping"—the delegation of all authority over land use and environmental issues to a single "czar"—cannot, realistically speaking, be accomplished. The issues are too complex; our political institutions, too varied.[44]

Some observers maintain that suburban growth regulations will succumb to a familiar process of regulatory capture, in which the regulated firms gradually come to dominate the agencies set up to supervise them. This argument assumes that those who are regulated have enough political power to force public agencies to bargain with them. It almost never happens that way in the suburbs where developers usually come from outside the community and have little power or even legitimacy in their dealings with local government. Far from capturing regulatory agencies, developers are forced to compromise with them at the expense of housing consumers. If anyone is capturing the process of growth regulation, it is the established residents and their environmental allies.

Suburban officials have the power to regulate homebuilding within their jurisdiction, but future homebuyers are excluded from the decision process. Since most homebuyers come from other places and have no connection to the local government that regulates their housing, the only way they can affect the outcome is by using their influence with the state and the federal government. These governments did try to intervene in suburban housing decisions on behalf of poor people, but they did not have enough political support to succeed at that time.

Now a larger constituency has a stake in opening up the suburbs. Young middle-income families and those who care about them could supply some of the political weight that was missing in the past. People with an economic stake in homebuilding might also join coalitions in support of suburban development. In California, for example, a group of corporations and labor unions have formed the Council for Environmental and Economic Balance to represent their moderately pro-development position on legislative and regulatory issues. Further, those groups that earlier fought suburban exclusion on behalf of the poor and minorities could lend both skills and legitimacy to a new campaign.

Some state officials are already searching for policies of moderation. In Massachusetts a recent growth strategy report suggests interesting state initiatives for this purpose. The Massachusetts report, unlike its counterpart in California, acknowledges openly that most suburbs in the state want to have slower growth than in the past, or want no growth at all. In order to induce them to accept a reasonable share of anticipated growth, the state proposes to offer them protection against exceptional development pressures. Each community would prepare a local growth program specifying the amount of housing it is prepared to take for several years ahead. State officials would review the program to determine whether it accommodates a reasonable share of the region's growth demand. If they approve the program, the community would be given the power to reject any housing proposal once the target for that year had been met. There would be a further bonus designed to encourage suburbs to accept low- and moderate-income housing: every moderately priced home would count as two housing units toward the community's target and every subsidized house or apartment would count as four units.

The state officials who prepared this strategy expected it to lead to less restrictive and less costly development controls. In their view many controls that have raised the cost of housing are actually intended to limit growth rather than to make housing more expensive. Since communities under the new program would be able to limit growth directly, they would no longer have to use large-lot zoning or excessive subdivision requirements in order to control the volume of growth.[45] Whether their reasoning is correct remains to be seen. In California the evidence is not encouraging, but the environmental movement in Massachusetts is still very moderate by comparison.

Recycling Environmental Groups?
Ingenious public policies can be helpful, but earlier efforts to overcome suburban exclusion did not fail for lack of good policy ideas. They failed for lack of an effective political constituency. Putting that constituency together will be a little easier now that exclusionary measures hit the middle class as well as the poor, but it will still be very hard. The main problem, noted earlier, is that rising home prices help more people than they hurt. Most families in metropolitan America already live in the suburbs and most in the entire country already own their homes. Higher housing prices raise the value of their property, and stopping homebuilding keeps their communities uncrowded and their scenery unspoiled.

Further, any coalition for suburban growth will constantly have to recruit new supporters to replace those whose outlook will change as soon as they buy their first home. Homeownership itself is a powerful force for suburban protectionism.

Like a speculator who buys in a rising market, the new homeowner who has just overpaid for his first house will want future buyers to overpay even more for theirs. The people who today want to freeze new development were outsiders themselves a few years ago. Now that they belong to the country club, they are eager to tighten admission standards and raise the entrance fees. The street wisdom of London bus-riders sums it up well: "Bang the bell, Jack, I'm on board."

Young families who want to buy homes will need all the political allies they can find. The prospects for successful coalition-building depend to a great extent on whether environmental groups will continue to work for suburban protectionism, or whether they will give more attention to the housing needs of the average citizen. Environmentalists can bring great strength to whichever side they join in a debate about suburban housing. Their vision of environmental quality attracts popular support, and they have shown exceptional skill in presenting their views to the media and to the courts.

Are the conflicts between environmentalism and the average homebuyer inevitable, or are there other ways of reaching environmental goals? Many of these conflicts are avoidable. If environmental groups were to start supporting growth management strategies for urban areas, instead of seizing easy opportunities to stop individual developments, they could make a positive contribution to the public environment at much lower cost to the nation's homebuyers.

An environmentally sound approach to growth management should mean supporting most infill developments near established communities and job centers. Environmental organizations should monitor infill developments to be sure that they do not generate objectionable side effects, such as waste disposal or drainage problems. And they should negotiate for reasonable provision of open space within new developments. If infill construction cannot supply enough new housing to take care of the increase in new families, environmentalists should also support planned and orderly development in fringe suburbs where open land is available. Their objective then would be good management of environmental impacts instead of blanket opposition to new housing. The environmental arsenal of growth-stopping tactics would be reserved for those scattered subdivisions beyond the urban fringe that are genuinely wasteful of land and of investments for new public services.

These policies would also serve the interests of environmentalists. Selective opposition to housing developments, and bargaining to improve but not eliminate those that fit within an efficient growth strategy, would conserve the limited political resources of environmental organizations for more important work on other fronts. This realignment would also help them build alliances with groups that care about the public environment but are unwilling to make consumers pay the heavy costs of environmental reform.

Leaders of national environmental organizations have begun to recognize a need to work more effectively with other groups. The Conservation Foundation, for example, has supported projects designed to improve relations between business people and their environmental adversaries. And Michael McCloskey, executive director of the Sierra Club, recently deplored the inability of environmentalists and industrialists to resolve their disputes through practical negotiation. He observed that both sides often take rigid positions that make limited disagreements into ideological battlegrounds, producing hollow victories: "Environmentalists have defeated projects on which they only really sought mitigation, while developers have been awarded permits for projects they did not originally envision."[46] McCloskey suggests that each side recognize the legitimacy of the other and that both try to find ways to settle resolvable issues.

If environmentalists reconsider their current strategies, they will have to decide which is more important, defending established suburbs or improving the environment for the public at large. If they decide in favor of the public environment, they will have to part company with their current suburban friends who are working to preserve their own social and fiscal advantages. But they could instead build alliances with middle-income families, labor unions, and minority groups who have a stake not only in homebuilding but also in those environmental issues that affect the public at large.

If environmental groups continue to disrupt homebuilding, the prospects for managing suburban growth equitably and at reasonable cost will be very poor. If they change course, those prospects will improve. In either case, reform of suburban development policies will not be easy because they have deep roots in our system of local government and our housing economy. Equally important, the age of environmentalism has already established the belief that each community has a right to decide how much or how little growth to accept. Even if environmentalists turn to new causes, this claim will not go away. As long as the suburbs are free to act on it, they will keep trying to pad the housing bill for newcomers in order to look after the interests of people who got there just ahead of them.

Regulatory Lessons

Experience with the new regulation of homebuilding should raise warning flags for other parts of the economy that are subject to the newly designed regulations of the 1970s. The regulatory process in this case turns out to be highly political, with the priorities and directions set mainly by influential suburbanites. In contrast to earlier capture of regulatory agencies by industry, this time the captors are local growth opponents and public officials guarding their own turf against newcomers.

The new homebuilding regulation is not so much a system for managing growth as it is for stopping it. Development reviews in practice seldom generate meaningful new information for decision-makers. Their main function is political: to give the opposition time to organize and repeated chances to block construction.

All this is not to say that there is no need for environmental regulation of community development. The public at large does have a legitimate stake in preventing pollution, protecting important natural resources, and minimizing the disruptions of growth. The basic case for regulation holds that if growth decisions are left to developers and consumers alone, they will give too little attention to the damage their own decisions might impose on the community at large. Since nearby residents and the public in general do have important interests in what is built, they should have a voice in establishing community growth policies. Building housing and protecting the environment are both valid goals, and it should be possible to reconcile the conflicts between them by making reasonable compromises.

The regulators, however, seldom act as though they are trying to balance two social goods against each other. Instead they view housing as at best a necessary evil, and protecting the existing environment as an unqualified good. Instead of adding the public as a third party to the interaction between developers and homebuyers, the regulatory system pushes out the consumer and leaves his interests in the hands of developers, local officials, and growth opponents. The regulators look narrowly at the local impact of new developments but give almost no attention to finding a desirable growth pattern for the region at large. This system protects certain places against change, but it shifts development to other places where there is less opposition. It stops compact, efficient development in established communities where the opposition is well organized, and it imposes a more objectionable pattern of sprawl on outlying places that are less populated and less regulated.

Regulatory policies are reducing the choices available to consumers and raising the cost of housing. They run counter to long-established national objectives of encouraging homeownership for families of average income and stimulating a large enough volume of homebuilding to take care of the growing number of families. Yet they are failing to produce environmental benefits for the public at large. Public regulation is achieving mainly private purposes.

The regulatory system is fundamentally unfair in the way it distributes costs and benefits. Opponents of growth make much of their assertion that people who buy inexpensive new houses do not "pay their own way" in property taxes—a conclusion that usually rests on shaky fiscal impact studies. Yet it is even clearer that environmentalists do not "pay their own way." Their favored techniques for preserving open space usually shift much of the cost of buying land or protecting farms to taxpayers outside the community. And their success in blocking homebuilding loads extra cost burdens on people who want to buy houses. Established residents get the benefits while outside taxpayers and people who want to buy homes get the bill.

Building a logical argument in favor of the present system would be very hard. It would somehow have to justify benefiting existing suburban residents at the expense of potential newcomers, encouraging sprawling development in lightly regulated places, and charging young families and taxpayers in general for the benefits that go to selected suburbanites. Nobody has yet made a persuasive case justifying these results.

No Room in the Lifeboat

The movement to stop suburban growth has done more than disrupt homebuilding. In attempting to justify its position on growth, it has begun to spread a new ideology of elitism through the country's political life. This ideology has served many different uses, but with one underlying theme: it supplies a ready rationale for the defense of privilege.

Is it fair to hold the environmental and anti-growth movement responsible for the uses of its ideology? When the movement was first struggling for recognition, critics overlooked its exaggerated rhetoric. Political movements create ideologies in order to drum up support for a cause, and realism or balance are not to be expected. Besides, most people thought the cause was a good one since environmentalists were fighting an uphill battle against entrenched economic and political power. If their rhetoric had elitist overtones, in which environmentalists were the guardians of higher values against the pressures of materialism, it was still no more than a slingshot for David to use against Goliath.

But now environmentalists and suburban growth opponents are no longer small and weak. As their movement has matured, however, it has acquired power and influence without leaving behind its rhetorical baggage. A turn away from ideology and toward pragmatism has yet to come. But mature movements must be held accountable for their rhetoric and its political uses. Otherwise, a good cause can easily promote bad public policy.

A recent airline dispute showed how the concept of environmental protection can preserve economic privileges even where no believable environmental issues are involved. For some time, a single airline offered the only nonstop service between Los Angeles and Miami. In 1972 the Civil Aeronautics Board (CAB) invited other airlines to propose competitive service on the same route. Almost all the domestic airlines filed applications, and a federal administrative judge decided in favor of one of them. National Airlines, which had been enjoying a monopoly on this route, then argued that additional flights would increase air and noise pollution in both Los Angeles and Miami. They demanded that the CAB prepare an environmental impact statement and rehear the case to consider environmental issues. Although the judge commented on National's "tardy enthusiasm for environmental matters," the CAB stopped the proceedings and delayed its decision more than two years while it investigated the alleged environmental impacts. Meanwhile National Airlines had two more years of monopoly profits.[47]

Using environmental arguments to defend privilege and restrict competition is a familiar enough story from the growth controversies of California. The concepts and methods perfected there are also flexible enough to help people resist change for reasons totally unrelated to community growth. In time even groups opposed to environmental protection will no doubt learn how to make use of what the environmentalists have created. And a close look at the latest anti-growth ideologies ought to persuade responsible environmentalists that their movement's rhetoric is bound to do more serious damage to the public in the future.

Environmental thinkers have begun to put together a new "lifeboat ethic" that outdoes even their own earlier efforts to justify protecting the privileged at everyone else's expense. Garrett Hardin, Professor of Human Ecology at the

University of California at Santa Barbara, has developed the lifeboat ethic as a reason to keep newcomers away from our scarce resources. His essay, "Living on a Lifeboat," presents a parable in which a lifeboat full of rich people represents each advanced nation of the world. The poor people of other countries live in more crowded lifeboats, and some of them keep falling into the water and swimming around, hoping to get into one of the rich lifeboats so that they can benefit from the good things on board.

In deciding whether to let them in, the rich passengers confront the central problem of the ethics of a lifeboat. They will be tempted to make their decision on the basis of the Christian ideal of brotherhood, or the Marxist ideal of "from each according to his abilities, to each according to his needs." But every lifeboat, even theirs, has a limited carrying capacity. If they admit all the needy to their boat, it will be swamped and everyone will be drowned. Complete justice will produce complete catastrophe, according to Hardin's scenario. The sensible solution, unjust though it may seem, is to admit no more people to the lifeboat so that those already inside may survive. Sharing would be suicidal.

Does the image of the lifeboat fit the situation in the United States, one of the least crowded of industrial countries? Hardin believes that it does: "The land of every nation has a limited carrying capacity. The exact limit is a matter for argument, but the energy crunch is convincing more people every day that we have already exceeded the carrying capacity of the land."[48]

The question of fairness remains troublesome, however. Hardin acknowledges that critics will ask how his prescription differs from the simple selfishness of slamming the door once you are safe inside. Since almost all Americans are descended from immigrants, how can they justify keeping their own place in the rich lifeboat while refusing to admit others? Doesn't a full and fair application of the lifeboat ethic require us to give the land back to the Indians and go somewhere else? Hardin concedes that his own logic offers no way to reject this proposal. "Yet," he says, "I am unwilling to live by it; and I know no one who is." Non-Indian Americans would have no place to go. Most came from Europe, but they would not be welcomed back there. Besides, Europeans also have no historical title to their lands; so they, too, would have to give up their homes.

The solution to this dilemma is an expedient one: "The law long ago invented statutes of limitations to justify the rejection of pure justice, in the interest of preventing massive disorder. The law zealously defends property rights—but only *recent* property rights. . . . Drawing a line in time may be unjust, but any other action is practically worse. We are all the descendents of thieves, and the world's resources are inequitably distributed, but we must begin the journey to tomorrow from the point where we are today. . . . We cannot safely divide the wealth equitably among all present peoples, . . . because to do so would guarantee that our grandchildren—everyone's grandchildren—would have only a ruined world to inhabit."[49]

An overriding concern for survival and for future generations justifies the lifeboat ethic. Whether the image on which it is based is at all applicable to the United States is doubtful since other industrial societies (Western Europe, Japan) have achieved high standards of living despite far greater population pressure on their limited land and resources. Making this argument about foreign immigration fit the local growth policies of American suburbs goes well beyond doubt, however, and into the theater of the absurd.

Yet environmentalists and other growth opponents have applied the lifeboat ethic in just that way. By declaring their land and environmental resources to be threatened by growth, and by appointing themselves guardians of finite resources, they conclude that it is time to draw the line against further urban development. In San Francisco a leading environmental organization calls for setting permanent boundaries to future urbanization on exactly this basis: "The time is at hand to apply an ethic of stewardship to our most precious resource— our finite land."[50] And environmental columnist Harold Gilliam has this to say about what continued population growth will do to the San Francisco area: "Ultimately, every conservation problem is a population problem. Every effort to save some vestige of California's pristine splendor, every campaign to preserve the bay or the hills or a natural coastline or a grove of redwoods, every attempt to curb galloping slurbanism or to save breathing space for the future, would be defeated by the unending advance of new hordes of population like a swarm of locusts devouring everything in sight."[51]

If the suburbs are lifeboats, they are exceptionally spacious and comfortable lifeboats, like Marin County with more than 90 percent of its land still open. Additional suburban growth poses no threat to anyone's survival. The only threat is to the pleasures of affluent living, including the enjoyment of not having unwanted neighbors. And indeed, the talk of survival, limited resources, and austerity does not crimp the life-style of suburban environmentalists, but only of the people they keep outside.

One Bay Area environmentalist recently showed how to honor the principles of ecological preservation while living in luxury within the lifeboat. A retired computer executive whose environmental awareness had been raised to a high level commissioned his architect to build a house that would use recycled materials as much as possible. The architect used river-washed rock from a dry stream bed on the client's 200-acre estate as the basic structural material. These large stones made attractive colonnades, terraces, and columns for the main house and a separate guest cottage and wine-storage room. They also made an unusual swimming pool. Rather than order newly cut lumber, the architect found an abandoned pier in northern California made of Douglas-fir timbers, which he disassembled and shipped to the building site. The weathered wood made handsome ceiling beams. Similarly, he used antique machine parts to make novel hardware for the doors. Further in the spirit of ecological preservation, the owner decided to recycle furniture from his last home, supplemented only with a few finds from countryside shops nearby.[52]

This house owes as much to the tradition of Hearst Castle, where William Randolph Hearst recycled whole rooms brought over from Europe, as it does to ecological awareness. It is characteristic of the environmental outlook in another way: these gestures of resource conservation involve no real sacrifice. They are flourishes that enhance an affluent way of life and make it even more prestigious. They are only another form of conspicuous consumption, masquerading as conspicuous nonconsumption. But environmentalists who admire this extravagant use of resources on a 200-acre spread in the Napa Valley will turn up their noses at the modest homes and small gardens of average families.

People who are well-off can use the lifeboat analogy to protect what they have at no cost to themselves: the call for sacrifice and austerity is directed only to outsiders. Meanwhile the same uncritical thinking that allows prosperous suburbanites to imagine themselves huddled in a lifeboat is also warping other political debates. Lifeboat thinkers argue against many types of aid for the have-nots, on the ground that finite tax dollars must go to the productive members of society if we are to survive. "No room in the lifeboat" slogans, based on superficial analysis plus a strong measure of self-interest, are undermining a basic sense of fairness and decency in public policy.[53]

The takeover of local growth controls for exclusionary purposes, and the selling of a lifeboat rhetoric to justify it, are both outstanding successes for the new elitism in our national politics. Recognition of this elitism will not trouble environmental purists, though. Fairness is not an important consideration for them.

But the movement's more responsible leadership will have to contend with an increasingly skeptical climate of opinion, as the public continues to question increasing regulation and as the flaws of environmental politics draw critical attention. For political effectiveness, if for no other reason, environmentalists are likely to move toward a more equitable strategy and a more considered ideology. If they want to keep a base of popular support, they will have to offer the average person something better than a rear view of a fleet of fat lifeboats sailing into the sunset while he flounders behind in the water.

Notes

Notes to Chapter 1

1. For data sources and related analyses of homeowner costs, see Bernard J. Frieden, Arthur P. Solomon, David L. Birch, and John Pitkin, *The Nation's Housing: 1975 to 1985* (Cambridge, Mass.: MIT-Harvard Joint Center for Urban Studies, 1977).

2. Quoted in Charles Abrams, *The City Is The Frontier* (New York: Harper & Row, 1965), p. 254.

3. Gallup Opinion Index, "Analysis: Managed Growth," August, 1974, Report 110.

4. See David Birch et al., *America's Housing Needs: 1970-1980* (Cambridge, Mass.: MIT-Harvard Joint Center for Urban Studies, 1973), pp. 5-3, 5-4, and pp. 5-21 to 5-23; and *Survey of AFL-CIO Members Housing: 1975* (Washington, D.C.: AFL-CIO, 1975).

5. See Frieden et al., *The Nation's Housing: 1975 to 1985,* chapter 2, which forecasts 8.8 million. The *lowest* comparable census bureau projection is for an increase of 9.3 million.

6. These estimates were prepared by the federal government, cited in Charles L. Schultze, *The Public Use of Private Interest* (Washington, D.C.: The Brookings Institution, 1977), pp. 7-8.

7. Aaron Wildavsky, "Economy and Environment/Rationality and Ritual: A Review of *The Uncertain Search for Environmental Quality,"* Working Paper No. 35, Graduate School of Public Policy, University of California, Berkeley, 1975, p. 2.

8. Michael Sterne, "Environmentalist Questions Priorities," *New York Times,* May 12, 1978, p. B1.

Notes to Chapter 2

1. Security Pacific Bank, *A Special Report on the Economy of the San Francisco Bay Area* (September 1975), statistical tables 1 and 2. Throughout this book, the San Francisco Bay Area refers to the following nine counties: Alameda, Contra Costa, Marin, Napa, San Francisco, San Mateo, Santa Clara, Solano, and Sonoma.

2. See Melvin M. Webber, "The BART Experience—What Have We Learned?" *The Public Interest,* no. 45 (Fall 1976): pp. 79-108.

3. Ibid., p. 93.

4. See Rice Odell, *The Saving of San Francisco Bay* (Washington, D.C.: The Conservation Foundation, 1972).

5. Quoted in Thomas R. Ferguson, "The Napa Study," Graduate School of Business Administration, Master of Business Administration report, University of California, Berkeley, June 1969, pp. 7-8.

6. Ibid., p. 9.

7. Ibid., pp. 24-25.

8. For an account of the Williamson Act and other California provisions for reduced assessments to preserve open space, see the following works: Gregory C. Gustafson and L. T. Wallace, "Differential Assessment as Land Use Policy: The California Case," *Journal of the American Institute of Planners* 41 (November 1975): 379–389; State of California Legislative Analyst, *Report on Open Space Taxation* (Sacramento, Calif., December 22, 1971); and Valerie C. Kircher, "The Legislative Battle Over Preserving Agricultural Land," *California Journal* 7 (May 1976): 155–157.

9. Quoted in Tom Harris, "Californians Are Saying 'No' to Growth in a Spreading Revolt That Makes Strange Allies," *California Journal* 4 (July 1973): 224–229; quotation from p. 227.

10. See Anne Jackson, "Agonizing Reappraisal for the Environmental Quality Act, *California Journal* 7 (February 1976): 59–61.

11. Gladwin Hill, "Environmental Impact Assessments, Practically a Revolution," *New York Times,* December 5, 1976, section 4, p. E14.

12. State of California Office of Planning and Research, *California Environmental Quality Act Litigation Study* (Sacramento, April 1976), p. 8.

13. Mary Cranston, Bryant Garth, Robert Plattner, and Jay Varon, *A Handbook for Controlling Local Growth* (Stanford, Calif.: Stanford Environmental Law Society, 1973), p. 77.

14. Quoted in Stanley Scott, *Governing California's Coast* (Berkeley: University of California Institute of Governmental Studies, 1975), p. 355.

15. See ibid., pp. 357, 360–361.

16. Both opposition quotations cited in Thomas Dickert and Jens Sorenson, "Social Equity in Coastal Zone Planning," *Coastal Zone Management Journal* 1 (1974): 141–150, quoted on p. 143.

17. Harris, "Californians Are Saying 'No' to Growth," p. 227.

18. See Joan Sweeney, "David vs. Goliath—Three Youths Challenge $13 Million Project," *Los Angeles Times,* August 23, 1974, p. 1.

19. See Cranston et al., *A Handbook for Controlling Local Growth,* pp. 90–93.

20. Information on Livermore's growth control methods from Associated Building Industry of Northern California vs. City of Livermore, Civil Action 74-1710RFP, U.S. District Court, Northern District of California, "Second Amended Complaint."

21. "California Court Approves Laws Limiting Building," *New York Times,* December 19, 1976, p. 26; and David F. Beatty, "California Supreme Court Upholds Livermore Growth Law," *Practicing Planner* 7 (September 1977): 12–13.

22. David Gebhard, Robert Montgomery, Robert Winter, John Woodbridge, and Sally Woodbridge, *A Guide to Architecture in San Francisco and Northern California* (Santa Barbara: Peregrine Smith, 1973), p. 166.

23. Robert C. Fellmeth, *Politics of Land* (New York: Grossman Publishers, 1973), p. 32.

24. Robert Feinbaum, "The Politics of Growth in the 'Valley of Heart's Delight,' " *California Journal* 7 (March 1976): 95–98, quotation from p. 98.

25. Research Division of the Urban Land Institute and Gruen Gruen + Associates, *Effects of Regulation on Housing Costs: Two Case Studies* (Washington, D.C.: Urban Land Institute, 1977), pp. 11–13.

26. Cranston et al., *A Handbook for Controlling Local Growth*, pp. 103–105.

27. Terry Christensen, "Slowing Growth in San Jose," *Urban Land* 34 (February 1975): 13–17.

28. Ibid.; and Feinbaum, "The Politics of Growth in the 'Valley of Heart's Delight,' " p. 97.

29. Information on the consequences of the initiative was collected by the San Francisco firm of Livingston and Blayney, consultants to the city of San Jose.

30. Research Division of the Urban Land Institute and Gruen Gruen + Associates, *Effects of Regulation on Housing Costs*, p. 12.

31. Ibid., pp. 14–18.

32. Quoted in E. S. Rolph, *Decision-Making by Residential Developers in Santa Clara County* (Santa Monica, Calif.: Rand Corporation, August 1973), p. 21.

33. Ibid., pp. 21–22.

34. Interview with Frank B. Gray, June 10, 1976.

35. Sources of information on Petaluma are: City of Petaluma, *Environmental Design Plans*, March 27, 1972; City of Petaluma, *Petaluma Housing Element*, July 10, 1972; Frank B. Gray, "The City of Petaluma: Residential Development Control," *Management and Control of Growth*, Randall W. Scott, ed. (Washington, D.C.: Urban Land Institute, 1975), 2: 149–159; John Hart, "The Petaluma Case," *Cry California* 9 (Spring 1974): 6–15; interview with Frank B. Gray, Director of Community Development, Petaluma, June 10, 1976.

Notes to Chapter 3

1. Marin County Planning Department, *The Marin Countywide Plan, Revision O, October 1973* (San Rafael, Calif., 1973), p. 1-6.

2. Ibid., pp. 2-11 to 2-19.

3. Ibid., p. 2-16.

4. Interview with Gary Giacomini, Marin County supervisor, June 30, 1976.

5. Marin County Planning Department, *The Marin Countywide Plan*, p. 4-12.

6. Ibid., p. 4-10.

7. Thomas G. Dickert and Robert H. Twiss, *Environmental Planning Study: Marin Municipal Water District* (Berkeley, Calif.: Craftsman Press, 1974), p. 51.

8. For a full account of this open space purchase, see Jean Fitzgerald, "Urban Open Space—Who Will Pay the Bill?" Master of Journalism project, Graduate Division, University of California, Berkeley, December, 1973.

9. W. Seeger, "Water Planning in a No-Growth County," *Management and Control of Growth*, ed. Randall W. Scott (Washington, D.C.: Urban Land Institute, 1975), 2: 459–460.

10. Ibid., p. 459.

11. See James Kimo Campbell, "The No-Growth Politics of Cutting Off Water," *California Journal* 6 (July 1975): 251–252.

12. See "Green Panthers vs. Marin Water Bonds," *San Francisco Chronicle*, November 2, 1973, p. 57; and "Is $7.5 Million Water Bond a 'Trojan Horse'?" *San Rafael Independent-Journal*, August 31, 1973, p. 44.

13. Interview, June 30, 1976.

14. Sonya Thompson, "Russian River Water Project," *The Yodeler*, October 1973, p. 8.

15. "California County Hit by Drought, Begins Tough Rationing of Water," *New York Times*, February 2, 1977, p. A8.

16. Letter from Ron Stafford, *Pacific Sun*, March 19–25, 1976, p. 2.

17. "Where Are They Now?" *Pacific Sun*, March 5–11, 1976, p. 8.

18. "Marin Water Rate Boost Is Assailed," *San Francisco Chronicle*, March 4, 1976, p. 3.

19. *Marin Conservation League Newsletter*, February 1976, p. 2.

20. "The Water Shortage: A Parched Bolinas Pulls in Welcome Mat," *San Francisco Sunday Examiner & Chronicle*, July 4, 1976, section A, p. 26; and "Bolinas Blockade Fizzles Out," *San Francisco Chronicle*, July 5, 1976, p. 2.

21. Interview, June 30, 1976.

22. Interview, May 27, 1976.

23. "Marin Move to Aid Dry Dairy Ranches," *San Francisco Chronicle*, March 17, 1976, p. 3.

24. Housing data for 1960–1962, from *Northern California Real Estate Report*, 1st quarter 1965; housing data for 1963–1976, from Security Pacific National Bank.

25. Real Estate Research Council of Northern California, *Sales Price Trends of Single-Family Residences in the San Francisco Bay Area, 1972-1973-1974* (San Francisco, 1976), p. 5.

26. "Survey of Tract Housing in the San Francisco Bay Area" in Real Estate Research Council of Northern California, *Northern California Real Estate Report* 27 (1st quarter 1975): 10.

27. Don Stanley, "Managing in Marin," *Pacific Sun,* March 12-18, 1976, p. 5.

28. "Homeowners Protest Marin Assessments," *San Francisco Chronicle,* April 30, 1976, p. 4.

29. "Kentfield Solution–They're Willing to Pay the Price," *San Francisco Chronicle,* July 6, 1976, p. 21; and "Preserving the Neighborhood," *Pacific Sun,* June 11-17, 1976, p. 11.

30. Cranston et al., *Handbook for Controlling Local Growth,* p. 101.

31. Harold Gilliam, "Marin Pays the Price for Growth Control," *San Francisco Examiner & Chronicle,* June 6, 1976, *This World,* p. 31.

Notes to Chapter 4

1. Oakland City Planning Department, "A Preliminary Assessment of the Impact of the Proposed Mountain Village Project on the Community," April 7, 1972.

2. Letter from Jerome Keithley, City Manager, to Oakland City Council, Subject: Mountain Village Cost-Revenue Study, June 8, 1972.

3. Letter from Alden W. Badal, Associate Superintendent, Oakland Public Schools, to Mr. Jerome Keithley, City Manager, May 31, 1972.

4. Citizens against Mountain Village vs. City Council of the City of Oakland, California Superior Court for Alameda County, Department 20, "Memorandum and Notice of Intended Decision," 430400, March 26, 1973.

5. Interview with T. J. Lannen, July 9, 1976.

6. Additional sources of information on Mountain Village: Articles in *The Yodeler,* newspaper published by the San Francisco Bay Chapter of the Sierra Club, May 1972, July 1972, August 1972, October 1972, November 1972, March 1973; Citizens against Mountain Village, "Facts About Mountain Village," mimeographed handout; Dan Coleman Associates, "Proposed Master Plan for Mountain Village," 1972; interviews with T.J. Lannen, Challenge Developments, Inc., Redwood City, Calif., March 30 and July 9, 1976.

Notes to Chapter 5

1. Letter from Maurice A. Garbell, aeronautical engineering consultant, to Ronald H. Cowen, President, Harbor Bay Isle Associates, August 29, 1972.

2. Letter from Maurice A. Garbell, President, Maurice A. Garbell, Inc., to Mr. Walter A. Abernathy, Deputy Executive Director, Port of Oakland, February 2, 1973.

3. Arthur D. Little, Inc., "Harbor Bay Isle: A Residential/Industrial Development on Bay Farm Island, City of Alameda, Environmental Impact Report: Draft," November 21,

1973, p. IV-51; and memo from Joseph E. Bodovitz, Executive Director, San Francisco Bay Conservation and Development Commission, to All Commissioners and Alternates, Subject: Regional Airport Plan Proposed by ABAG Airport Study Committee, June 23, 1972.

4.   Arthur D. Little, Inc., "Harbor Bay Isle," p. IV-129.

5.   Ibid., pp. IV-198, 199 and VI-9-10.

6.   City of Alameda and Harbor Bay Isle Associates vs. City of Oakland, California Superior Court for City and County of San Francisco, 687–726, "Findings of Material Facts and Conclusions of Law," April 6, 1976.

7.   City of Oakland vs. City of Alameda and Harbor Bay Isle Associates, California Superior Court, County of Alameda, 450083-0, "Request for Clarification of Court's Opinion," filed August 19, 1975.

8.   City of Oakland vs. City of Alameda and Harbor Bay Isle Associates, California Superior Court for Alameda County, 450083-0, "Response by the Court to Request for Clarification," August 29, 1975.

9.   "Four-Year Hassle Ends: Bay Farm Project Approval," *Oakland Tribune,* July 22, 1976, p. 15.

10.   Memo from Joseph E. Bodovitz, Executive Director, San Francisco Bay Conservation and Development Commission, to all Commissioners and alternates, Subject: Regional Airport Plan Proposed by ABAG Airport Study Committee, June 23, 1972.

11.   Additional sources of information on Harbor Bay Isle are: "Environmental Impact Report: Harbor Bay Isle, A Doric-Planned Development on Bay Farm Island, Alameda," Prepared by the technical consultants to Harbor Bay Isle Associates, October 3, 1972; Marshall Kaplan, Gans, and Kahn, "Revised Draft Environmental Impact Report on Harbor Bay Isle," April 1976; City of Oaklana vs. City of Alameda and Harbor Bay Isle Associates, California Superior Court for Alameda County, 450083-0, "Memorandum Opinion: Announcement of Intended Decision," August 11, 1975; City of Alameda and Harbor Bay Isle Associates vs. City of Oakland, California Superior Court for City and County of San Francisco, 687-726, "Findings of Material Facts and Conclusions of Law," April 6, 1976; interviews with Sheldon Gans, Ted Dienstfrey, and Peter Grenell of Marshall Kaplan, Gans, and Kahn, April 1976; interview with Oscar Barry, Harbor Bay Isle Associates, March 30, 1976.

Notes to Chapter 6

1.   Business agent of a teamsters local, Daly City, at San Mateo County Board of Supervisors hearing, February 13, 1976.

2.   Development Research Associates and Eckbo, Dean, Austin, and Williams, "Visitacion Rancho: Sphere of Influence Study," prepared for San Mateo Local Agency Formation Commission, October 1972, pp. I-9, I-10.

3.   Richard DeLeon and David Tabb, "Brisbane Citizen Attitude Survey," San Francisco State University, June 1975.

4.   Letter from Marjorie Sutton, Chairwoman, Loma Prieta Chapter, Sierra Club, to San Mateo County Planning Commission, April 18, 1975.

5. URS Research Company, *Draft Environmental Impact Report: Application for a General Plan Amendment: Crocker Hills,* prepared for the San Mateo County Planning Department, January 1975, vol. 1, p. 18.

6. San Mateo County Planning Department, *Staff Report: San Bruno Mountain* (Redwood City, Calif., June 1975), p. IV-2 and IV-3.

7. Thomas W. Schnetlage, "Ecological Impacts of Development in the Saddle Area and the Impacts of Using the Saddle as a Park/Open Space," paper prepared for Department of City and Regional Planning, University of California, Berkeley, 1975.

8. San Mateo County Planning Commission hearing, July 10, 1975.

9. Planning commission hearing, August 14, 1975.

10. Planning commission hearing, July 10, 1975.

11. Planning commission hearing, July 28, 1975.

12. Planning commission hearing, August 14, 1975.

13. Planning commission hearing, July 23, 1975.

14. Planning commission hearing, September 17, 1975.

15. Planning commission hearing, November 26, 1975.

16. San Mateo County Board of Supervisors hearing, January 22, 1976.

17. Board of supervisors hearing, January 29, 1976.

18. Williams-Kuebelbeck and Associates, "Fiscal Impact Analysis of the Proposed Crocker Hills Development," prepared for the county of San Mateo, Redwood City, Calif., April 14, 1975.

19. San Mateo County Planning Department, *Summary Staff Report: San Bruno Mountain,* November 1975, Appendix A.

20. Board of supervisors hearing, January 22, 1976.

21. Board of supervisors hearing, January 29, 1976.

22. Board of supervisors hearing, January 29, 1976.

23. Board of supervisors hearing, January 22, 1976.

24. Board of supervisors hearing, January 22, 1976.

25. Letter from Polly Roberts to William H. Royer, Chairman, San Mateo County Board of Supervisors, January 27, 1976.

26. San Mateo County Planning Department, *Summary Staff Report: San Bruno Mountain,* November 1975, p. 17.

27. Board of supervisors hearing, February 23, 1976.

28. Board of supervisors hearing, January 22, 1976.

29. San Mateo County Planning Commission, "Initial Housing Plan—A General Plan Element," January 16, 1975, pp. 4, 6.

30. See Lorene Wilson et al. vs. County of San Mateo, California Superior Court, San Mateo County, 185034, "Amended Petition for Mandamus and/or Complaint for Injunctive and Declaratory Relief," July 15, 1975.

31. San Mateo County Planning Commission, "Initial Housing Plan—A General Plan Element," pp. 3, 4.

32. Board of supervisors hearing, February 23, 1976.

33. Sources of information on the San Bruno Mountain controversy in addition to those cited in preceding footnotes are: Visitacion Associates, "Visitacion Rancho Planning Recommendations," December 5, 1973; Visitacion Associates, "Visitacion Rancho: Recommendation for General Plan Amendment, San Mateo County, California," June 1974; Visitacion Associates, "Crocker Hills: The South San Francisco Area, Recommendations for General Plan Amendment, San Mateo County, California," September 1974; Economics Research Associates, "Summary and Update of the Fiscal Impact of the Proposed Crocker Hills Development, prepared for Visitacion Associates," January 14, 1976; San Mateo County Planning Commission, *Proposed Crocker Hills General Plan Amendment for San Bruno Mountain,* 1975; San Mateo County Planning Commission, "General Plan Amendment for San Bruno Mountain," April 20, 1976; San Mateo County Planning Commission, "EIR Analysis and Comments," 1975; interview with Thomas R. Adams, Legal Aid Society of San Mateo County, Daly City, California, July 13, 1976; interview with James Augustino, member of Committee to Save San Bruno Mountain, July 6, 1976; interview with Geraldine Bolter, Brisbane, Calif., July 1, 1976; interview with Howard Ellman, counsel to Visitacion Associates, San Francisco, July 2, 1976; interview with Ronald J. Grudzinski, Project Manager, Visitacion Associates, May 12, 1976; letter from Ronald J. Grudzinski, November 10, 1976; interview with Marc Mihaly, former staff member, San Mateo County Legal Aid Society, July 6, 1976; interview with Geraldine Steere, staff member, San Mateo County Planning Department, April 30, 1976; transcripts and tapes of planning commission and board of supervisors' hearings made available by Visitacion Associates.

Notes to Chapter 7

1. Contra Costa County Planning Department, "Blackhawk Ranch Environmental Impact Report," 1840-RZ, February 6, 1974, p. 52. The prior technical reports were James A. Roberts Associates, "Blackhawk Ranch: Draft Environmental Impact Report," August 28, 1973; and Ecological Impact Studies, Inc., "Final Environmental Impact Report for Contra Costa County," January 1974.

2. Contra Costa County Planning Department, "Blackhawk Ranch Environmental Impact Report," p. 52.

3. James A. Roberts Associates, "Blackhawk Ranch: Draft Environmental Impact Report," p. 85; and Ecological Impact Studies, Inc., "Final Environmental Impact Report for Contra Costa County," p. 53.

4. Contra Costa County Planning Department, "Blackhawk Ranch Environmental Impact Report," p. 52.

5. James A. Roberts Associates, "Blackhawk Ranch Environmental Impact Report," p. 85.

6. Contra Costa County Planning Department, "Blackhawk Ranch Environmental Impact Report," p. 52.

7. Ibid., p. 54.

8. Ibid., p. 53.

9. James A. Roberts Associates, "Blackhawk Ranch: Draft Environmental Impact Report," August 28, 1973, appendix memo on economic impact.

10. Gruen Gruen + Associates, "The Economic Impact of the Blackhawk Ranch Project," San Francisco, December 1973.

11. "Economic Supplement, Application 1840-RZ, Environmental Impact Report," prepared by Contra Costa County Planning Department, April 11, 1974.

12. Ibid., p. 26.

13. Ibid., pp. 1–2.

14. Ibid., pp. 39–40.

15. Interview with Anthony Dehaesus, Director of Planning, Contra Costa County, April 26, 1976.

16. Systems Planning Corporation, "San Ramon Valley Unified School District: Fiscal Impact of the Blackhawk Ranch Development," June 1974.

17. Contra Costa County Planning Commission public hearing, March 26, 1974.

18. Amigos de Diablo, "Summary of Position on Blackhawk," July 19, 1974.

19. Contra Costa County Board of Supervisors, "Further Response to Comments to Draft EIR [1840-RZ]," September 3, 1974.

20. Sierra Club et al. vs. Contra Costa County, California Superior Court, 147,426, "Memorandum of Decision," September 5, 1975.

21. Interview with Susan Watson, People for Open Space, May 13, 1976.

22. Additional sources of information on Blackhawk Ranch not cited above were: Susan Watson, "An Old Mountain with a Modern Problem: Mount Diablo and the Planning Issue," People for Open Space, *Regional Exchange,* November 1975, pp. 1–3; and interview with Larry Silver, Sierra Club Legal Defense Fund, San Francisco, July 1, 1976.

Notes to Chapter 8

1. Livingston and Blayney, *Foothills Environmental Design Study: Report No. 2 to the City of Palo Alto* (December 1969), pp. 1–2.

2. Livingston and Blayney, *Foothills Environmental Design Study: Report No. 1 to the City of Palo Alto* (October 1969), p. 32.

3. Livingston and Blayney, *Report No. 2*, p. 2.

4. State of California Office of the Controller, *Annual Report of Financial Transactions Concerning Cities of California: Fiscal Year 1972-73* (Sacramento, 1974).

5. Livingston and Blayney, *Foothills Environmental Design Study: Report No. 3 to the City of Palo Alto* (May 1970), pp. 28–29.

6. Livingston and Blayney, *Report No. 3*, pp. 51–52, 58–60.

7. Livingston and Blayney, *Report No. 3*, pp. 51–52.

8. Livingston and Blayney, *Report No. 3*, p. 52.

9. Ibid., p. 59.

10. Ibid., p. 60.

11. Palo Alto Planning Department, "The Problem of Housing in Palo Alto," July 23, 1970, p. 2.

12. Council of the City of Palo Alto, Committee of the Whole, "Minutes of the meeting of July 27, 1970," pp. 5–6.

13. Ibid., pp. 4–5.

14. Livingston and Blayney, *Report No. 3*, p. 58.

15. G. Christopher Davis, Economics Research Associates, Los Angeles, letter to Brett La Shelle, Vice President, Land Resources Corporation, Beverly Hills, October 29, 1969.

16. Arastra Limited Partnership vs. City of Palo Alto, U.S. District Court for Northern California, C-72-2305 RHS, "Decision," September 15, 1975, pp. 34–35.

17. Palo Alto Department of Planning and Community Development, "The Open Space Element of the General Plan," April 5, 1972, p. B-1.

18. Arastra Limited Partnership vs. City of Palo Alto, pp. 35–36.

19. Ibid., p. 37.

20. Ibid., p. 37.

21. Professor William Alonso, then at the University of California, Berkeley, and now at Harvard University, generously made available an extensive collection of material on Palo Alto that he had assembled. Principal sources in addition to those cited above are the following: Jay Thorwaldson, "The Palo Alto Experience," *Cry California* 8 (Spring 1973): 5-17; Cranston et al., *A Handbook for Controlling Local Growth*, pp. 86–89; Livingston and Blayney, *Foothills Environmental Design Study: Report No. 4 to the City of Palo Alto* (February 1971), and *Final Report, Open Space vs. Development* (February 1971); Palo

Alto Housing Advisory Committee, "Toward a Housing Plan for Palo Alto," January 25, 1973; Palo Alto Planning Commission, "Minutes," meetings of February 4, March 4, and July 1, 1970; Palo Alto City Council, "Minutes," meeting of November 9, 1970; interview with Robert Webber, of Fulop, Rolston, Burns and McKittrick, attorneys for Arastra Limited Partnership, July 12, 1976.

Notes to Chapter 9

1. "Is This Bridge Necessary?", *The Yodeler* (newspaper published by the San Francisco chapter of the Sierra Club), January 1974, p. 3.

2. *The Yodeler,* November, 1972, p. 2.

3. *The Yodeler,* June 1972.

4. Letter from Marjorie Sutton, Chairwoman, Loma Prieta Chapter, Sierra Club, Palo Alto, California to San Mateo County Planning Commission, April 18, 1975.

5. People for Open Space, *Regional Exchange,* April 1970, p. 2, and March 1975, p. 3.

6. People for Open Space, *Regional Exchange,* September 1972, p. 3.

7. People for Open Space, *Regional Exchange,* April 1970, p. 2, and March 1975, p. 2.

8. People for Open Space, *Regional Exchange,* March 1975, p. 2.

9. William K. Reilly, ed., *The Use of Land: A Citizen's Policy Guide to Urban Growth* (New York: Thomas Y. Crowell Co., 1973), p. 13.

10. See Editors of *Fortune, The Exploding Metropolis* (Garden City, N.Y.: Doubleday Anchor Books, 1958) for a good summary of the 1950s critique.

11. See Herbert J. Gans, *The Levittowners* (New York: Pantheon Books, 1967); William Michelson, "Most People Don't Want What Architects Want," *Trans-action* 5 (July–August 1968): 37–43; Jack Lessinger, "The Case for Scatteration," *Journal of the American Institute of Planners* 28 (August 1962): 159–169; Scott Donaldson, *The Suburban Myth* (New York: Columbia University Press, 1969).

12. Gallup Opinion Index, "Analysis: Managed Growth," August 1974, Report 110.

13. Reilly, ed., *The Use of Land,* p. 55.

14. Ibid., p. 257.

15. Ibid., pp. 209–210.

16. Ibid., p. 123.

17. Ibid., p. 111.

18. Ibid., p. 123.

19. Ibid., pp. 136–137.

20. Ibid., p. 137.

21. California Coastal Zone Conservation Commissions, *California Coastal Plan* (Sacramento: Documents and Publications Branch, 1975), p. 22.

22. Ibid., p. 79.

23. Ibid., pp. 79–80.

24. Ibid., p. 77.

25. Ibid., p. 80.

26. Ibid., p. 81.

27. Ibid., p. 55.

28. Ibid., pp. 57, 424.

29. Alfred Heller, ed., "The California Tomorrow Plan, Revised Edition," *Cry California* 7 (Summer, 1972): entire issue; quotation from p. 59.

30. Ibid.

31. Quoted in Samuel P. Hays, *Conservation and the Gospel of Efficiency* (Cambridge, Mass.: Harvard University Press, 1959), pp. 41–42. This work is the source of the historical interpretation presented here.

32. Ibid., p. 145.

33. Ibid., pp. 193–194.

34. California Coastal Zone Conservation Commissions, *California Coastal Plan*, p. 99.

35. Ibid., p. 115.

36. Contra Costa County Planning Department, "Blackhawk Ranch Environmental Impact Report," 1840-RZ, February 6, 1974, p. 51.

37. See Robert C. Wood, *1400 Governments* (Cambridge, Mass.: Harvard University Press, 1961), pp. 93–113; and Richard F. Babcock, *The Zoning Game* (Madison, Wis.: University of Wisconsin Press, 1969).

38. Mary Cranston, Bryant Garth, Robert Plattner, and Jay Varon, *A Handbook for Controlling Local Growth* (Stanford, Calif.: Stanford University Law School, Environmental Law Society,1973), p. 71.

39. People for Open Space, *Regional Exchange,* April 1970, p. 2

40. People for Open Space, *Regional Exchange,* March 1975, pp. 3–4.

41. "The Club Looks at Itself," *Sierra Club Bulletin* 57 (July–August 1972):35–39.

42. Ibid., p. 37.

43. John Zierold, "This Time the Wolf Is Really Here." *Perspective,* no. 1, supplement to *The Yodeler* [Sierra Club newsletter], December 1975, p. 4.

44. State of California Office of Planning and Research, *Prime Agricultural Lands Report,* October 1974, pp. 4-5.

45. Ibid., p. 7.

46. U.S. Department of Agriculture Economic Research Service, *Major Uses of Land in the United States: Summary for 1969,* Agricultural Economic Report No. 247 (Washington, D.C., 1973), p. 2.

47. George E. Peterson and Harvey Yampolsky, *Urban Development and the Protection of Metropolitan Farmland* (Washington, D.C.: The Urban Institute, 1975), p. 6.

48. Kathryn A. Zeimetz, Elizabeth Dillon, Ernest E. Hardy, Robert C. Otte, *Dynamics of Land Use in Fast Growth Areas,* U.S. Department of Agriculture, Economic Research Service, Agricultural Economic Report No. 325 (Washington, D.C., 1976), pp. 7, 24.

49. Peterson and Yampolsky, *Urban Development and the Protection of Metropolitan Farmland,* p. 15.

50. See, for example, Sterling Wortman, "Food and Agriculture," *Scientific American* 235 (September 1976): 30-39; and Earl O. Heady, "The Agriculture of the United States," *Scientific American* 235 (September 1976): 106-127.

51. Heady, "The Agriculture of the United States," pp. 126-127.

52. "Sierra Club Agriculture Policy," adopted February 22, 1976 (San Francisco: Sierra Club, 1976), p. 4.

53. See *Perspective,* no. 1, pp. 1-3.

54. See Gregory C. Gustafson and L.T. Wallace, "Differential Assessment as Land Use Policy: The California Case," *Journal of the American Institute of Planners* 41 (November 1975); 379-389; and Robert C. Fellmeth, *Politics of Land* (New York: Grossman Publishers, 1973), pp. 36-43.

55. *Perspective,* no. 1, p. 1.

56. People for Open Space, *Regional Exchange,* March 1974, p. 4.

57. Harold Gilliam, *For Better or for Worse* (San Francisco: Chronicle Books, 1972), p. 43.

58. T. J. Kent, Jr., "Metropolitan Open Space and Regional Government," essay prepared for the Institute of Governmental Studies, University of California, Berkeley, August 1969, pp. 13-14.

59. J. Clarence Davies III and Barbara S. Davies, *The Politics of Pollution* (Indianapolis: Bobbs-Merrill, 1976), p. 91; and Gladwin Hill, "Environmentalists Map Biggest Political Year," *New York Times,* February 15, 1976, p. 56.

60. Davies and Davies, *The Politics of Pollution,* pp. 90, 95.

61. Gallup poll release, February 5, 1976.

62. Gallup poll release, March 11, 1973; see also Matthew A. Crenson, *The Un-Politics of Air Pollution* (Baltimore: Johns Hopkins University Press, 1971), pp. 13–16; and Davies and Davies, *The Politics of Pollution,* pp. 80–85.

63. People for Open Space, *Regional Exchange,* April 1970, p. 2.

Notes to Chapter 10

1. Real Estate Research Council of Northern California, "Survey of Tract Housing in the San Francisco Bay Area," *Northern California Real Estate Report* 27 (1st quarter, 1975): 4–11.

2. State of California Office of Planning and Research, *California Environmental Quality Act Litigation Study* (Sacramento, April, 1976), p. 1.

3. Ibid., p. 8.

4. See ibid., Appendix B. The seven cases have the following identifying numbers: 73-2-10; 73-3-01; 74-2-02; 74-4-02; 75-1-02; 75-2-19; 75-4-02.

5. Ibid., p. 8.

6. State of California Assembly Committee on Local Government, *The California Environmental Quality Act: An Evaluation . . .* (November, 1975), 1: 40.

7. Ibid., 1: 62

8. Ibid., 3: 37.

9. Ibid., 1: 41.

10. Data supplied by the Statistical Division, Office of Economic Research, Federal Home Loan Bank Board, Washington, D. C. The Federal Home Loan Bank Board, in cooperation with the Federal Deposit Insurance Corporation, compiles average prices each month from individual statistics for conventional mortagages reported by a sample of savings and loan associations, mortgage bankers, commercial banks, and mutual savings banks. The Federal Home Loan Bank Board survey covers the San Francisco-Oakland Standard Metropolitan Statistical Area, consisting of Alameda, Contra Costa, Marin, San Francisco, and San Mateo counties. Other data in this book on the San Francisco Bay Area include four additional counties: Napa, Santa Clara, Solano, and Sonoma.
Independent surveys of San Francisco area housing prices made by the Real Estate Research Council of Northern California and the California Association of Realtors are in close agreement with the Federal Home Loan Bank Board data.

11. Real Estate Research Council of Northern California, *Sales Price Trends of Single Family Residences in the San Francisco Bay Area: 1972-1973-1974* (San Francisco, 1976).

12. Maurice P. Abraham, "The Availability and Geographical Distribution of New Median Income Housing in the San Francisco Bay Area 1970–1975" (San Jose: George S. Nolte and Associates, December 1975).

13. Interview with William Leonard, Executive Director, Associated Building Industry of Northern California, March 26, 1976.

14. Interview with Gerson Bakar, July 15, 1976.

15. Richard F. Babcock and Fred P. Bosselman, *Exclusionary Zoning: Land Use Regulation and Housing in the 1970s* (New York: Praeger, 1973), p. 15.

16. Robert Lindsey, "How Government is Pushing up the Cost of Housing," *New York Times,* July 18, 1976, section 3, p. 1.

17. James Robert and Robert Bush, "Managed Growth Overview and Analysis," *Environmental Comment,* no. 19 (March 1975): 4.

18. International City Management Association, "Local Government Techniques for Managing Growth," *Management Information Service Report* 6 (May, 1974): 8.

19. Advance Mortgage Corporation "Housing Boom Outpaces Supply of Lots; Crunch Will Come Next Year in Third of Markets," *U.S. Housing Markets* (Detroit, October 21, 1977), p. 2.

20. Letter to the author from Michael Towbes, Michael Towbes Construction and Development Inc., Santa Barbara, Calif., July 20, 1977; and personal interview, July 13, 1977.

21. Gladwin Hill, "Housing Rules Adopted on Coast to Aid Salamander," *New York Times,* December 5, 1976, p. 26.

22. See Federal Home Loan Bank of San Francisco, *Commentary,* vol. 2 (February 1976).

23. Robert Lindsey, "Home Demand: Torrid and Strong in Some Regions, Weak in Others," *New York Times,* September 24, 1976, p. D1.

24. Maurice Mann, "The California Housing Boom—Where is it Going?", remarks at the Quarterly UCLA Business Forecast Update Conference, July 16, 1977, Los Angeles, p. 6.

25. A. Richard Immel, "A Bursting Bubble? Experts Predict an End to Speculative Boom in California Housing," *Wall Street Journal,* June 2, 1977, p. 1.

26. Data from Statistical Division, Office of Economic Research, Federal Home Loan Bank Board.

27. See Robert Lindsey, "California to Vote on Plan to Limit Property Taxes; Schools and Local Governments Fear Revenue Loss," *New York Times,* January 5, 1978, p. A14; and Robert Lindsey, "Budget Cuts Begun After Californians Vote to Curb Taxes," *New York Times,* June 8, 1978, p. 1.

28. John Herbers, "California Tax Revolt Is Expected To Bring More Dependence on U.S.," *New York Times,* June 11, 1978, p. 1.

29. Advance Mortgage Corporation, "Housing Boom Outpaces Supply of Lots; Crunch will Come Next Year in Third of Markets," *U.S. Housing Markets,* (Detroit, October 21, 1977).

30. State of California Office of Planning and Research, *Urban Development Strategy for California: Review Draft* (Sacramento, May 1977), p. 35.

31. See ibid., pp. 34-36.

32. Ibid., p. 29.

33. Ibid., pp. 48-49.

34. State of California Office of Planning and Research, *An Urban Strategy for California* (Sacramento, February 1978), p. 11.

35. Ibid., p. 10.

36. Ibid., p. 14.

Notes to Chapter 11

1. International City Management Association, *Management Information Service Report* 7 (June 1975): 2.

2. Council of State Governments, *State Growth Management: May 1976* (Washington, D.C.: U.S. Department of Housing and Urban Development, 1976), pp. 24-26.

3. See Michael N. Danielson, *The Politics of Exclusion* (New York: Columbia University Press, 1976), p. 287.

4. Richard F. Babcock, *The Zoning Game* (Madison, Wis.: University of Wisconsin Press, 1969), pp. 115-116.

5. U.S., National Commission on Urban Problems, *Building the American City: Report to the Congress and the President of the United States* (Washington, D.C.: Government Printing Office, 1969), p. 204.

6. Ibid., p. 211.

7. U.S. President's Committee on Urban Housing, *Report: A Decent Home* (Washington, D.C.: Government Printing Office, 1969), p. 142.

8. Ibid., p. 143

9. Norman Williams, Jr., and Thomas Norman, "Exclusionary Land Use Controls: The Case of North-Eastern New Jersey," *Land Use Controls, Present Problems and Future Reform,* David Listokin, ed. (New Brunswick, N.J.: Rutgers University Center for Urban Policy Research, 1974), pp. 105-130; citation from p. 127.

10. Babcock, *The Zoning Game,* pp. 92-93.

11. International City Management Association, *Management Information Service Report* 6 (May 1974): 9.

12. See ibid., p. 8; and John DeGrove, *Land Management: New Directions for the States* (Columbus, Ohio: Academy for Contemporary Problems, 1976), p. 131.

13. International City Management Association, *Management Information Service Report* 6 (May 1974): 8.

14. John T. Hazel, Jr., "Growth Management through Litigation: A Case Study of Fairfax County, Virginia," *Urban Land* 35 (November 1976): 10.

15. See David Falk and Herbert M. Franklin, *Local Growth Management Policy: A Legal Primer* (Washington, D.C.: The Potomac Institute, 1975), pp. 13-16.

16. International City Management Association, *Management Information Service Report* 6 (May 1974): 12-13.

17. Ibid., pp. 13-14; and James Roberts and Larry Bush, "Managed Growth Overview and Analysis," *Environmental Comment*, no. 19 (March 1975): 2-3.

18. Falk and Franklin, *Local Growth Management Policy*, p. 19.

19. International City Management Association, *Management Information Service Report* 6 (May 1974): 16.

20. "Vote to Limit Growth Cuts Housing Permits," *New York Times*, December 13, 1976, p. 25; and "Boulder, Colorado Moves to Curb Its Growth," *New York Times*, September 11, 1977, p. 47.

21. International City Management Association, *Management Information Service Report* 6 (May 1974): 7-8.

22. Ibid., p. 8.

23. Letter from George E. Winzer, Chief, Environment and Land Use Research Group, Department of Housing and Urban Development, Washington, D.C., to the author, February 1, 1977.

24. Malcolm D. Rivkin, "Growth Control via Sewer Moratoria," *Urban Land* 33 (March 1974): 14.

25. Stephen R. Seidel, *Housing Costs and Government Regulations* (New Brunswick, N.J.: Rutgers University Center for Urban Policy Research, 1978), pp. 27-29.

26. U.S., National Commission on Urban Problems, *Building the American City*, p. 422.

27. Michael Sumichrast and Sara A. Frankel, *Profile of the Builder and His Industry* (Washington, D.C.: National Association of Home Builders, 1970), p. 25; and National Association of Home Builders, *Economic News Notes* 21 (May 1975): 3-4.

28. Advance Mortgage Corporation "Housing Boom Outpaces Supply of Lots; Crunch Will Come Next Year in Third of Markets," *U.S. Housing Markets* (Detroit, October 21, 1977).

29. See National Association of Home Builders, *Economic News Notes* 31 (May 1975): 4; and Michael Sumichrast [Chief Economist, National Association of Home Builders], "Housing Costs," *Washington Star*, series of articles published March 4-April 15, 1977.

30. Seidel, *Housing Costs and Government Regulations,* p. 243.

31. Thomas Muller with Kathleen Christensen, "State-Mandated Impact Evaluation: A Preliminary Assessment," Land Use Center Contract Report 0217-01 (Washington, D.C.: The Urban Institute, April 1976), pp. 23, 30-31, 37.

32. Ibid., p. 36.

33. Seidel, *Housing Costs and Government Regulations,* pp. 33-34.

34. Malcolm D. Rivkin, "Growth Control Via Sewer Moratoria," *Urban Land* 33 (March 1974): 14.

35. AFL-CIO, *Survey of AFL-CIO Members Housing: 1975* (Washington, D.C.: AFL-CIO, 1975), p. 4.

36. Danielson, *The Politics of Exclusion,* p. 325.

37. "Closing of Five Palo Alto Schools Asked by Santee," *Palo Alto Times,* November 5, 1974, p. 1.

38. Michael Knight, "Suburbs Losing Control of Schools," *New York Times,* July 18, 1977, p. 1.

39. Franklin J. James, Jr. with Oliver Duane Windsor, "Fiscal Zoning, Fiscal Reform, and Exclusionary Land Use Controls," *Journal of the American Institute of Planners* 42 (April 1976): 130-141.

40. Ben A. Franklin, "Rockefeller Irks Well-to-Do Neighbors," *New York Times,* October 29, 1977, p. 25.

41. Alan Altshuler, "Review of *The Costs of Sprawl,*" *Journal of the American Institute of Planners* 43 (April 1977): 207-209.

42. State of California Office of Planning and Research, *Urban Development Strategy for California: Review Draft* (May 1977), p. 11.

43. See Martha Derthick, *New Towns In-Town* (Washington, D.C.: The Urban Institute, 1972).

44. Fred Bosselman, Duayne A. Feurer, and Charles L. Siemon, *The Permit Explosion* (Washington, D.C.: The Urban Land Institute, 1976), p. 5.

45. State of Massachusetts Office of State Planning, *City and Town Centers: A Program for Growth* (September 1977), pp. 78-79.

46. Michael McCloskey, "On Loggerheadedness," *New York Times,* September 20, 1977, p. 41.

47. James M. Burger, "Deregulation's Foggy Future," *New York Times,* May 22, 1977, section 3, p. 1.

48. Garrett Hardin, "Living on a Lifeboat," *Managing the Commons,* Garrett Hardin and John Baden, eds. (San Francisco: W.H. Freeman and Co., 1977), pp. 262–263.

49. Ibid., p. 276.

50. People for Open Space, "A Greenbelt for the Bay Area," 1978, p. 2.

51. Harold Gilliam, *For Better or For Worse* (San Francisco: Chronicle Books, 1972), p. 150.

52. Lois Wagner Green, "Second Time Around," *New York Times Magazine,* March 7, 1976, pp. 68–69.

53. See Richard J. Barnet, "No Room in the Lifeboats," *New York Times Magazine,* April 16, 1978, pp. 32–38.

The Joint Center for Urban Studies, a cooperative venture of the Massachusetts Institute of Technology and Harvard University, was founded in 1959 to organize and encourage research on urban and regional problems. Participants have included scholars from the fields of anthropology, architecture, business, city planning, economics, education, engineering, history, law, philosophy, political science, and sociology.

The findings and conclusions of this book are, as with all Joint Center publications, solely the responsibility of the author.

Published by Harvard University Press

The Intellectual versus the City: From Thomas Jefferson to Frank Lloyd Wright, by Morton and Lucia White, 1962

Streetcar Suburbs: The Process of Growth in Boston, 1870–1900, by Sam B. Warner, Jr., 1962

City Politics, by Edward C. Banfield and James Q. Wilson, 1963

Law and Land: Anglo-American Planning Practice, edited by Charles M. Haar, 1964

Location and Land Use: Toward a General Theory of Land Rent, by William Alonso, 1964

Poverty and Progress: Social Mobility in a Nineteenth Century City, by Stephan Thernstrom, 1964

Boston: The Job Ahead, by Martin Meyerson and Edward C. Banfield, 1966

The Myth and Reality of Our Urban Problems, by Raymond Vernon, 1966

Muslin Cities in the Later Middle Ages, by Ira Marvin Lapidus, 1967

The Fragmented Metropolis: Los Angeles, 1850–1930, by Robert M. Fogelson, 1967

Law and Equal Opportunity: A Study of the Massachusetts Commission Against Discrimination, by Leon H. Mayhew, 1968

Varieties of Police Behavior: The Management of Law and Order in Eight Communities, by James Q. Wilson, 1968

The Metropolitan Enigma: Inquiries into the Nature and Dimensions of America's "Urban Crisis," edited by James Q. Wilson, revised edition, 1968

Traffic and The Police: Variations in Law-Enforcement Policy, by John A. Gardiner, 1969

The Influence of Federal Grants: Public Assistance in Massachusetts, by Martha Derthick, 1970

The Arts in Boston, by Bernard Taper, 1970

Families Against the City: Middle Class Homes of Industrial Chicago, 1872–1890, by Richard Sennett, 1970

The Political Economy of Urban Schools, by Martin T. Katzman, 1971

Origins of the Urban School: Public Education in Massachusetts, 1870–1915, by Marvin Lazerson, 1971

The Other Bostonians: Poverty and Progress in the American Metropolis, 1880–1970, by Stephan Thernstrom, 1973

Published by the MIT Press

The Image of the City, by Kevin Lynch, 1960

Housing and Economic Progress: A Study of the Housing Experiences of Boston's Middle-Income Families, by Lloyd Rodwin, 1961

The Historian and the City, edited by Oscar Handlin and John Burchard,, 1963

The Federal Bulldozer: A Critical Analysis of Urban Renewal, 1949-1962, by Martin Anderson, 1964

The Future of Old Neighborhoods: Rebuilding for a Changing Population, by Bernard J. Frieden, 1964

Man's Struggle for Shelter in an Urbanizing World, by Charles Abrams, 1964

The View from the Road, by Donald Appleyard, Kevin Lynch, and John R. Myer, 1964

The Public Library and the City, edited by Ralph W. Conant, 1965

Regional Development Policy: A Case Study of Venezuela, by John Friedmann, 1966

Urban Renewal: The Record and the Controversy, edited by James Q. Wilson, 1965

Transport Technology for Developing Regions: A Study of Road Transportation in Venezuela, by Richard M. Soberman, 1966

Computer Methods in the Analysis of Large-Scale Social Systems, edited by James M. Beshers, 1968

Planning Urban Growth and Regional Development: The Experience of the Guayana Programs of Venezuela, by Lloyd Rodwin and Associates, 1969

Build a Mill, Build a City, Build a School: Industrialization, Urbanization, and Education in Ciudad Guayana, by Noel F. McGinn and Russell G. Davis, 1969

Land-Use Controls in the United States, by John Delafons, second edition, 1969

Beyond the Melting Pot: The Negroes, Puerto Ricans, Jews, Italians, and Irish of New York City, by Nathan Glazer and Daniel Patrick Moynihan, revised eidition, 1970

Bargaining: Monopoly Power versus Union Power, by George de Menil, 1971

Housing the Urban Poor: A Critical Evaluation of Federal Housing Polocy, by Arthur P. Solomon, 1974

The Politics of Neglect: Urban Aid from Model Cities to Revenue Sharing, by Bernard J. Frieden and Marshall Kaplan, 1975

The Urban Transportation System: Politics and Policy Innovation, by Alan A. Altshuler with James P. Womack and John R. Pucher, 1979

The Joint Center also publishes monographs and reports.

Index